Hockey
Bantam to Pro

Jack Kelley
GENERAL MANAGER,
NEW ENGLAND WHALERS

Milt Schmidt
COACH AND GENERAL MANAGER,
WASHINGTON CAPITOLS

with Al Hirshberg

ALLYN and BACON, Inc. • BOSTON

Library of Congress Cataloging in Publication Data

Kelley, Jack.
  Hockey: bantam to pro.

  Bibliography: p.
  1. Hockey. I. Schmidt, Milt, joint author.
II. Hirshberg, Albert, 1909-1973, joint author.
III. Title.
GV847.K43   796.9′62   74-9688

Acknowledgments

We would like to acknowledge our indebtedness to Jim Fullerton, scout for the New York Islanders, who devoted much time and effort to this publication.

The authors are also grateful to, and wish to thank, John Bucyk, Terry Caffery, Wayne Cashman, Ed Johnson, Bruce Landon, Brad Selwood, Fred Stanfield, and Tom Webster for posing for the skill shots in Chapter 2. We are also indebted to the National Hockey League for allowing us to base Chapter 9 on Bill Head's NHL *Conditioning Manual*.

The photographs on pages 1, 2, 20, 22, 56, 72, 80, 88, 90, 126, 144, 174, and 184 are courtesy of *The Boston Globe*. The photograph on page 182 is a United Press International Photo, and the photograph on page 158 is by Joseph Connolly. The frontispiece (Romeyn de Hooghe's "Hockey Player") is reproduced by permission of The Metropolitan Museum of Art (Harris Brisbane Dick Fund, 1941).

Contents

Contents

Foreword

THE ALLYN AND BACON
SPORTS EDUCATION SERIES

Arthur G. Miller, Consulting Editor

Sports play a major role in the lives of practically everyone—the players, the coaches, the officials, and the spectators! Interest in sports is the result of several factors.

There is increased emphasis on *personal physical fitness*. Formal exercises or calisthenics, while worthwhile, are not as popular nor as motivating to the promotion of fitness as participation in sports. Through *sports participation*, children and adults gain fitness but also develop skills, group and personal satisfactions, and enjoyment.

Another factor in the growing interest in sports is the increase in television and radio broadcasts of sporting events. Team sports such as baseball, football, basketball, soccer, and hockey are seasonally covered by pratically all channels. The lifetime sports including bowling, golf, tennis, and skiing are also receiving more air time. Activities such as gymnastics, swimming, and other aquatic sports have, and will continue to receive,

more expanded coverage. The analysis of skills and strategy within each sport by knowledgeable commentators using instant video replay and stop-action techniques, makes the game or activity more interesting to the viewer.

The Allyn and Bacon Sports Education Series has been created to meet the need for players, coaches, and spectators to be informed about the basic and advanced skills, techniques, tactics, and strategies of sports. Each book in the Series is designed to provide an in-depth treatment of a selected sport or activity. Players find the individual skills and accompanying picture sequences very valuable. Coaches gain basic and advanced knowledge of individual and team play along with techniques of coaching. Sports fans are provided information about the activities and are thus able to become more knowledgeable about and appreciative of the basic and finer aspects of sports.

The authors of the *Sports Education*

Series have been carefully selected. They include experienced teachers, coaches, and managers of college and professional teams. Some books represent the combined effort of two or more authors, each with a different background and each contributing particular strengths to the text. For other books, a single author has been selected, whose background offers a breadth of knowledge and experience in the sport being covered.

Among the authors and titles of some of the team-sport books is George Allen, successful coach of the Washington Redskins, who collaborated with Don Weiskopf on the information book *Inside Football*. Weiskopf also wrote with Walter Alston, of the Los Angeles Dodgers, the *Complete Baseball Handbook*. The book *Basketball—Concepts and Techniques,* by Bob Cousy, former coach of the Sun Kings, and Frank Power, presents the game for men. *Women's Basketball,* by Mildred Barnes of Central Missouri State University, covers the "new" five-player game for girls. Dr. Barnes also wrote the book *Field Hockey. The Challenge of Soccer* is by Hubert Vogelsinger, coach of the Boston Minutemen, and the book *Winning Volleyball* was written by Allen Scates of UCLA. A group of authors including General Managers Jack Kelley of the New England Whalers and Milt Schmidt of the Washington Hockey Club collaborated on the book *Hockey—Bantam to Pro.*

Individual sports included in the series are: *Racket Work,* Second Edition, by Jack Barnaby of Harvard University, and *Modern Track and Field for Girls and Women* by Donnis Thompson of the University of Hawaii. The book on *Gymnastics* is by Kitty Kjeldsen of the University of Massachusetts.

Tom Tutko and Jack Richards collaborated on the meaningful book, *Psychology of Coaching.* And Tutko joined with Patsy Neal to write *Coaching Girls and Women: Psychological Perspectives.*

This Sports Series enables readers to experience the thrills of the sport from the point of view of participants and coaches, to learn some of the reasons for success and causes of failure, and to receive basic information about teaching and coaching techniques.

Each volume in the series reflects the philosophy of the authors, but a common theme runs through all: the desire to instill in the reader a knowledge and appreciation of sports and physical activity which will carry over throughout his life as a participant or a spectator. Pictures, drawings, and diagrams are used throughout each book to clarify and illustrate the discussion.

The reader, whether a beginner or one experienced in sports, will gain much from each book in this Allyn and Bacon Sports Education Series.

Arthur G. Miller
Chairman, Department of Human
    Movement and Health Education
Boston University

Foreword

AL HIRSHBERG

We were just talking about Al Hirshberg the other night. We hadn't seen each other for awhile and there we were all together at this party, and we were remembering Al Hirshberg.

What we remembered was "the Old Master" (that's what he liked to be called) sitting in a beach chair in front of his house on Indian Rocks Beach, Florida. He had a golf hat on his head, and he was wearing blue swimming trunks and a shirt because of the skin cancer. He was sitting on that beach chair, plopped on the sand, refereeing a touch football game.

My wife and I were playing John and Barbara Devaney. Lenny and Lee Greene were standing by ready to come in if any one of us was struck by injuries, or exhaustion. And Al Hirshberg was sitting there making outrageous calls against our side. The Devaneys, you see, were so much taller than the Silvermans. It wasn't fair.

"Hey, Hirsh," I hollered once, "you stink."

"Shut up," he said, all business, "or you'll be out of the game."

All through it he was laughing so hard, and so were we, and it was the best of times that warm March day in Florida.

So we talked about Al Hirshberg at the party—Lenny and Lee, Barbara and John, and Rosa and myself. We talked about the touch football game, about our days with the Hirshbergs in Florida. We often gathered together in Florida in March during the 1960's and 70's. We were allegedly down there on business, it being spring training time for the major-league baseball teams. We did some work, but mainly it was an excuse to get in the sun and visit the Hirshbergs.

We remembered those good times. We talked about Al and his jollity and his good nature and his sharp tongue. And even though he had been gone over a year, none of us felt sad. The memories of Al Hirshberg are joyful ones. We think of him today with regret, of course, that he is no longer with us. But the talk always ends in smiles.

He had to walk slowly in his last years because he had angina and he took pills for his heart. He had to be careful. I remember a grand October day in Baltimore, before a World Series game. Al was covering the series for the magazine I was editing, and we spent most of our free time together. We walked from my hotel to his, about a half mile. It took us maybe an hour because Al couldn't walk very fast. But time never dragged when you were with Al. He always kept you going.

He would question you about the business or about your personal life, and he always had a story to tell you about his own experiences. He was a marvelous story teller. The stories were good and warm. They were often racy, too, but always full of the zest that marked his whole life.

My memories of the Old Master go way back. I was a kid growing up in a suburb of Boston and every night my Dad brought home two newspapers. One was the morning *Boston Post*. Al Hirshberg was a sportswriter for the *Post* and I always loved reading his stories. It seemed to me that he covered everything in those days, in the late 1930's. He would be on the road with the Boston Red Sox one day, attending a Boston College football game the next, looking in on the Boston Bruins another day. His attraction for the Bruins is where he got his knowledge and love of hockey, which are so evident in this book.

In those days I had faint dreams of becoming a sportswriter myself. Just before World War II, when I was in high school, I wrote a sports column for a Jewish Community Center newspaper. It was called "Pegging 'Em Over." I swear I was copying the brisk, tart, peppy journalism of Al Hirshberg.

After the war I attended Boston University, which was Al Hirshberg's alma mater. I was editor of the college newspaper my senior year and one day I went to the *Post* with a friend who was working there and he introduced me to Hirshberg.

Al had that cocky look on his face that was his trademark. He had a ruddy complexion, dimples when he smiled, and an easy way of making you feel right at home. I felt so much at home with him, in fact, that I asked him about a job.

"I'll be looking for work soon," I said.

"What kind of work, Pally?" he asked. (From that moment on, he always called me *Pally.*)

"Newspaper work, I guess. Maybe sports."

"Get into something else," he announced quickly. "The hours are long and the pay is rotten."

"I'd like to try it," I said. "If you know of anything. . . ." My words trailed off in embarrassment at being so forward.

"I'll see what I can do," he said.

Well, it turned out he couldn't do anything for me right off, but when I went to New York to seek my fortune he did help me. He gave me the name of a man to see at *SPORT Magazine*—Ed Fitzgerald, who was the managing editor of this new magazine. Al Hirshberg was writing a lot for *SPORT*.

So I presented myself to Fitzgerald and told him Hirshberg had sent me, and that was like a gold lifetime pass to any major-league ballpark.

Soon after, I went to work for *SPORT*.

And then Hirsh and I became good friends.

The Boston *Post* died a sad death and Al was out of work. One day he came to New York. I told him he should become a full-time freelance writer. I introduced him, in fact, to the man who became his agent, Sterling Lord. Lord became not only a strong fiscal influence on Al but an important spiritual influence in Al's life. And Al did become a freelance writer, and one of the most successful ones of the day.

I moved around a little bit in the 1950's. I left *SPORT,* went to work for a couple of other magazines, then became a freelance writer myself—but not as successful as Hirshberg. Early in the fifties he wrote a book that touched millions of people. It was called *Fear Strikes Out,* co-authored with Jim Piersall. It was the story of Piersall's mental breakdown while playing baseball for the Boston Red Sox. *Fear Strikes Out* became an enormous hit and was made into a movie. The book is still being read today.

So Al wrote books and magazine articles. (Last time we counted it up together, he told me he had written 400 magazine articles and 32 books.) He mingled with the greats of the day—Ted Williams, Rocky Marciano, Bob Cousy. Name a great athlete of that era and Hirshberg had done something on him—

either a magazine story or a book.

In 1960 I went back to *SPORT* as editor of the magazine, and for the next twelve years Al wrote as much for *SPORT* as any other writer did.

We had one gentleman's agreement between us in those years. We would always find a World Series story for Al. The Old Master never said so but he aldays missed being on the beat, working as a baseball writer for a daily newspaper. The World Series was at least a chance for him to mingle with his old friends. He was a great mingler. But he also worked down at the games—worked hard—and never once turned in a bad story for us.

And then, one night, in the spring of 1973, the phone call came from Sterling Lord. Al had died that morning. A peaceful death.

A few days later some of his friends met in a New York restaurant. We met to drink a toast to Al Hirshberg. It should have been a sad affair, I suppose, a solemn affair. But it wasn't. Because we all told the stories that we knew about Al Hirshberg. And we retold the stories that the Old Master had told us. And there was laughter and no tears. And that's the way it will always be when we remember Al Hirshberg. And that's the way it should be.

Al Silverman
Editorial Director
Book-of-the-Month Club

I

Introduction

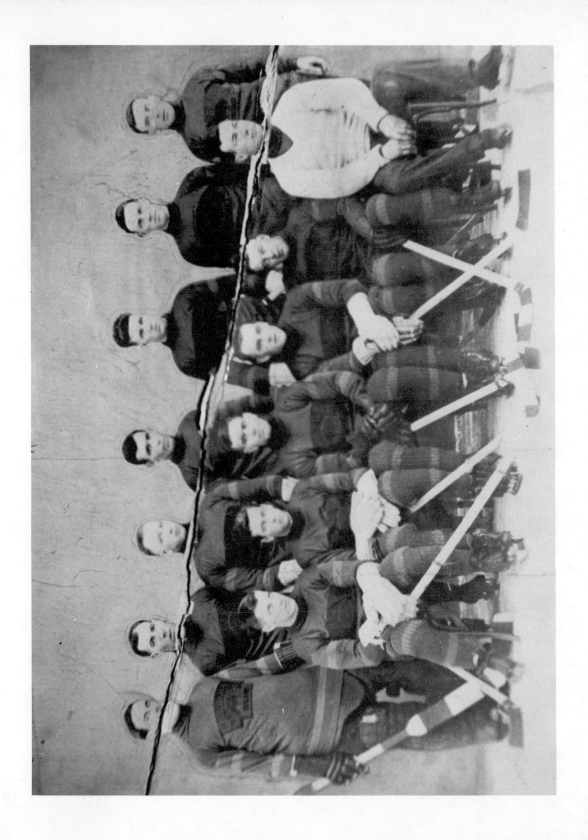

1

History of Ice Hockey

ORIGINS OF THE GAME

Probably no game now commonly accepted as a major professional sport in North America produces more confusion about its origins than ice hockey. Some historians consider it a direct descendant of an old European pastime known as bandy. Others believe it an ice version of hurling, a wild Irish game with rules so loose that practically anything goes, and injuries so commonplace that few pay much attention to them. Still others see ice hockey as an offshoot of field hockey, once a man's game but now played almost exclusively by women, at least in the United States.

Although field hockey resembles ice hockey in that both games are played with sticks and employ goals into which a missile must be shot past a goal-tender, not many people adhere to the theory that there ever was any real relationship between the two sports. It is considered more likely that the history of ice hockey, shrouded in the obscurity of the ages, is closely intertwined with the history of ice-skating, which goes all the way back to the years before the birth of Christ. Ice-skating itself probably started in the Scandinavian countries as a by-product of skiing, which is even older. There is evidence that the first skates were made from the shank or rib bone of elks, oxen, reindeer, and other animals long before the discovery of iron. Some of the world's natural history museums have bone skates believed to date back twenty centuries.

There are some indications of ice-skating in the mountains of Greece somewhere around 500 B.C. Whether or not this was true, since Greece is hardly a country noted for its ice, there is no question that skating is the only modern sport with a patron saint. In 1396 a young woman in Scheidam, Holland, was grievously injured skating; after living a long life devoted to others, she was canonized as St. Siedwi.

People have been ice-skating on the canals of Holland since the Middle Ages, and the sport appears to have reached England at least by the seventeenth century. An entry in the diary of Samuel

3

Pepys reads: "On December 1, 1662, on the canal in St. James Park, where first in my life did see people skiding in the skeetes, which is a very pretty art." Although there seems to have been a game vaguely resembling ice hockey back in the second century, the first concrete signs of anything like it as we know it today appear in sixteenth and seventeenth century paintings depicting bandy. Played on ice with sticks and a ball, bandy seems once to have been popular in Belgium, Holland, and Luxembourg. Northern Europeans apparently played bandy—or something similar—for about five centuries before ice hockey was modernized.

The one definitely known fact about modern ice hockey's background is that it was developed, codified, and popularized in Canada. There is some evidence that Canadian Iroquois Indians played a game like it centuries ago, but not until the nineteenth century was ice hockey given anything like the form it presently takes. So, for all practical purposes, Canada must be considered the true cradle of the game, which is quite rightly accepted as the Dominion's national sport.

There is no question that an ice game known as shinny was played in Canada as recently as the 1830's. Shinny is the only vestige of hockey's old days left in the English-speaking world. It is, in fact, to modern hockey what "scrub" is to modern baseball—a formless, higgeldy-piggeldy sort of game with indeterminate rules and no particular pattern. Youngsters play it to this day, using any ice surface that seems handy, with every lad for himself, and the devil take the hindmost. Shinny was probably the direct ancestor of ice hockey as we know it today.

Although no one knows definitely, it is said that the word "hockey" is an anglicized version of "hoquet," a French term for a shepherd's stick, which, with its curved end, resembles a hockey stick. This could also account for the term "field hockey," in which the stick bears a much closer resemblance to a shepherd's stick than does a modern ice hockey stick.

Although organized ice hockey is universally recognized as having been born in Canada, there is still great confusion over where the game was first played. Three widely separated Canadian cities, all in different provinces, have long demanded credit for establishment of the game's foundation. They are Montreal (Quebec), Kingston (Ontario), and Halifax (Nova Scotia). Kingston was so sure the credit belonged to it that it battled for—and won—recognition from the Canadian Amateur Hockey Association as the location of hockey's Hall of Fame, established in 1943. However, modern hockey people consider it a greater honor to win a place in the more prestigious hockey Hall of Fame in Toronto.

One Canadian hockey historian, making no attempt to claim his own country as the birthplace of the game, insisted that "the game of hockey dates back to the first time that men put runners on their feet to glide on the ice."

Another wrote the following reference to hockey in his diary, under the date of 1846–47: "Most of the soldier boys were quite at home on skates. They could cut the figure eight and other fancy figures, but shinny was their great delight. Groups would be placed at Shoal Tower and Point Frederick (Kingston) and 50 or more players on each side would be in the game."

The puck developed, as did many other

facets of modern ice hockey, at McGill University. The most widely accepted story is that one day in the late 1870's, a player, sick of chasing a rubber ball skidding hundreds of yards beyond the playing area, cut the ball into two flat surfaces. Just who first called this a "puck" is unknown, but there is little doubt that the player's ingenious invention cut down the speed of the missile so that when it moved flatly on the ice surface it went more slowly and stopped sooner. This has long since been offset by the ability of modern hockey players to lift the puck off the ice and scale it on a line like a baseball. By getting it into the air, professionals can shoot a puck anywhere from ninety to one hundred and twenty miles per hour. It is highly doubtful that, between the days of Her Majesty's Royal Canadian Rifles and the change from a round ball to a flat puck, anyone could shoot faster, but the change was undoubtedly one of the most significant developments in the game.

How the codification and modernization of hockey as we know it today evolved was discussed in a December, 1963, sports column in the Montreal *Gazette* by D. A. L. McDonald: "There were definite rules for the game, and the code was fashioned, in the main, after the rules of field hockey, the Field Hockey Association being formed in 1875." This would agree with the earlier reports that field hockey rules were first codified in that year. However, field hockey rules were at that time set up only in England. Although they might have quickly been brought across the Atlantic, it would not seem likely that ice hockey rules would be modeled after them in the very same year.

In summing up his report on the origins of hockey, Orlick made several claims favoring Montreal and McGill as the game's real birthplace. Some of these were (1) The first time the term "ice hockey" was used in a formal game was at the Victoria Skating Rink when two teams of McGill students met on March 3, 1875. (However, as noted above, reference to "shinny" was made as early as 1846.) (2) Since the game was on indoor ice, each team was limited to nine men. (3) In 1884, nine years later, this was reduced to seven. (The reduction to six men, three forwards, two defensemen, and a goal-keeper did not come until long after the turn of the century.) The forwards were always a center and two wingmen. The defensemen were called the "point" and the "cover-point." The seventh man was the "rover," whose job was exactly what the name implies—he wandered around the ice filling in wherever he was needed, sometimes playing forward, sometimes joining the point and cover-point on defense. Reference to the cover-point and the rover can be found in early twentieth century sports books for boys, such as the Frank Merriwell and the Rover Boys series. Although the term "cover-point" went out of style with "rover," defensemen are still referred to as "points."

DEVELOPMENT OF THE GAME

In the old shinny game, the playing object was a rubber ball. This was found unsuitable for indoor play, and a flat, circular piece of wood was first substituted, which was superseded by today's rubber puck. (This point *is* debatable, since the cutting down of the rubber ball to the puck—a disc-like object, flat on top and bottom and round in shape— probably occurred before hockey was played indoors. The purpose of transforming the ball to a disc—to keep it from going so far so fast—would have been automatically eliminated in the confines of an indoor rink.)

Regular goals, giving height and width and specifying a cloth net to form the back, were first used in the game of ice hockey in Montreal, and a goal-keeper (now formally known as the "goaler," but more familiarly known as the "goalie") was introduced into the game. (Goal-keepers did not exist in shinny.) Other innovations that differentiated ice hockey from shinny were the introduction of playing uniforms, definite playing positions and the names of those positions, hockey officials, and a set of codified rules for ice hockey (drawn up and put into use by McGill students).

The first known ice hockey association was organized in Montreal, and within a year of the first recorded game there were at least five organized ice hockey teams there.

The first known published account of an ice hockey game appeared in a December, 1877, issue of the McGill University *Gazette,* under the by-line of F. S. Van Wagner, a member of the McGill faculty. This reads in part: "Hockey— what is the thing like? How many of those coming from the country ever heard of it, to say nothing of playing it? Yet hockey, at McGill, is a recognized game, and the fact that the club of last year defeated the crack club of this city (Montreal) in the first match, and was beaten only after a severe struggle by one goal to nothing, should give students in general the idea that it is worth supporting."

The article goes on to introduce a new wrinkle—that the codification of ice hockey was modeled after football (soccer) rules. Two rules in common between the games were actually cited—that going offside was illegal and that charging from behind was permitted. Both terms (offside and charging) are in use to this day in hockey, although their interpretations are somewhat different from the original rules. These and other present-day rules will be discussed in detail in later chapters.

There is a reference in the 1877 *Gazette* report to checking, now a common ice hockey term. Checking is, in effect, guarding an opposing player, usually by trying to stop him from getting or holding possession of the puck. There are several types of checking, all of which will also be discussed later. An interesting feature of the *Gazette* study was an offhand remark of no particular significance then, but now extremely important to those interested in hockey's background: ". . . The pluck and skill of our team was wonderful, and in point of checking, *to use the lacrosse word,* they far excelled their opponents." Obviously, in those days, lacrosse, an ancient North American Indian game, was much better known to Canadian sports lovers than was hockey.

Kingston had the first truly organized ice hockey league, established in 1885. Up to then, even in Montreal, where the most hockey was played, clubs met each other indiscriminately—in answer to challenges or simply in games arranged on the spur of the moment. Kingston's league had four clubs—the Royal Military College, Queen's University, the Kingston Athletics, and the Kingston Hockey Club—and they played out a prearranged season's schedule.

One intriguing feature of ice hockey teams in the game's earliest days was that most of the goalies were not good skaters because they did not have to be. Some were so bad they needed help to reach their own nets, and, once there, had to steady themselves by leaning against the posts. The standard technique for a goal-tender was to stay in front of the net and wait for the puck to come to him, a pattern of defense that lasted many years. Since the net was only six feet wide and four feet high, anyone but a midget could cover all of it by lying prone across the front.

Skating became more and more important to goal-tenders as refinements were brought into ice hockey. Soon after the turn of the century, men who had trouble standing upright on skates were replaced by more skillful skaters because goal-tenders had to move around more. Even covering the six-foot area in front of the net required skaters who not only could glide smoothly back and forth, but also could scramble quickly enough to their feet from a prone position to defend against rebounds of the shots they had already stopped by dropping to their knees or lying across the ice. Even today, many goals are scored on rebounds. After the goalie has made one stop he must immediately be prepared to make another, with the puck usually coming from a different direction. Thus good skating became as essential to goalies as to everyone else on the ice.

By 1953, goalies were forced to become far better than average skaters. That was the year Jacques Plante, beginning his National Hockey League career with the Montreal Canadiens, added some innovations that have become standard procedure for professional goalies today. Perhaps the greatest student of goal-tending who ever lived, Plante was the first to wander more than a few feet from his net. It was he who devised the technique of trying to stop a score by skating out to meet an on-coming puck carrier, thus narrowing the angle of his shot. Plante, a fast, competent skater, sometimes carried the puck out as far as center ice, occasionally taking shots at the opposing goal. He was the cause of a rules change which now penalizes goalies from going beyond their blue lines (the limits of their own defensive zone). Plante, who among other things invented the protective mask that is now standard equipment for goalies, was also the first to skate around behind his net to pick up a loose puck and shoot it out to a teammate for a quicker start on an offensive play. Plante's techniques wiped out the hope of below-par skaters ever becoming effective goalies.

Hockey's Stanley Cup, one of the most famous of championship emblems, is the oldest trophy in professional sports. Generally described as a battered old mug whose intrinsic value probably was not much greater than the ten pounds ($48.67) Lord Stanley of Preston paid for it, it actually has become a pretty expensive item. Up to 1946, it *was* a battered old mug. Since then, however, alterations in its basic structure have cost over $6,000 and another $8,000 has been spent on engraving costs, dating back to 1912. Now a handsome trophy, an important segment of professional ice hockey's history is an integral part of it. Even its present intrinsic worth of about $15,000 is low, for its historical and sentimental value is incalculable.

The first team to win the Stanley Cup in 1893 was the Montreal Amateur Athletic Association. In the years immediately following, the cup was emblematic of the amateur hockey championship of Canada only because there were no recognized professional teams. In the late 1890's, monied citizens of various Canadian communities put up cash inducements to draw star players, but they were never considered professionals. Stanley Cup winners and the players on Stanley Cup competing teams retained their amateur standings up to and including 1911, although by then they were no more amateur in character than are the Davis Cup tennis players.

The Stanley Cup went professional in name as well as fact in 1912, when it was awarded to the winners of a series between the champions of the East and the West. From 1912 through 1925, competition for the cup remained coast-to-coast in character, with the eastern teams winning the trophy most often. But Pacific Coast League champions won several times in that period. One of them, the Seattle Metropolitans, was the first American team to take the trophy. For some years, Seattle and Portland had teams in the Pacific Coast League, but they went out of existence when the league was bought by Charles F. Adams, owner of the Boston Bruins, in 1926. Since then, the Stanley Cup has always gone to the National Hockey League champions.

HOCKEY TODAY

Through most of the first two decades of the twentieth century, amateur ice hockey, even when the Stanley Cup left its hands, enjoyed nearly as much prestige in Canada as did professional

hockey. The first seeds of professional hockey as we know it today were sown when the forerunner of the National Hockey League, the National Hockey Association, was formed. It has never been confirmed, but, according to rumors of the time, the NHL was set up in 1917 from the NHA as a ruse to get rid of an unwanted owner. Whatever the reason, the NHL dates back only to 1917. It gained strength and prestige after World War I, and was brought to the United States by Adams when he established the Bruins in Boston. Within two years there were more American than Canadian teams in the NHL, and such has been the case ever since.

In the meantime, amateur hockey, while thriving in Canada, had its ups and downs in the United States. Oddly enough, Baltimore, one of the first cities in the United States to have hockey, was among the first to abandon the game. Perhaps in the 1890's and the years immediately after the turn of the century, Baltimore's weather was colder than it is today. Undoubtedly, the only reason the city did not continue its interest in ice hockey was its shortage of ice. Too many winters failed to produce enough cold weather lasting long enough to form natural outdoor ice for a reliable period of time.

Even with indoor arenas and artificial ice, the game of ice hockey was never universally popular in the United States until recently. Only Boston, New York, Detroit, and Chicago had NHL teams for years. Although minor leagues were in existence and got by financially, they could not engender the general enthusiasm that major-league clubs did. Thus, hockey was a spot sport in this country, popular only in the four big-league cities and in northern and mountain locales such as Minnesota and Colorado, where natural ice was plentiful enough for young players to practice with reasonable consistency.

Weather was also responsible for the shortage of American-born big-league hockey players. Only a handful were ever good enough to make it in the NHL, and most of these were from Minnesota. To this day, hockey's big leagues have an overwhelming majority of Canadian-born players who grew up in cold climates where they could play outdoors six or seven months a year. American youngsters, on the other hand, confined their informal sports to baseball, football, and basketball while they were growing up.

The situation changed somewhat after World War II, when so-called Peewee hockey leagues (similar to Little League baseball) were formed in some northern sections of the United States. Peewee hockey has since become so popular that kids play it in almost every city and town with an indoor rink and artificial ice. Yet hockey never really caught on as a childhood game here until 1967 when the NHL expanded to twelve teams. All six of the new clubs—Los Angeles, Minnesota, Oakland, Philadelphia, Pittsburgh, and St. Louis—are in the United States. Three years later two more teams, in Vancouver and Buffalo, New York, expanded the league to fourteen teams, eleven in the United States and three in Canada. A second New York team, the Islanders, and a new club in Atlanta were added in 1972, and there is a possibility of still more expansion in the future.

In the meantime, a rival league to the NHL, called the World Hockey Association, began operating with twelve teams in the 1972–73 season. Owners in this circuit raided the NHL, enticing many of its players with huge financial bait. The WHA, which has some teams in direct competition with NHL clubs in established cities and some teams in new cities, may eventually become strong enough to provide a genuine challenge to the NHL for the Stanley Cup.

Another new development was the showing of a Russian hockey team in a series against Team Canada, made up of selected NHL stars. Instead of winning easily, as they expected, the Canadians barely beat the Russians (by winning four of eight games). The Russians won three and one game was tied. There is little question that they, too, eventually may challenge for the international cup.

New teams in an old league, an entire new league, competition from the Soviet Union and other countries, along with nation-wide television in the United States and Canada have made ice hockey the fastest growing sport in the western hemisphere and one of the fastest growing sports in the world. In the United States it now ranks with baseball, football, and basketball in popularity. Once confined to Canada, then the United States, hockey is now truly international in scope. The game is played all over the world, and since 1920 has been a regular part of the world Olympic games, held every four years. Although the professional teams are still dominated by Canadian-born players, and Canadian amateur teams won every Olympic championship between 1920 and 1932, England was the 1936 winner, and since the end of World War II, European teams have won more and more Olympic and world championships.

There is no question that the professional leagues will see greater numbers of American players as the years go on.

Wherever big-league hockey is played in the United States, potential big-league players are growing up, soon to be ready to take their places as established professionals. Some are in the minor leagues now and may soon move into the top ranks of the game.

Hockey, spawned centuries ago in Europe, codified in Canada, and perfected there and in the United States, is rapidly becoming one of the world's most popular sports.

HOCKEY STARS

Although hockey had several outstanding stars in its early years, the man who first did more than anyone else to popularize the game in American NHL cities was Eddie Shore, who played thirteen years for the Boston Bruins, starting in 1927, and an additional season for the New York Americans before his retirement. Shore, a tough, spectacular, ruthless, hard-hitting skater and an amazing stick-handler, was the first high-scoring defenseman. Only Bobby Orr, the current Bruins star and the only defenseman ever to lead the NHL in scoring, has been considered his superior by experts who have seen both men play. Professional hockey has several immortal names that predate Shore. One is Howie Morenz, a great Montreal Canadien forward who died prematurely after he was traded to the Chicago Black Hawks. Another is Georges Vezina, an outstanding goalie who also died prematurely while still playing in the league. It is possible that the lustre of some of these figures was brightened by their early deaths, but all of Shore's was

earned on the ice. Other great stars of past and present had to be rated either as skaters or goalies. The best defensive goalie wins a trophy named for Vezina. The man who has won it most often is Glenn Hall, who has played for Detroit, Chicago, and St. Louis in a brilliant career.

The pressures of transcontinental travel, increased schedules, larger playing squads, and the continually accelerating speed of a game that was one of the world's fastest to begin with, has made goal-tending an impossible chore for one man. Although the Vezina Cup was still awarded to one man—Ken Dryden of the Montreal Canadiens—in the 1972–1973 season, hockey experts feel that the day is near, if it has not arrived already, when the trophy will have to be divided between two goalies. No NHL team depends completely on one, and all NHL teams now dress two for every game.

Many teams either alternate their goalies or play them only a few games at a time. It was only a short time ago that, with only one goalie in uniform, the game had to be held up if he got hurt. On the rare occasions when his injury was serious enough to keep him out of action for the rest of the game, a spare goalie would have to be rushed into uniform.

Prior to the days when spare goalies were carried for just such emergencies, finding a spare goalie to replace an injured one was a major job on all teams. Sometimes a former goalie long since retired had to be called back into action. Lester Patrick once filled in at goal while in his late forties. Although he had not played in an NHL game for over ten years, he shut out the opposition, then hung up his pads for good.

There was a time when a spare goalie had to be recruited from the opposing team, a system that was put into effect only as a last resort. Spare goalies have been known to shut out their own teammates, for the code of every goalie is, as it was then, to do the best job he could, even if it cost his own team a game. Indeed, the ties that bind goalies together were once as close as the ties that bound teammates together. It takes a strong, heroic character to stand in front of a hockey net and spend pressure-packed hours being shot at by pucks traveling upwards of 100 miles an hour. This is why the brotherhood of professional goalies is a mutual admiration society. Hockey goalies have more empathy with each other than men playing the same position have in any other sport.

One of the greatest skaters who ever lived, and certainly the most colorful, was Maurice Richard of the Canadiens. A fiery forward who made the first or second NHL All-Star teams practically every year for a decade and a half, he was a flashy, fearless, fantastically fast and clever skater who dominated the game through the 1940's and 1950's. After his retirement, the league's outstanding skater who, like Hall, is still active as these lines are written, was for years considered to be Bobby Hull of the Chicago Black Hawks. His 1972 defection to the WHA gave the new league its first big boost.

Modern-day hockey experts feel that before he is through, Bobby Orr of the Boston Bruins will prove to be greater than any of his predecessors. A defenseman who can shoot from both sides with equal facility, Orr can do anything required of a professional player. He is a defenseman only because the Bruins wanted him to be one, since they saw in him the second coming of Eddie Shore. But Orr is, in effect, a fourth forward whenever he is on the ice, which is an enormous part of the time. He is faster than Shore, has the most murderous shot the league has ever known, and may be the greatest skater in hockey history. During recent seasons, he became the seventh NHL defenseman to win the Hart Memorial Trophy as the league's most valuable player. Barring injury, he is likely to win it many more times before he ends a career begun as spectacularly as any in the game.

Professional hockey is now the fastest and one of the most bruising contact sports in the world. Although professional football players pride themselves on their toughness and their emphasis on hitting each other as hard as humanly possible, even they lack the durability and ferocity of hockey players. The professionals have considered nothing short of broken bones an excuse for leaving the scene of action. Hockey players have taken as many as twenty-five stitches to sew up cuts sustained in one period and returned to action in another period of the same game. Yet, although the game is highly dangerous because of the very nature of its action, the NHL has had only one fatality in more than half a century, and that may not have been due to the game itself. In 1968, Bill Masterson of the Minnesota North Stars fractured his skull in a fall on the ice and died that night. It was later determined, however, that Masterson had a heart weakness that was aggravated by his hockey participation. Whether it was his heart or the skull fracture that killed him will probably never be known.

The only other NHL players who ever flirted with death in hockey were Ace Bailey of Toronto and Teddy Green of

Boston, both of whom suffered serious skull fractures. Bailey pulled through but never played again. Green, at death's door for a week after being hit in an exhibition game at Ottawa, not only pulled through but made one of the most remarkable comebacks in sports history. Within a year after his injury, he was back with the Bruins, and enjoying an outstanding season in the 1970–71 campaign. He, too, joined the WHA in 1972.

THE MAKINGS OF A
PROFESSIONAL PLAYER

Every sport has its fundamentals, and ice hockey is no exception. They may be developed as early as so-called "Squirt" hockey, from age levels of six to ten. Some fundamentals come naturally, some must be demonstrated to an exact degree, and some must be taught. None can be learned by everyone. There are certain people who, because of their physical build, lack of coordination, grace, motivation, or interest, will never excel in any sport.

Sports at any age are fun, and ice hockey is truly a fun sport. Naturally as a player advances from a boyhood interest in it to a point where he has high school, junior, or college possibilities, he will run into certain pressures, but pressure is part of competitive sports. There is a point where fun, while not superseded, lessens in importance and bows to pressure. Many hockey players find pressure itself fun—the more at stake, the more they enjoy it. A team fighting for a championship at any level is almost always made up of boys who are fundamentally enjoying themselves.

But the boy who becomes an accomplished hockey player does not reach this level just because he is looking for fun. It takes work—hard, steady, dedicated effort. Hockey is a complicated game; regardless of the degree of his natural ability, a young hockey player has much to learn. The distance between the neighborhood rink and a championship game depends on how much and how well he develops his skills during his growing-up years.

Nobody becomes a star overnight; nobody becomes a star without proper instruction; and nobody becomes a star by accident. From his earliest days of shinny and street hockey, a young player must think in terms of development. The transformation from beginner to star is as dramatic as the transformation from child to adult.

Although an established sport in Canada for more than a century, hockey is in its infancy elsewhere. In the United States, for example, only very few segments of the country—the Northeast, Michigan, Minnesota, and Colorado, where the weather is consistently cold enough for outdoor hockey—had any sort of teaching programs until recent years.

This was partly because the National Hockey League was small—until its expansion in 1962 it had but six teams, two in Canada and four in the United States—and partly because the game went undiscovered for years in many parts of the country. There is a definite correlation between major-league hockey and the development of popular interest in the sport.

Of the four original American cities in the NHL, three were good hockey areas for years—Boston, New York, and Detroit. The fourth, Chicago, lagged behind.

Although interest in the Black Hawks seldom flagged, there were comparatively few young aspirants for organized, and possibly professional, participation. In the eyes of most people, even in American cities, hockey was meant to be watched, not played.

The situation changed rapidly after a slow but perceptible start in the years immediately following World War II. The big acceleration came with the first NHL expansion. New interest was kindled in many American cities, which is why ice hockey is now the fastest growing sport in the United States.

But the growth has barely begun. Amateur programs at all age levels, beginning as young as six, will produce more and more fine American hockey players in future years. In the meantime, a good job of setting up these programs is essential.

Cold weather is not a prerequisite for interest in hockey development. The fact that California is now one of the hotbeds of the sport is concrete proof of that. Even before major-league hockey reached California, hockey rinks were beginning to spring up there. It now is almost certain that future years will find many professionals who learned their hockey in a state where the only natural ice is in the mountains.

Until recently, young American boys with hockey talent went to Canada for advanced training. The Canadian system of teaching the game is excellent. For the United States to copy at least parts of the system is perfectly natural and makes eminently good sense.

The United States' hockey system is modeled after the Canadian system in the earlier stages. The youngest age group are the Squirts, from six to ten. Next come the Peewees, from ten to twelve, fol-

lowed by the Bantams, from twelve to fourteen, and the Midgets, at fifteen. It is at the Midget stage that a deviation occurs, for the American system puts a heavy emphasis on high school hockey and the Canadian system does not.

In Canada, the sixteen-year-old group is the Juveniles, with the Juniors ranging from seventeen to twenty. Except for the older Juniors, this overlaps the normal American high school age group.

Junior hockey is very important in Canada. Divided into categories such as Junior A and Junior B, it is the final step before moving into professional hockey. Junior teams and leagues are often affiliated with professional teams. Until the professional teams installed a hockey draft system, every major-league hockey team had, among others, at least one Junior club in each Canadian province. Most of its members were committed to the professional club that sponsored it.

In the United States, hockey players of high school age play high school hockey, which is virtually nonexistent in Canada. Good young hockey players attend high schools there, but most play for local amateur teams in accordance with their age brackets. Many American high schools are just beginning to build hockey programs; to replace them in favor of Junior programs hardly seems logical.

Until recent years, the only American high schools with hockey programs were those in or near communities where hockey was played at the college level. As college hockey expanded, high school hockey expanded with it, a process that is still going on. In the early 1940's there were perhaps twenty colleges in the whole country that supported varsity hockey programs. By the early seventies there were over 100, with many colleges taking up the sport every year.

The domination of high school hockey in the United States thus becomes increasingly stronger. This means that the Midgets, at fifteen, close out the Canadian-type hockey development program in the United States. Whether this is good or bad depends upon one's point of view.

For the better hockey player who looks forward to college before getting involved professionally—if he is potential professional material—this is probably good. At the high school and college levels, he gets excellent instruction in the United States. The majority of American high school and college coaches know the game well and are fine professional teachers.

However, the American system tends to cut down hockey participation on the part of boys who play the game for fun. Once they have gone through the Midget class, they have nowhere to go if they lack the ability to make it in high school. The high schools can handle only a limited number of boys, leaving the vast majority of interested youths stranded without possibilities of further hockey play.

Fortunately, American hockey enthusiasts are well aware of the problem, with the result that more and more cities are building rinks for public use. Junior hockey has just been introduced in two or three cities in the United States and probably will become an important part of the American program, as it is in Canada, thus opening new horizons to all young hockey players in this country.

The ideal would be to have high school *and* Junior hockey. Both Canada and the United States are slowly moving in that direction. Some Canadian high schools are beginning to develop hockey

programs to give boys unable to break into organized amateur ranks a chance to play regularly. In the United States, the amateur system for younger boys is going forward. The result may be an interesting contrast between the two countries. Good young Canadian players will continue to develop in Juvenile and Junior circles, as well as in the high schools. Good young American players will continue to develop in high schools and colleges, as well as in organized amateur circles.

There is room everywhere for both high school and amateur hockey programs. In the United States, many players in younger age groups are involved in amateur hockey at one level or another below high school. The most fully developed programs are in the communities that have fostered hockey the longest. In other communities, the big problem is how and where to start.

Often the answer lies with the high school coach. He can and should be the leader and organizing sponsor of amateur hockey at all levels. As a professional coach, his primary job is to coach his high school team. However, he can help himself, his team, and his community if he takes the initiative in building good programs of development for young people from the Squirt class onward.

It does not matter whether he coaches in a small town or a big city. If he is in a small town with only one high school, his job will be easier and the results more obvious. In a large city, a program can be built that will foster hockey, help dedicated, unpaid coaches teach the game properly, and give both junior high and high schools rich sources from which to draw new talent.

In the natural course of events, those

boys most interested in hockey will go to one of the schools that have good hockey programs. The coaches who supervise the beginning and developmental stages of youth hockey programs will get their share of boys when they reach high school age. Those who go elsewhere will take with them years of experience gained from participation in the program as youngsters.

In the United States the question of where to play was once a serious problem, but this, too, is gradually being solved. Today, most northern and western cities have several hockey rinks and many smaller towns have at least one or two. This is true even in some southern communities that never had outdoor hockey. Their interest has increased with the national interest in the sport.

Television, which brings top-quality hockey into living rooms all over America, has accelerated the interest in, and the growth of, the game. Even in areas where there is no professional hockey, this tremendously fast and exciting sport has begun to catch on. More and more youngsters want hockey and are trying to play it in their formative years, as they do baseball, football, and basketball, the three major spectator sports.

More and more boys are asking for and getting hockey sticks as gifts from parents, relatives, or friends. Many young boys are playing street hockey, an off-season, fun game that helps develop stick-handling. Even major-league stars can remember their street hockey days, for many mature hockey players once turned to street hockey in the absence of ice.

To play street hockey, only sticks and a puck are necessary. With this equipment, it is surprising how much young boys can learn about stick-handling, es-

pecially if they have had a little formal training. Street hockey also needs goalies; goals can easily be made or designated by cones or other types of uprights.

Street hockey is probably the simplest form of hockey, but it can be a beginning, just as other sports have their simple interpretations for youths without formal facilities or refinements. Any type of hockey is good for young boys who love the game once they have been exposed to it.

Formal hockey is played in rinks, with dimensions that allow some variations in size. Without a rink, a budding young hockey player has no way of knowing how to play when definite dimensions (boards) are imposed. A boy who has spent too many years playing hockey in open areas has to learn the game all over again when he is first introduced to rink hockey. Unused to its confines, he is almost as much in need of special instruction as a beginner, except that he does know how to skate.

The dedicated high school coach will try not to let young hockey aspirants go too long without instruction. This is where he can be of as much value as he is within the confines of his own school, for he can be the catalyst in building up hockey in a community or a section of a city.

One of the coach's first jobs is to find dedicated men to assist in starting youth leagues and supervise the teams when they are established. The primary place to find the dedicated teachers of the young are within the families of the boys who are trying to play the game or in the schools or colleges where hockey is being played.

Squirt, Peewee, Bantam, and Midget leagues are not hard to start if ice is available. The job facing the leader is teaching young fathers, older brothers, or dedicated men who like working with boys the fundamentals of the game. Potential teachers, all amateurs who are interested in building and fostering interest among children and early teenagers, should be the key to full programs of amateur hockey.

The buildup of leagues may be similar to the buildup of baseball's Little Leagues. The difference, of course, is that baseball has been established in the United States for many years, whereas hockey is new. The Squirt coaches may be starting from scratch. Many have never played hockey and need instruction. Not knowing too much about the game, they will learn from reading about fundamentals and watching games what they can do, how much they can expect from boys in the age brackets they will serve, and how they can prevent young boys from developing bad habits that must later be broken if they are to become good hockey players.

Young amateur coaches with some hockey experience behind them are ahead of inexperienced coaches. In developing a youth hockey program, it does not much matter whether the budding teacher knows the game or not. He can learn the fundamentals quickly and, having done that, pass them along to his charges.

Where does he find these charges? In the rinks. Any community that has hockey rinks—and there are more and more of these every year—will have young boys skating on them. And any young boy who can skate is likely to have a hockey stick. Put a boy on skates and give him a stick, and you have a potential hockey player of possible high quality. This, of course, depends on his

growing dedication to the game, his natural ability, his physical build, and the intensity of his desire. In the very early stages—the Squirt hockey leagues—the only factor is that the boy must like hockey and want to play it.

Every boy is by nature an imitator of those whom he most admires. Since boys have become exposed to hockey, many already have their idols among the professionals or, perhaps, even among players in college or high school. A boy with an idol will try to do as his idol does. If his idol is a hockey player, then it is best for the boy that he be taught the game properly instead of trying to learn it on his own. This is why supervision is so important. Granted, a new coach of limited knowledge can only scratch the surface in learning hockey fundamentals for teaching purposes, but anyone of reasonable intelligence *can* learn enough to know the basic differences between right and wrong techniques. With no more knowledge even than that, he can help correct basic mistakes.

After the establishment of a hockey program, the school coach should follow it up by checking personally on its progress. From time to time, he should watch young players in action. Having seen them, he can then call attention to elementary errors not previously noted by the volunteer coach. This does not have to be carried to the extreme of looking for refinements in the earliest years of a young player's life. These boys will not have developed to the point where refinements are necessary. That will come at more advanced age groups. The Squirts, particularly, are not expected to learn those things a finished hockey player knows. Playing the game for fun, they will require only a minimum of instruction.

The higher they go in age class, the more precise their coaching. Peewees and Bantams should know more than Squirts, and Midgets will be pretty well-defined as to the quality of hockey they might play, although a great deal of this progression depends on the individual. Bobby Orr, for example, was an outstanding hockey player at age twelve, the oldest year of Peewee hockey.

Since Orrs are few and far between and even players good enough for advanced hockey are in the minority, it should always be borne in mind that the game is the thing and the quality of the player incidental to the whole picture. The point is to permit as many boys as possible to play. If a few star, so much the better. But there must be room for everyone who wants to play.

Thus the day will come in this country, as it has in Canada, when men can play hockey for fun, just as men play other popular sports for fun. Not everyone can play pro football but any healthy person who likes it can play tag football. Not everyone can play pro baseball, but any healthy person who likes it can play softball. Not everyone can play top-quality hockey, but there is no reason why any healthy person who likes it cannot play the game as a recreational activity.

This is not to minimize the possibilities of developing good players, or even players of professional stature. The National Hockey League, which rarely had more than one or two top Americans at a time, had at least half a dozen by the opening of the 1972–73 season, with more on their way up through minor league and Canadian Junior A hockey circles. And the World Hockey Association had a score or more of Americans on their teams.

In California, which had no hockey at all until after World War II, the game has grown faster than in any other state in the Union. With two NHL teams in Oakland and Los Angeles and a WHA team in Los Angeles, the Golden State is now a real hockey center. California sent a Midget team all the way to New England for a tournament, and several eastern college teams have varsity players who learned their hockey in California, and there will be more as time goes on. The hockey traffic is going in both directions. Several coaches went to California from the northeastern part of the United States, the cradle of hockey in this country. Even some Canadian hockey men have settled in California, where they, and now their sons, are helping to popularize the game.

Until a few years ago, almost every professional player went through the Canadian ranks, jumping to the pros from Junior A hockey. This included all but a handful of the Americans who have ever played major-league hockey.

Now that trend is turning. A good many Canadian and American boys are playing hockey in American colleges and may go on to professional ranks after receiving their degrees. The future will undoubtedly bring more and more young men like Ken Dryden into hockey's major-league circles. Dryden, a Canadian, was a great college goalie at Cornell, who led his team to one American intercollegiate hockey championship and brought it close two other times during his three years of varsity hockey eligibility. Less than a year after receiving his Cornell degree, Dryden led the Montreal Canadiens to the 1971 Stanley Cup and was voted the outstanding man in the play-offs.

There are other student-athletes attending college in the United States. More and more, like Dryden, will reach the National Hockey League. Each new man will give an additional boost to the American college system, which has produced over 200 professional players since 1963. In 1973 alone, the NHL drafted over sixty players from the collegiate ranks.

In the meantime, with new amateur leagues springing up from the Squirt level on, all over the United States, hockey is now a major spectator sport, rapidly attaining a place for itself alongside baseball, football, and basketball in that respect. With its great growth, there is a real need for educational books on hockey. This one is designed to help players, coaches, and fans in developing an appreciation of the fastest game on the North American sporting scene.

II

Individual Play

2
Skating

Skating is to hockey what throwing is to baseball, what running is to football, what shooting is to basketball. It is without question hockey's most important fundamental. Anyone who can skate well is mastering the first step toward excelling in hockey.

Hockey followers are so well-indoctrinated into seeing players on skates that they are inclined to overlook what skilled skaters they are watching. The higher the level of play, the better the skater. Even in the very youngest classification, the Squirt class, the best players are almost always the best skaters.

Although not really a natural function like walking, skating comes easiest to those who grow up near ice. Professional hockey players had to be taught certain refinements, but most learned to skate by themselves. Bobby Orr of the Boston Bruins, for example, cannot remember when he first learned to skate. He is universally recognized as the best player in the National Hockey League, but what many do not realize is that he is probably the best skater as well. It is

primarily this which makes him such an outstanding hockey player.

How does one become a good enough skater to progress up the hockey ladder? Where does he start? If he has hockey promise, how does he develop his skills? More and more fathers and young sons have asked these questions with the passing of the years. Because hockey is one of the world's fastest growing sports (over a dozen North American, European, and Asian countries entered teams in the 1972 winter Olympics), more and more fathers and young sons will ask the same questions in future years.

There are sound reasons why hockey requires unusual skating skill. Depending upon how much ice time he puts in during a game, a hockey player will skate about three miles—forward and backward. If nothing else, this spotlights the need for stamina. It takes more of that, to say nothing of strength and skill, to skate three miles during a hockey game than, say, to race three miles on skates on a measured track. A racer has no one in his way. He is, in effect, battling only the clock. Any contact that occurs in speed racing is accidental—in fact, it would call for disciplinary action against the responsible contestant. Hockey, on the other hand, is a contact sport. It has penalties for breaking set rules, but most legal checks (although not all) require contact. Every hockey player, therefore, always has someone in his way, someone he must avoid, get around, push past, or, if he is on the defensive, stop—usually by sheer physical force.

This is why *his* three miles or so are so much harder than a speed racer's. Unlike the speed skater, he must at all times be prepared for a quick stop, a sudden turn, a lightning-fast change of direction. Even if he shows great promise

Figure 2-1. *Side view of stance, left-hand shot. Note head up (showing good balance) and left arm away from body.*

in executing these movements, he almost always needs instruction of some kind somewhere between childhood and maturity. And never may he forget the need for constant practice, a need that will always be present, even if he reaches the eminence of the professional leagues.

At the outset, then, what must he do? To find some of the answers, it is first necessary to study the equipment—the skates.

SKATES AND THEIR CARE

Hockey is a precise game. The skates must always be right—not for anyone but for each individual skater. Most good hockey players are aware of this, but some are not. The proper skates worn in the proper way can make an aspiring young player (just as improper skates worn improperly can break him). It is better to get inexpensive skates that fit properly than expensive ones that do not.

If the ankles are to be strong and steady, the skates must fit well. A player veers over on his ankles—a common fault among experienced skaters as well as novices—usually only when the skates are too large or too loosely laced. It makes no more sense to buy skates without first trying them on than to buy shoes. Before buying skates, one should put them on, lace them up, and walk around on them. There must be no slipping in the heel. A good boot has thick leather support around the ankles. The blade should be of good steel. The rocker of the blade—the center part—should not be too long; its size should be limited to the needs of the skater. The skates

Figure 2-2. *Side view of stance, right-hand shot. Note head position for split vision, bent knees, and right hand away from body.*

should be firmly laced; when pulled snug the eyelets should be at least an inch and a half apart (see Figure 2-3).

Today's hockey players generally do not wear high boots. Their equipment is much better and the low boot is fine. The professional players' skates are very expensive—upwards of ~~ninety dollars a~~ $200.00 ~~pair~~—but for a young player, it makes no sense to spend that much money. Many manufacturers make good skates at lower prices, and the cost of the skates, even the quality, is not nearly as important as the size. If the skates fit, one should wear them. Again, it is better to

have an inexpensive good fit than an expensive poor one.

Professional players have their skates sharpened in accordance with the position they play. Just how sharp or dull skates should be is up to the individual. Generally, the forwards' skates are sharpest, the defensemen's less, and the goalies' least of all. Everyone dulls his skates some after having them sharpened, because if they are too sharp they have a tendency to stick to the ice and the skater does not have enough freedom of stride. If skates are too sharp the user will have trouble, especially in turning fast. All skaters, even at the college, high

Figure 2-3. *Lacing. Note the proper spread between eyelets (not too close together) and the absorbent cotton at top of boots to cushion pressure on ligaments.*

school, or Junior level, need this touch of dullness. Anyone reaching a rink early enough before a hockey game will see the skaters, on first coming out to the ice, rub the blades of their skates on their sticks, or skate over to the side where they can rub their skates on wood to dull them. This cuts the edges a little and keeps the blades from sticking. Of course, really dull skates must be sharpened. The forwards need the sharpness to skate faster and, after going through their own little dulling process, to maneuver more easily. Dull skates cause slipping and, to a skater who must move fast, this means losing precious seconds. The forward, therefore, dulls his skates the least, but he must dull them some.

A defenseman's skates are sharpened flatter than a forward's, because defensemen need more of the blade on the ice since they must have a more solid foundation underneath. When they bodycheck a man, their feet must be planted pretty firmly; they are often practically standing still when they hit the puck carrier bearing down on them. Defensemen normally do not have to turn as sharply as forwards do. Where a forward will have his skates rockered so that they may have only two or three inches of blade on the ice, a defenseman may need four inches or so. Under normal conditions, a defenseman's skates do not need to be as sharp as a forward's.

The dullest skates of all are the goalie's. Specialists in so many other ways, goalies dislike having their skates sharpened too often because they do a lot of sliding from post to post as they stand in front of the nets. If their skates are too sharp they cannot slide. Goalies spend more time dulling their skates than other players.

SKATING TECHNIQUES

There are three basic types of skating skills. One is straight power, or forward skating. The second is agility skating—mobility, proficiency in changing direction without losing balance, and proper maneuverability when turning. The third is backward skating, which is often overlooked by young coaches. As hockey is played today, a man must be equally adept at skating backward as well as forward.

Forward Skating

For the front start, the skates should be shoulder-width apart, the knees flat, and the body bent forward over the skate (see Figure 2-4). The skate is bent slightly inward with a strong leg drive. To start, use short, quick strides with the knee of the front leg well-bent. Forward skating begins with little or no slide, with the thrust coming from the toe of the skate. Start in the basic position—feet apart, knees flat, body upright. To start quickly, lean in the direction of the start. With the thrust from the ball of the skate, acceleration is obtained in five or six short strides.

Lengthen the stride after the start, keep the body leaning forward, and use good long strides to maintain easy body rhythm. The upper part of the body, well-over the front leg, should be at about a forty-five-degree angle. The rear leg should push to the full extent down to the toe of the skate. The rhythm of the arm drive and the leg drive will contribute to both speed and agility. At full

Figure 2-4. *Skating—initial drive forward. Note use of inside edge of right skate and position of left skate (pointing forward) prior to contact with ice. Note also looseness of arms.*

would belong to a player with his chest held high, his stomach drawn in, his hips free and unrestricted, his shoulders relaxed, and his knees somewhat bent. The body would have a natural tendency to lean ahead of the hips, but not so far as to throw the skater off-balance. The head, relaxed and not straining forward, should be up so the player can see what is going on around him: where his teammates are, if they are forming a play pattern, and where the opposition is. If he looks down at all, it should be only for a fraction of a second to make sure he has control of the puck. A good hockey player will rarely have to look down because he develops a "feel" for the puck—in other words, he knows

forward power, the long, graceful stride and the full drive of the rear leg will be noted (see Figure 2-5).

Once under way, a minimum of physical effort is required to keep going at top speed. Many players, failing to realize this, work too hard and are soon exhausted. Power skating is actually skating from the hips down. The player who skates from the legs or knees will tire faster than the one who uses his hips. Since hockey requires so much stamina and strength, it is essential that the player use his body properly to get the most out of the physical equipment with which nature has provided him.

The posture of a good skating habit

Figure 2-5. *Skating forward, driving off the inside edge of left skate. Arms and elbows are loose and away from body.*

where it is without actually having to look at it.

One possible pitfall is a tendency to use a forward *body* motion. In some cases a boy will lean way over when skating. This cuts off his wind and tends to tire him quickly. The knee position should be flexible and relaxed. The only time the leg is straight is when it is used on the thrust that drives the skater from a stationary position. The flexible knee, which should be ahead of the feet, gives balance.

The weight is always on the forward foot, but when the leg drives on, the thrust of the weight shifts to the other foot. The foot action has the leg going to the outside in a forty-degree angle. The point where the weight changes from one foot to the other comes when the initial thrust is in a downward drive.

The arm and shoulder action is diametrically opposite from that of a runner, and its importance is more than people realize. The arm and shoulder should move with the leg, not, as with a runner, opposite from the leg. For example, when a runner sets down his right foot, he swings his left arm. When a hockey player sets down his right foot, he should swing his right arm. If he moves arms and shoulders as a runner does, he loses a great deal of speed and hampers his rhythm. This is why a skater might often be seen working hard on the ice but lacking in speed and drive. Not properly synchronizing hips, shoulders, arms, and legs, he is not getting the maximum speed and power out of his skating technique.

Agility Skating

Some of the most important jobs for a hockey player are stops, turns, and quick changes of direction. The two-foot stop (Figure 2-6) is the quickest and most effective. In making it, the knees are bent and the feet are staggered and close together. The body leans back and pressure is applied with the toes. The skater is poised and properly balanced so that he is ready to move in any direction (see Figure 2-7).

There is also the front-foot stop (Figure 2-8) and the rear-foot stop (Figure 2-9). The front-foot stop has the weight on the toes of the front skate. The feet are apart, the knees flexed. In the rear-foot stop, the weight is on the back skate and there is more leanage on the body. Both front- and back-foot stops are acceptable when, because split seconds are of the essence, there is no time

Figure 2-6.   *Stopping using both feet. Note the balance.*

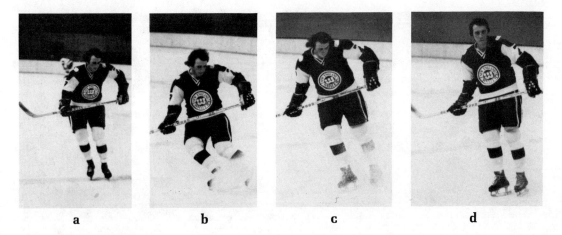

a   b   c   d

Figure 2-7.   *Skating and stopping series. (a) Note parallel blades. (b) In the stop: arms are relaxed and away from the body; balanced use of skate edges. (c) Recovery: prior to turn, knees have slightly straightened. (d) Finishing off: in motion to the right.*

for an alternative. Whenever possible, however, the two-foot stop is recommended.

Turns should be a common ability for all good hockey players. Sharp turns are very useful when perfectly mastered, but executing proper turns takes endless practice and some good hockey players never learn the technique. In a sharp turn, the inside skate precedes the outside skate, with the angle of the body toward the inside of the circle. The pressure is applied on the back of the blade, and the weight of the body is forward to permit fast emergence from the turn.

To prevent loss of speed the crossover turn is recommended. This is a very graceful thing to watch when it is properly executed. As the player makes his turn, the outside leg continuously crosses over the inside leg, with the pressure applied to the back of the blade. Eventually, when he becomes proficient, a player should learn to do the crossover turn by running on the toes of his skates in the interest of speed.

Backward Skating

There is a tendency on the part of some young coaches to forget that everyone on the ice, including the goalie, must know how to skate backward. The

a   b

Figure 2-8.   *Stopping—single front-foot series. (a) Good balance with knees bent and weight on front leg. (b) Use of inside edge of front skate to stop, with right toe pointing in direction of next move.*

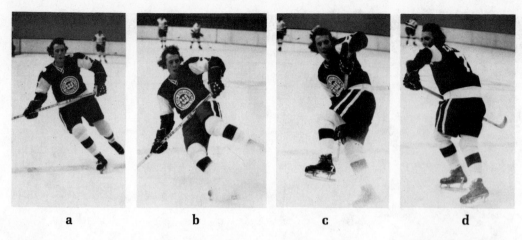

    a   **b**   **c**   **d**

Figure 2-9. *Single rear-foot stop. (a) Arms out, weight on rear foot outside edge. (b) Arms out, hands spread, weight nearer toe of contact foot. (c) Front foot brought around. (d) Good balance with left leg pointing to next skating direction.*

goalie's technique is peculiar to him-self and will be discussed later. Con-trary to the apparent belief of some in-experienced coaches, who seem to think that only defensemen must learn to skate backward, *everyone* should be able.

The defenseman is responsible for protecting the goalie and stopping the charge of an oncoming puck carrier. With the puck carrier heading toward him, the defenseman must back-pedal in order to hit at the proper angle and to keep the opposing forward from fak-ing him out of position or skating around him.

All hockey players, including forwards, must be expert in skating backward be-cause there are frequent occasions when it is necessary. In execution, backward skating begins by starting in a sitting position with the knee bent and the body leaning slightly forward. The feet are shoulder-width apart. Place the weight on the pushing foot and thrust off. (See Figures 2-10 through 2-13.)

Backward crossovers are necessary for shadowing or checking an opposing player. The movement consists of cross-ing the leg while skating backward. In backward crossovers, the weight of the body should be maintained on the front of the blade, with the power coming from the push of each lower leg. The body is relatively straight and the knees slightly bent. The weight is transferred from one knee to the other, giving the impression of small arcs. The stick is always in front to be sure the skater is ready to forecheck.

In certain cases, depending upon the situation, both forward and backward crossovers precede rotation of the legs, allowing a more rapid change of direc-tion for the skater. Before any turn, the skates should be fairly close together, the strides short and rapid. While lean-ing to pivot, the body should be lowered by bending the knees. Once the basic technique is learned, an attempt should be made to turn faster.

a   b   c

Figure 2-10.   *Skating backward series. Stick in front, legs apart, knees bent, head up, arms away from body, blades parallel.*

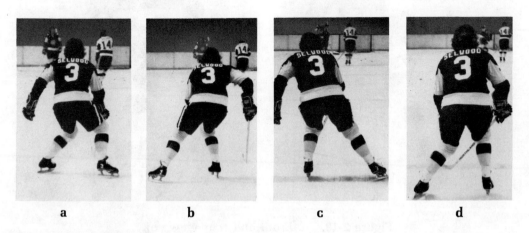

a   b   c   d

Figure 2-11.   *Rear view of skating backward series. Exaggerated bending of knees, shifting weight, and drive from inside edges keeping blades parallel.*

a   b   c   d

Figure 2-12.   *Front view of skating backward series. Arms away from body, elbow on stick hand side bent, head up.*

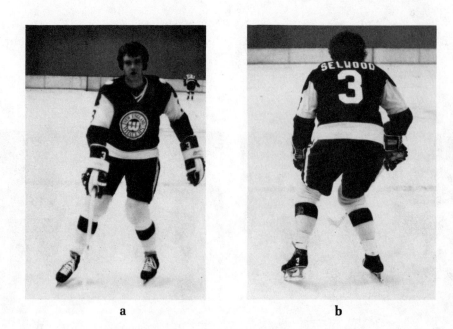

a   b

Figure 2-13.   *Front and rear views of backward skating in stride. Note push-off with right leg, inside edge.*

Other Skating Techniques

All turns, backward, forward, or sideways, must be mastered on both the left and right sides.

To turn from back to front, or vice versa, the feet should be kept together, the weight on one foot, and the elbow and shoulder thrust in the opposite direction. The free foot should be brought around as close to a 180-degree angle as possible. The turn is best made by concentrating on the thrust of the elbow and shoulders.

When practicing, always skate clockwise and counterclockwise, both forward and backward. Practice stopping facing first to the left, then to the right. Then do the same thing going forward and backward. This is important in that it teaches players to get back into play immediately rather than having to make a big, time-consuming circle.

Under "Skating," one of the more important phases was omitted—i.e., the pacing or better still "changing of pace." Pacing separates the good players from the "also ran."

The Stick

There seems to be a popular misconception that a hockey stick should be as tall as the man using it. On the contrary, it should not be longer than the distance between the ice with the stick flat on it and the chin of the player on his skates. Both length and lie are factors. A player who skates straight up will need a longer stick than the one who skates stooped over (in a crouch).

The rules are flexible as to the dimensions of the stick. It may be fifty-five inches or less in length. The blade (that part which lies on the ice) may curve as much as half an inch. The tip of the blade may curve up to two inches (see Figure 2-14.)

The stick is second only to skates in importance, and its lie on the ice is perhaps its most important factor. The lie of the stick, which is its angle with relation to the ice, is numbered. The higher the number, the flatter the stick; the lower the number, the higher the stick. The lie is determined by whether the stick is closer or farther away from the player.

Figure 2-14. *Hockey stick curves. Stick on left has very slight curve. Stick on right shows greater curve. (A half inch is maximum.)*

A stooped over skater, for example, will use a low lie and a straight up-and-down skater a high one. Milt Schmidt skated stooped over, which meant he held the stick farther away from his body than a straight up skater. He used a 5 lie, which is about average for a stooped skater in pro hockey.

As a general rule, tall men are straight up skaters and shorter ones stoop over. The more exaggerated the stoop, the farther away from the body the stick and the lower the lie. A stooped skater does not want as much of the stick flat on the ice as a straight up skater.

From the standpoint of efficiency, it does not matter if a skater is straight up or stooped over any more than it matters to a baseball batter how he stands at the plate. Some outstanding hitters look awkward as they take their batting stance, but they are quite comfortable, as their averages testify. The same is true of straight up or stooped skaters.

Figure 2-15.   *Front view of stance, left-hand shot. Note right arm and elbow are loose and away from the body. Left hand is at knee level.*

Stick-handling Technique

Good stick-handling is one of the most important skills for a hockey player at any level. This skill will improve with age and experience, but the sooner proper techniques are taught the better. Bad habits in the earliest stages become more and more difficult to break as the years pass. Difficult, but not impossible: at the college or Canadian Junior hockey level, they can be broken by an intelligent player who wants to learn to do his job correctly.

Unlike skating, which does not necessarily have to be taught to boys who grow up on skates, stick-handling has fundamental techniques that will not always come naturally even to a boy who cannot remember when he was not trying to play hockey. There are definitely right and wrong ways to hold and manipulate a hockey stick.

A sound hockey player uses the same grip for stick-handling as for passing. The stick is held firmly with the fingers of the lower hand and the thumb is placed on the side of the handle. The top hand should be on the butt end of the stick. The finger grip should be firm, with the thumb on the side. *Pressure* is placed on the stick with the *thumb*. The wrists should be fluid, not locked, as too tight a grip will seriously interfere with maneuverability. The stance should be easy and natural.

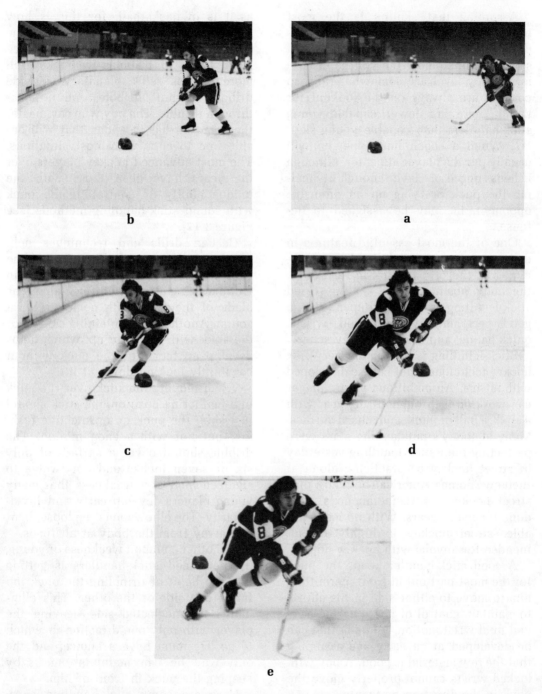

Figure 2-16. *Skating and stick-handling around pylons. (a) Balance. (b) Head up, knees bent. (c) Body between pylon and cushioned puck. (d) Head up, ready to shoot or pass. (e) Follow through.*

Assuming that skating is the most important phase of hockey, stick-handling is second in importance. Good stick-handlers below the college or Junior hockey level are somewhat rare, so coaches are always on the lookout for them. There are fewer capable young stick-handlers than capable young skaters. When a coach finds one, he will usually put the player at center, although if he is rugged or clever enough at stealing the puck or tying up an offensive opponent, he may be assigned to defense.

One of the most essential features in developing good stick-handling techniques is the proper stick in relation to the body position while skating. Good stick-handling is heavily dependent on good peripheral vision, fluid wrists, quick hands, and a keen hockey sense.

Stick-handling is one of the very few hockey techniques that can be developed without ice. An ambitious young player can work on it throughout the year with a stick, a ball or puck, and a hard surface. Many of today's outstanding stars were perfecting their stick-handling yesterday in street hockey or practicing alone at their own homes. American boys now play street hockey, as Canadian boys have done for many years. With no ice available, street hockey is highly recommended for anyone with hockey hopes.

A good stick-handler keeps the puck for the most part out in front, permitting him to move to either side in his efforts to maintain control of it. He has an easy and fluid wrist motion, a knack that can be developed at an early age assuming that the raw material is good. A boy with locked wrists cannot properly move the puck in the direction he wants.

"Dribbling" is as important in hockey as it is in basketball, for this is how a player keeps control of the puck as he moves down the ice. There are three basic types of dribbles in hockey, all more or less self-explanatory—a wide dribble, a short dribble, and a push-through dribble. The boy who can master these moves has weapons that will enable him to cope with most situations. The most advanced hockey players over the years have been those with the unique ability of controlling the puck with sound stick-handling methods (see Figure 2-17).

Certain drills and techniques help develop good stick-handling. One of the simplest is to feather the puck out in front, moving it back and forth along the blade of the stick with complete wrist action. Another is maintaining control of the stick with the head up, which helps develop a "feel" for the puck without constantly looking down at it.

When moving the stick over the puck in a feathering position, the stick should just skim the puck in a protective fashion, but not with a chop motion. The dribble should cover a surface of only six or seven inches and not twelve to eighteen inches, a weakness that many young players develop early and involuntarily. The elbows must be loose, bent and away from the body at all times.

One other common weakness of young, inexperienced stick-handlers is getting into the habit of dribbling the puck too far to one side or the other. This eliminates the neglected side, leaving the player with only one direction in which to go. He must have a choice, and the only way he can maintain one is by keeping the puck in front of him.

Here are some stick-handling exercises suitable for practice sessions:

Figure 2-17. *Stick-handling— front dribble series. (a) Head up, puck near heel of blade. (b) Puck brought from right to left, weight shifts, elbows are bent and away from body. (c) Puck directly in front of stick. (d) Dribble from left to right. (e) Puck cushioned on stick.*

1. Divide players into three zones, each with one puck. Let a player see how long he can maintain possession on his own.
2. Form a large circle and have each player slowly carry the puck inside the circle, while he looks straight ahead—not at the puck.
3. Station one player at center ice, one on the blue line, and one midway between the blue line and the goal. Then have each of the other players take turns carrying the puck from the opposite end of the ice, weaving in and out of the stationary players *with his head up.*

Keeping the head up while carrying the puck cannot be emphasized too strongly. For success in hockey, this is *basic.*

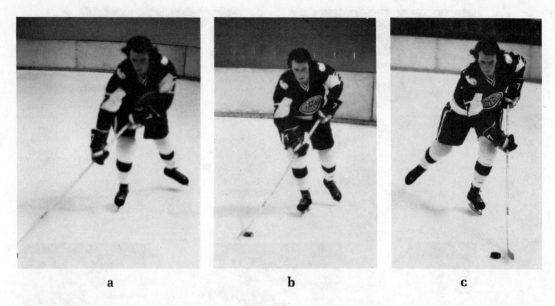

a   b   c

Figure 2-18.   *Wide dribble series—the most important stick-handling maneuver in hockey. (a) Head up, stick extended wide to the right. (b) Puck being brought in front toward other side. (c) Cushioning puck on backhand side to player's left.*

PASSING

In passing and receiving the puck, every good hockey player must develop proficiency in the following shots.

The Forehand Pass

A basic maneuver, the forehand pass should be easy to learn. Put the puck near the heel of the stick and watch the target, not the puck. Transfer the weight from the rear foot to the front foot; the weight should always be slightly ahead. There should be a pull and then a push of the top hand. As this takes place, the puck slowly spins to the middle of the blade. Keep the blade flat on the ice and slightly tilted over the puck. For accuracy at the stick, follow through in a straight line, low and crisp to the target. Remember the follow through of the lower hand, which helps give the puck enough spin for accuracy. Otherwise, control is lost and the puck might go almost anywhere in the general direction it is shot. The pass should be aimed at a point just ahead of the receiver's stick.

The Backhand Pass

This pass is similar to the forehand pass. Look at the target and sweep in a straight line to it. Give a good forward push of the lower hand and follow through with both hands. The backhand pass is executed with both arms. There is no upper body rotation. A common weakness with the backhand pass is too much pull with the bottom hand. The lower elbow should be kept bent. The passer should lead his receiver. Since the backhand pass is the hardest to learn and control, many outstanding hockey players unknowingly avoid it whenever possible. Few players really like to use it or find it their most effective pass. Even professionals, while they require good backhands, will often try to turn in order to pass on their forehands, which normally is everyone's natural move. Hockey is so fast, however, that there is not always time to make such a turn. Like it or not, a good backhand is essential to prevent the loss of many good opportunities.

The Flip Pass

This pass is executed with a quick upward and forward movement of the wrist. The weight is on the forward foot. The blade of the stick is tilted up and the puck is rolled off the top of the blade. There should be a spin as the puck leaves the stick. If there is not, passing is not being done properly. Eyes should be kept on the target with a shift in weight to the forward foot, using the easy wrist flip and a high follow through. Both the forward and the backward flip passes are excellent ways to pass the puck over an obstacle—usually a member of the opposing team—to a teammate. A good flip will sail over an opponent's stick before he can get it up high enough to intercept it.

The Drop Pass

Like the flip pass, the drop pass is executed mainly with the wrist. The player skates forward, places the blade in front of the puck, does not move it too far, and keeps it in line with a trailing teammate. Properly executed, it could set the latter up for a shot on goal, but a badly placed drop pass can mean disaster, for it can give the puck to the opposition. The important thing is to leave it exactly where a teammate sees it and can easily reach it. There are, of course, numerous hazards. The puck should be left precisely where the trailing teammate can get it without changing direction. If it is moved three or four feet to one side or the other, the teammate is probably going too fast to pick it up. A good stick-handler will put enough pressure to the puck for a tail, which will keep it in a stationary position for the man behind to pick it up. Sometimes a player, in trying to leave a drop pass, is going so fast himself that his own momentum carries the puck with him. It is most important that he put enough backspin to the puck to keep it in a dead position and not let it carry away.

The Clearing Pass

The one function of the clearing pass is to get the puck out of the defensive zone. In executing it, the weight starts on the rear foot and goes to the front as the puck is reached. The blade of the stick is wide open and the follow through high. Every move must be lightning-fast,

39

for the job is to get the puck away from that danger zone within range of a player's own goal.

Off-the-Board Passes

Sometimes the only solution to moving the puck when trying to keep possession while momentarily stymied is an off-the-board pass. Many players fail to take advantage of the boards because they do not know how to use them. Learning to do so is difficult but, once mastered, is a good weapon both on defense and offense. Too often, a young player will try to stick-handle around an opponent when a pass off the boards will easily accomplish the same purpose with much less danger of losing the puck. Of course, it is imperative that the action of the boards is familiar in order to determine how hard to pass the puck. Lively boards will get a player in trouble if the pass is made into them with full power. By the same token, dead boards could cost a player the puck if he does not pass hard enough into them. In a strange rink, the boards should be tested in pregame practice to know how much power is needed in using them to advantage. A board carom is not the type of pass that should be overused, but a player should be prepared to resort to it when the situation calls for it. By playing the puck off the boards he may save himself the trouble of having to play through an opponent. A man with the puck going forward must be able to judge the speed of his shot. As long as the opponent does not have possession, he is always on the defensive, so the offensive player has him at a disadvantage. This edge

can be maintained with an off-the-board pass either to oneself or to a teammate, but it should not be used unless necessary. When it is used, the player using it should be sure he knows where the puck is most likely to ricochet after it caroms off the boards.

A man should never pass if he does not have control of the puck. He should never pass (except to himself off the boards) unless he sees a teammate either close or in a position to get clear and reach the puck as he moves forward. He should never pass if his opponent is in a better position to reach the puck than his teammate.

The Fast or Straight Pass

This pass is executed in the same manner as taking a shot, although not as hard. The upper hand is worked against the lower, the latter acting as a lever. With players moving at top speed, the pass must be made ahead of the receiver.

The Push Pass

A slow pass, the push puss is executed by pushing both hands forward. This keeps the puck from spinning. It becomes a "dead puck" and much easier to handle. The pass can be made straight ahead, as it will be slow enough when properly executed to enable the wingman to outspeed his check (opponent) and "skate into it." It should be used when the defense is standing on or over the blue line and the wings are covered.

RECEIVING

In *receiving a pass*, the receiver should have his stick on the ice and out in front, giving his teammate a target for passing. He must bear in mind that his stick, not he himself, is the prime objective of any pass. If the puck misses his stick, goes into his skates, or misses him altogether, it is going to be up for grabs with everyone, including himself, fighting for possession. Too often, a player skates with his stick up off the ice —a common habit with young players— and cannot react fast enough to get the stick down where it belongs to take a quick pass. By keeping the stick on the ice, the would-be receiver makes it that much easier for his teammate to place a perfect pass. When in possession of the puck, a player's stick is on the ice. When a man is not in possession but involved in an offensive play he must keep his stick on the ice, too. If he fails, he might either miss the puck altogether or see it bounce off his stick as he belatedly brings it down to accept the pass.

When receiving a pass, a player should catch the puck as he would catch a baseball. He should cushion the puck as

Figure 2-19.   *Receiving. Note position of player near crease, expecting pass or rebound; head up; stick on ice with pressure on blade; good body balance.*

Figure 2-20.   *Shot on goal.*

it hits the stick just as a ballplayer does in accepting a throw or fielding a fly ball or grounder. With the curved stick, taking passes on the forehand is much easier than with a straight stick, but harder on the backhand. As always, it is imperative that a player not have a stiff stick (held too tightly), but one that will ride with the puck.

In general, it might be noted that the longer players play together, the more they learn about the habits or preferences of their teammates. A player should know his teammates so well that he sometimes will hardly even have to look before passing, just to make sure his teammate is not covered, but this would be necessary only if he has just taken the puck from the opposition. When starting a drive up the ice from his own zone, however, the center usually will not have to worry. His wings will automatically pick him up, and their

passing back and forth will also be almost automatic.

Sometimes, when asked by his coach why he did not pass when given the chance, a player will reply, "I didn't see him." This is no excuse. If he kept his head up, he would have seen the player open for a pass. When a player says he did not see an open player, he is, in effect, admitting his head was down. He *must* keep his head up. This is a cardinal rule when carrying out the puck, although the puck carrier has to find his way around opponents. Some responsibility is therefore on the free man to speak, holler, whistle, or in some way let the puck carrier know that he is free and ready to accept a pass.

SHOOTING

All the instruction in the world, all the talent that may blossom into stardom, all the moves and counter-moves executed in the rink, everything that is done in hockey zeroes in on one basic fact—that the team that scores the most goals wins the game. The primary objective is to get the puck into the opposing team's goal. This automatically makes the goalie the most important man on any team. A good team with a poor goalie will lose more games than a mediocre team with a good goalie. This brings hockey down to a battle between the shooters on the one hand and the goalies on the other.

No matter what the game, everyone likes to score or be the person setting up the score. The baseball hitter likes to drive in runs or, better still, hit home runs. The football passer likes to throw the long "bombs" and the receiver likes to catch them and carry the ball over the goal line. The basketball player likes to shoot the ball through the hoop. And the hockey player likes to shoot the puck past the goalie and into the nets.

As in all specialties, there is a technique in shooting for goals. In making the shot, the player should hold the puck as close to the heel of the stick as possible (see Figure 2-21). In order to get maximum speed and greater accuracy, a follow through must be made. In order to keep the goalie from knowing which way to look for the scoring attempt, it is essential that the intent to shoot not be telegraphed by means of dropping the lower hand or winding up. Since the bulk of the goalie's protection and his easiest maneuverability are above the knees, the best shots are low. In order to handle them, the goalie must use his feet instead of his body and glove, with which he can most easily make a stop. In order to make a low shot,

a

b

Figure 2-21.   *Shooting series. (a) Note position of puck on blade, near heel; head up; hands spread; knees bent; weight on rear foot. (b) Follow through.*

43

the shooter must "cup" his stick, which he can learn to do through constant practice.

If a low shot is not possible because of the speed of the action or the necessity of getting the shot away before a player skates himself out of range of the net, then his only alternative is a high shot. In making this type of shot, he must open the blade of his stick. The more open the blade, the higher the shot, so it is important that the blade not be opened too far. The result would be a shot that clears the net altogether.

Although anything that gets the puck past the goalie and into his net is good, there are six basic shots on goal.

The *power shot* should be made from behind the body. The bottom hand should be lowered and the weight of the body thrown forward. For a left-hand shot, the right foot must be forward, and for a right-hand shot the left.

The *close-in shot* should best be made from in front of the body where it is less likely to be telegraphed. In moving in on the goalie, either foot may be forward or both may be together. The head must be up, as in passing, dribbling, or handling the puck in any other way. If the head is down, the goalie can know exactly to which spot the shooter is aiming. If the head is up and the shooter looks straight ahead, the goalie can be kept in doubt as to which side of the net he intends to snap his shot.

The *slap shot* (Figures 2-22 and 2-23) is one of the best in hockey when done properly *and* at the proper time. It is most effective because it is a surprise shot that can catch the goalie completely off guard. It is best executed by slapping a pass from some other player. The shooter should stand facing the puck, throwing all the weight on the back

leg—the left leg if the shot is a left shot, the right leg if a right shot. The slap at the puck should be made with a flip of the wrists, with the stick hitting the ice about four inches behind the puck. It is *most* important that the stick hit the ice in back of the puck, as a golfer might hit behind the ball when shooting out of a sand trap. Although the slap shot is unreliable—it is not only hard to control but does tricks that, with few exceptions, most players cannot anticipate—many goals are scored with it. Although unreliable, it is always dangerous and goalies hate to see it coming.

Today's players slap the puck by letting it sit on the ice for a split second while they pull their curved sticks back to their shoulders or above, and then swing down at the puck like a golfer. If they hit the ice at the proper spot and make the puck move in the right direction, it will travel at the goalie at speeds upwards of one hundred and twenty miles an hour. The only way to learn to control the slap shot is by practice, and even then there is no guarantee that a player will be successful. That is why there are so few in the professional leagues who can tell for sure where their slap shot, propelled with such speed by their curved sticks, is going.

In the *wrist shot* (Figure 2-24), the shooter starts with the puck on his stick, holding it slightly behind him, then dragging it along the ice and snapping his wrists as he lets it go. Unlike the slap shot, the wrist shot is made without lifting the stick off the ice. The shot is easy to control, easy to learn, and easy to perfect. With the curved stick, it can move the puck somewhere around ninety miles an hour.

The *snap shot,* which seems to be going out of style, has the elements of both

Figure 2-22.   *Slap shot—rear view series. (a) Body balanced, looking at target. (b) Weight shifts, stick is raised, eye on puck. (c) Puck contact, left toe points to target. (d) Follow through, blade on net.*

the slap shot and the wrist shot. Its slap-shot action is leaving the puck unprotected on the ice for a split second. But instead of winding up and bringing the stick up to the shoulders or higher, as slap shooters do, the snap shot requires the shooter to bring his stick back only about two feet from the puck. He then quickly comes forward and snaps the shot in a movement that is all wrist.

The snap shot has an element of surprise which is present in neither the slap nor the wrist shot. The reason is that when the shooter brings his stick back such a short distance, it does not appear that he intends to shoot at all. It is a good shot to master under any conditions.

It is, of course, a much safer shot than a slap shot because the puck is left unprotected on the ice for a much shorter time. More than one National Hockey League player has had the puck stolen right from under him while he prepared to shoot a slap shot. The puck is seldom stolen when a player makes a snap shot. There simply is not time.

The *backhand shot* is uncomfortable, but it is effective when properly exe-

Figure 2-23.   *Slap shot—side view series. (a) Body balanced, looking at target. (b) Weight shifts, stick is raised, eye on puck. (c) Puck contact, left toe points to target. (d) Follow through, blade on net.*

cuted. It requires a good deal of wrist action, coupled with a turning, sweeping motion of the body.

Although one of the most feared shots in hockey, the backhand shot is almost a lost art. Unquestionably more difficult to control than a forehand shot, it is nevertheless a great shot because it catches the goalie completely by surprise.

Of course, the curved stick discourages backhand shooting because the curve is designed for more speed with the forehand shot. There are a few players who have cut down the curve of

their sticks who will occasionally try backhanders with some success. The best is Stan Mikita. Phil Esposito has a good backhand, but the curve on his stick is not as sharp as Mikita's. Bobby Hull is one of the only players with a perceptible stick curve who can backhand.

Wrist and slap shots are probably most effective because the shooter does not have to be on top of the goalie to get the puck by him. Deception is important, too. Sometimes the goalie can be faked out of position, with the result that it takes only an easy shot to slip the puck past him. Pucks are refrigerated, making them almost as hard as bullets. The curved stick and the slap shot add speed and deception to shots on goal.

There is always room for a good little man but a good big man has a better chance. Every team is looking for the big man who can station himself at the goalmouth, fight off opposing defensemen trying to get him out of there, and slam the puck home when it lands on his stick. This is one of the greatest assets Esposito has—he is big and rugged, almost impossible to move once he gets into position. His size gives him the strength he needs to fight off the opposition. That he also has an assortment of great shots and is very quick with his hands are bonuses that add to his remarkable effectiveness.

The way the puck is shot in today's game, sixty feet does not mean a thing. Many a goal is scored from that distance because the puck moves like lightning and so many shots are screened that the goalie has little more than a fair chance to see the puck, let alone stop it. There are more and more left shots playing right wing and vice versa, and this situation will continue as time goes on. Hockey coaches and players have learned that the advantages of playing the off side far outweigh the disadvantages.

A left shot coming in on the goalie from the right side has more of the net to shoot at, and of course the same is true when a right shot comes in from the left side. When a goalie comes out to meet a right shot coming from the right side, for example, he can cut the angle and the puck must be shot between him and the post. But when he meets a right shot coming from the left side, the shooter has all the way from the center of the net to the far post as a

target, so he is much harder to stop.

Some players are better than others at going in on the goalie alone and beating him to the punch. Phil Esposito is a great example of this. He stations himself close to the goal and when the puck lands on his stick after a pass from a teammate, he smashes it home before the goalie can get set. Esposito has a very wide shift, which is confusing to the goalie.

When going in on a goalie alone, it is not advisable to go in too close because that interferes with maneuverability. The best distance is about ten or fifteen feet, which leaves room for options. There is enough ice space to maneuver around the goalie, yet the skater is close enough to take a shot (which at that distance would be very difficult to stop). No matter what type of shot is employed, more goals are likely to be scored from ten or fifteen feet than from any other distance.

A great deal depends on the goalie. Each one is different. Shooters must be-

Figure 2-24. *Flip or wrist shot near crease. Note stick has followed direction of flight of puck, feet are in proper position.*

        a   b

        d   c

Figure 2-25.   *Deking goalie series. (a) Skater watches goalie who is in front of crease. (b) Skater brings puck from left to right hoping to make goalie move right. (c) Puck carrier moves left. (d) Puck carrier prepares to shoot.*

come as familiar with goalies as goalies are with them. Each goalie has his pet moves and his pet hates. The skater must learn that hate—or weakness—before he can know exactly how to play goalies. No goalie is perfect. Each has a weakness that will come out sooner or later. And each has moves that can be anticipated, just as each shooter has moves that the goalie can anticipate.

Sometimes the skater can surprise the goalie so much that even a poor shot might trickle past him into the net. A good stick-handler can overcome a goal-ie's moves by saving his own for the last split second.

Players may develop styles similar to those they admire, but they should not try to do the impossible. A budding hockey player can find no better example of how the game should be played than by watching selected professional players.

CHECKING

Checking is one of the most commonly used and least understood aspects of hockey. Its importance cannot be emphasized too greatly, for it is probably outranked only by skating, stick-handling, and shooting. Every player except the goalie must know when checks are legal and should be used, and when they are illegal and should not. Even the goalie must be able to tell the difference, although he himself should never be involved in checking, either as a checker or as the recipient of a check.

During virtually every minute of every game somebody on the ice is checking or preparing to check somebody else in one way or another. It does not matter who has the puck or in which direction it is being carried. It does not matter if the checker or the man being checked is a forward or a defenseman. In hockey parlance, the very term "check" can mean either a man or a maneuver. The *individual* opponent of a skater is often referred to as his "check." When a player is instructed to cover his "check" it means to cover the man he must watch. The "check" may change as the game progresses, for a man may temporarily take over the duties of a teammate. When that happens, the player must cover his mate's "check." When he resumes his regular duties, he picks up his original "check."

A checking maneuver may be legal or illegal. There are specified times when it is one or the other. (Illegal checks will be explained in Chapter 4.) The legal checks, a legitimate and important part of hockey, include the two most often used—*forechecking* and *backchecking.*

Forechecking is going into the offensive zone after the man with the puck. To keep the team from having too many men caught at the wrong end of the ice, only one attacking player should try to forecheck the puck carrier. A second

man should be ready to pick up a loose puck. (See Figure 2-26.) A third should be in front of the net ready to take a pass for a shot on goal. Only one man heads for the puck carrier, as more than one would leave an assignment uncovered and thus open the possibility of more than one being left helpless when the defensive team becomes offensive as its forwards head for the opposite net in possession of the puck.

Figure 2-26. *Checking the puck carrier with the second defensive man ready to assist.*

The purpose of forechecking is to keep the opposition from moving the puck out of its own zone. When a forechecker goes after the puck carrier—usually a defenseman—he must look at the man, not the puck. He must also be careful with his check to be sure it is a legal one. If he charges the man with the puck against the boards he is asking for two minutes in the penalty box. The same is true if he moves in with his stick too high or if he tries to grab the man with one hand.

The most important thing to remember in forechecking is its primary objective—*to take the puck carrier out of the play.* A good forechecker does not

PART II   *Individual Play*

even have to touch his man. All the fore-checker must do is get in front of him, making sure he cannot get by. This should be enough to keep him from getting rid of the puck or moving into position to receive a return pass. Watch his chest or his hips: one or the other will tell the forechecker what he must know —if the puck carrier will move, and in what direction. By watching and playing his body, the forechecker can tie him up by making sure he has nowhere to go. If the forechecker plays the puck, the defenseman might stick-handle around him. If he plays the body, there is no way the man with the puck can do this.

When more than one man is in the attacking zone with an opposing defenseman in possession of the puck, the man closest to the puck carrier should forecheck. If the puck goes around the boards from left to right, the right wing will be in the best position to make the check and the left wing to take the puck. The third man will be in front of the net. Although the ideal situation would be for the actual right or left wing to be forechecking or fighting for the puck and the center to be stationed in front of the net, these situations might change because of the circumstances of the moment. If the center has had to cover for a wing, for example, and the wing has had to move into the center's position, then that wing might be in the slot near the net while the center is working with the wing on the defenseman. There might also be a situation where, for example, the center has had to move to the right wing's position because the wing has gone in to forecheck. This would prevent the opposition from moving up unopposed on the right side if the defenseman succeeds in getting the puck out to one of his forwards. The same

precaution must be taken by the center when the left wing goes in to forecheck. This is why all three forwards must know each other's jobs, with the center as the key man. He in particular must be ready to go either to his right or left to cover for a forechecking wing.

When forechecking a defenseman, it is best to try to maneuver at him from an angle with the aim of forcing him toward the boards. In other words, the forechecker should give him only one way to go. By going in straight at him, he gives his man a choice of moving either to the right or to the left.

Forechecking must be teamwork on the part of all three forwards. One might be caught in the offensive zone without the puck, or even two—but *never* all three. The center is usually in the best position to forecheck. If he fails, the two wings should peel-off and come in with their checks. "Peeling-off" is when the offensive wings pick up their "checks"— their opposing counterparts—so that if one receives a pass from the defense-man and starts up the ice, the wing covering him might be able to check, or even intercept the pass. Care is essential in doing this because it is illegal to interfere with an opponent's skating if he does not have the puck; to do so draws a penalty.

If the "check" has the puck, *body-checking* is legal, but it is not possible to bodycheck when the would-be checker is chasing his "check." To hit him from behind is charging and calls for a penalty under most conditions. Therefore, body-checking should always be done from the front or side. It is possible to body-check legally from behind, but not easy. Any time a checker goes at a man from behind, the chances are he will hit him and do something illegal, like crashing

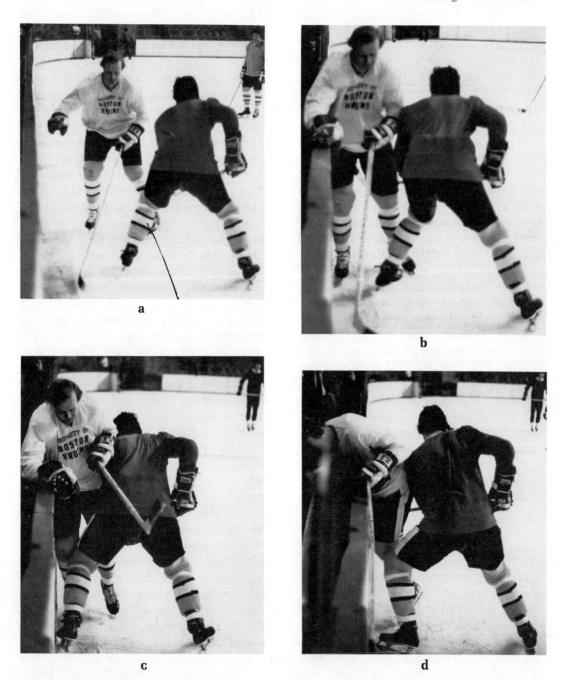

Figure 2-27.   *Boarding sequence series. Note the defenseman. (a) Skating backward. (b) Making contact; has good low stance. (c) Shoulder applied to midriff of opponent; good use of right skate edge for balance. (d) Follow through, maintaining contact.*

him into the boards, knocking him flat, or hitting him after taking more than two strides. (There is no provision in the rule book that actually specifies that more than two strides from behind constitutes charging, but it is a judgment call nearly always invoked by the referee.)

A straight bodycheck is usually a *shoulder check*. Normally, the chances of hitting a man legally are much better with a shoulder check than any other kind of bodycheck. There is less guesswork on the one hand and less chance of missing the man altogether on the other. (See Figure 2-27.)

When bodychecking, it is often advisable to *hip check*—get into a sitting position and stick out one hip or the other, depending upon which way the puck carrier appears about to move. The checker can tell by watching his opponent's hips or chest. If the man appears to be moving left, throw out the left hip; if right, the right hip. Either way, it is a legal hip check. This, of course, is another example of the necessity of *always* keeping the head up. The puck is on the ice, but the action is triggered by the players. It is impossible to see what anyone on the ice is doing unless the head is up.

The *hook check,* which is legal and effective, is almost a lost art in hockey today. It is executed by going down on one knee and laying the stick flat on the ice. A left-hander hooks to his right and vice versa. But before attempting a hook check, the forechecker must force the puck carrier to his right, then drop to his left knee, moving him toward the checker's right leg and laying the stick on the ice. The hook check has, apparently, gone almost completely out of style in modern professional hockey. It

used to be a common maneuver, and there is no reason it should not continue to be.

The *poke check* is exclusively a stick maneuver. This is one of the few that can be—and occasionally is—effectively used by goalies. It is an easily learned and most effective check that should be in the repertoire of every hockey player. It is executed by meeting the opponent face to face and shooting the stick straight forward with the top hand.

Whatever check is used, it must always be borne in mind that any legal check, whether the opponent is touched or not, is an integral part of hockey. The name of the game may be scoring, but the name of one of the essentials in trying to score is forechecking. The good forechecking team will score. The poor forechecking team is never out of trouble.

Backchecking is fully as important as forechecking. This is one of the best defensive maneuvers in hockey, but young offensive-minded players often do not even bother to do more with it than go through the motions. More goals are scored because of poor or nonexistent backchecking than for any other reason.

Backchecking is simply getting back to a defensive position following an offensive surge in time to stop the opposition from doing serious damage after it has gained possession of the puck. One minute an entire team (except the goalie) is at or inside the opposition's blue line. The next, opposing skaters are dashing madly down the ice in possession of the puck. If the team that so suddenly has been transformed from attackers to defenders fails to backcheck properly, the opposition could conceivably be bearing down with one, two, or three men on an unprotected goalie.

Backchecking is really anticipating trouble. The first to backcheck should be the defensemen. They are normally stationed at the offensive blue line to keep the puck from going out of that zone while their teammates are in close trying to score. They must keep their eyes open so they can tell when their own mates have lost the puck and the other team is starting a drive toward their goal.

If the defensemen do not backcheck at the right time the whole team is in trouble. The forwards must also backcheck, of course, but if the defensemen do their job, the worst that can happen is a three-on-two situation. In this, there will be three skaters moving down, passing the puck back and forth between them, while the two defensemen, having backchecked in time to protect their zone, are ready to keep the attackers from getting too close to their own goal.

This is why in forechecking, and trying to get the puck in the offensive zone, no more than two forwards should be directly involved in offensive action deep in opposing territory. The third forward should always be in a position to backcheck if necessary. Normally, this forward would be the center. While the wings are either forechecking or ready to pounce on a loose puck, the center is in front of the opposing net waiting for a pass that he might convert into a goal. When he sees that his pass is never coming because the other team will move the puck, he must forget the goal he could not score and think defensively, backchecking at once, in order to help the defensemen who are themselves backchecking to get into defensive positions within their own zone.

In many ways, hockey is a game of forechecking and backchecking. The puck

moves so quickly from end to end that everyone but the goalies is doing one or the other a good part of the time. Backchecking is a natural maneuver on the part of defensemen, but when a forward does it, it is an art, although some forwards do not know how to backcheck properly. Even in the professional leagues this is often true. A forward can help his team defensively if he backchecks.

As in forechecking, a good backchecker can stop an opponent by being in the right place at the right time, often not even having to touch his man in order to check him. Fans delight in the body contact that makes hockey, by its very nature, a rough game. It is rare for a nonhitting checking player to draw a penalty. The man who hits is nearly always the one caught doing something illegal. He is most often the man who is involved in controversy, which invariably leads to penalties.

The more a player knows about legal checks the more he can help his team. A great rule of thumb in backchecking is always to keep a man between the checker and the puck carrier. If a player backchecks without touching his "check" he is breaking no rules. All he has to do is stay in his "check's" way. He constitutes an obstacle to his "check." With him there, the "check" cannot take a pass easily, cannot go where he pleases, and cannot set himself up for a shot on goal or any other offensive maneuver.

When the checker does his job properly without laying a hand on his "check," he is being fully as effective as though he had actually knocked his "check" down—more so, in fact. If a player backchecks without touching a man who does not have possession of the puck he will draw no penalty. But if the checker hits his "check" when the "check" does not have the puck, he will in most cases be penalized.

It is advisable to bear in mind that very often the puck carrier is the *least* dangerous man on the ice. The most dangerous is the trailing man looking for a pass. Therefore, it is the wing's responsibility in backchecking to take the nearest man *not* in possession of the puck. By doing that, he makes life easier both for himself and his defensemen. The job of the defensemen is to take care of the puck carrier. If they know the *potential* carriers are covered, they can concentrate on the man with the puck.

There is some difference of opinion on how to cover a wing in backchecking. One approach is to have the checker on the inside and half a stride ahead of his "check." He may not be able to see the puck, but if he has his man covered, that man still has to beat him if the puck is passed to him. If the checker plays on the outside and his man gets the puck, the checker is already beaten.

Another important point to remember in checking is that a bodycheck is illegal only if in the act of bodychecking a player does something that calls for a penalty. Although he cannot bodycheck a man who does not have the puck, the checker has a good deal of latitude in

bodychecking a man with the puck. Some bodychecks may be borderline cases as to legality, in which case it is up to the referee to decide.

When a player disagrees with a referee's call, it is safest to keep quiet and simply go to the penalty box. Except in the most flagrant miscarriages of justice—and in the major hockey leagues there are very few because big-league officials know their business—it must be assumed that the referee is right. He will usually give the checker the benefit of the doubt. Even if he does not, it makes little sense to argue. If the penalized man is so upset that his temper gets the better of him, he may say something inviting a five-minute misconduct penalty.

The best solution is to know the rules. It is amazing how many major-league hockey players have never read them. Granted the rules are sometimes couched in ponderous language, but they are really quite clear. The better a player knows the rules, the less chance he has of breaking them. It is basic, of course, that the coach know them. It should be basic that players know them, too. Knowledge of the rules may not help a man curb his temper, but at least it will keep him from breaking too many rules.

3

Position Play

PLAY OF THE CENTER

The *center* must not only be one of the best all-round hockey players on the team, but also have strength, brains, leadership qualities, and adaptability. If this seems too large a collection of qualities, it is only because the perfect center has one of the most demanding jobs on the team. He must literally be almost all things to all men.

He must be a great all-round hockey player because, although his primary job is center, he must know how to play either wing. He must be a fast, outstanding skater, a smart, well-rounded stickhandler, and the best playmaker on the team. He must know all the shots—either for passing or for scoring purposes—and must be at home shooting forehand and backhand, shooting left and right, passing left and right.

He must have enough strength to hold off the defensive concentration that is often leveled in his direction. Of all the men on the team, the center is considered most dangerous by the opposition—

everyone is therefore gunning for him and he must be strong enough to cope.

He must have brains because he is often called upon to make key, split-second decisions. On the attack, the center is the one man who cannot falter. If a wing is a little slow coming up, it will hurt but not be fatal. If the center is slow, it can ruin a promising possibility of a shot or series of shots on goal.

He must have leadership qualities because, in effect, he *is* the team leader. On offense, the team takes its cue from the center. If he does not set up the attack, someone else must. The center, in taking the lead, makes the first move and sets the pace of the attacking team.

On the center's adaptability rests all major shifts that come with an attack on the opponent's goal. He is the man who moves from side to side, who, by whatever step he takes, decides the moves of the wings. If he sees that a wing is better able to go in than he is, he might swap positions with that wing. Thus, for the moment, he actually is the wing.

Contrary to some popular thought, the center should have a good scoring shot

Figure 3-1.   *The faceoff. Note good position by official and players; left arm of official signals timer.*

but does not necessarily have to be the team's best scorer. However, since he is always in the thick of the action, he will often be close enough to the opposing goal to be in the best position to shoot. In the natural course of events, the center will have many more scoring chances than anyone else on the team. This is why centers often lead their teams in scoring—not because they are outstanding shots, but because they have the most and best opportunities to shoot. They have so many other functions, however, that shooting is only one.

It has sometimes been said that centers are born, not made, but this is not necessarily true. Any fast, clever skater who knows how to stick-handle well and effectively can be made into a center. Some coaches naturally gravitate to a man with basic abilities as a prime candidate for center. But that man is not *born* to the job. He must be taught. All he has to start with are the tools, which does not always mean he knows how to use them. But given those tools, there is no reason he cannot be taught to be-

come a good center. If he can be made to understand the myriad requirements for the job—and any intelligent young player with those tools can learn to use them properly—he should be a good center.

One of the first things he must understand is that any center is most often thought of as the team's *playmaker*. Although he should have a hard shot to be able to score goals when opportunities arise, his job is primarily to set up and develop the play for his particular line. He needs good hockey sense, good ability in handling the puck and the stick, good passing proficiency with either forehand or backhand, good timing, and good scoring techniques.

A good center today is a strong forechecker who can go into the attacking zone and force the play. His skating balance must be good enough to enable him to change direction without looping around and taking himself out of the play. He should be able to stop, change direction immediately, and stay on top of the action.

One of hockey's biggest changes in recent years is that forechecking has become an important feature. No longer do centers always drop off and just pick up wings to come back with the play, as they used to. Now the team in possession of the puck dumps it into the attacking zone and then forechecks to force defensive players into mistakes. This takes great teamwork from the five skaters on the ice, particularly the forwards. The key to a good checking line is the center, who should possess all these abilities.

Some centers are not effective until they get beyond the attacking blue line into the opponents' defensive zone. The center who is in the habit of trying to wind up and rush the length of the ice can almost always be played or easily defensed by opposing coaches. The center who not only can carry the puck but also move it to breaking wings, is tougher to defense and far more dangerous in the scoring zone. This is why the best centers rarely keep the puck for long as they go down the ice. They are constantly passing off to linemates and looking for return passes as the play develops. Of special importance is that the center always be cognizant of head men and pass to them if they are open or if they shake their cover.

The center must sometimes shift to a wing because the teammate who regularly plays there has voluntarily drifted to center, due to the fluid motion of the game. When the wing comes in on the puck to take over the center's job of forechecking, the center must back him up and play the wing until the progress of the game results in a change back to the original assignments.

In effect, this means that the center must know the job of both his wings and be prepared, if necessary, to take the place of one. The wings must know the center's job in the attacking zone at least as well as their own. A good line is always interchangeable; in daily practices the players should exchange positions on the same line.

Because the center will so often find himself in many different types of scoring positions, he should learn to shoot his backhand as well as his forehand. Of all the men on the team, the center's backhand is most important. In the tight scrambles close to the opposing net, he has no time to maneuver himself into position for a forehand shot or pass. If he has no backhand shot or pass or can not develop one, he should not play center.

As the scoring play develops, it is the center who must be stationed in the slot directly in front of the opposing net, ready to convert any pass, from wherever it comes, into a shot on goal—all in one motion. The best center is therefore a big man with the size and strength to hold off the checking defensemen trying to beat him away from the goalmouth and to keep him out of the play.

Centers should concentrate on scoring, if in the slot, know where the puck is at all times, and *not* wrestle with their opponent who is covering or checking them.

Because he is the focal point in forechecking, the center often is the last man back in the defensive zone when opponents have the puck. Each coach has his own preference on the center's defensive role, but in most cases coaches expect the center to be able to come back, pick up the open wings, and not skate by them, leaving them uncovered. A center moving in behind the play must watch for the trailing wing. If his own wing was forechecking and he in turn was backing up and checking behind his teammate, he must play the wing's position and cover him at his own end of the ice.

On working the puck out of his defensive zone, the center must maneuver himself into a free position to receive passes from his defensemen or his wings, or whoever is carrying the puck. A key point for all centers is to be moving constantly into open ice where a teammate may successfully complete a breakout pass to him. He must know when to stay in deep or, if the occasion demands, when to move toward his blue line. This depends on the situation at hand. His basic hockey sense will dictate his reactions.

The center's job has changed in the last twenty years. The primary function of the center used to be to lead his line into the attacking zone, which, of course, it still is. Today, however, the puck is dumped in just anywhere and then followed.

In modern hockey anyone in a position to shoot the puck in does so—in fact, a shot on goal from the opponents' blue line is not uncommon. This makes for a faster game, but a more dangerous one, for once the puck is in, the center and everyone else must go in to try to get it away from the opposition.

In the Russian-Canadian games of 1972, the Russian attack was based on the pre-World War II game, with more emphasis on passing and stick-handling and less on the Canadian attack of dumping the puck in the opponents' end and following up.

The center's function is to hover around the goalmouth in hopes of taking a pass he can convert into a shot. The modern center should be rugged. When in the slot he has to take a pretty good physical beating from opposing defenders trying to get him out of there.

This is one quality that has made Phil Esposito of the Bruins the outstanding center of modern times. It was no accident that up through the 1972 season he was the only National Hockey League player other than Bobby Hull to have scored fifty or more goals in more than one season.

A rugged 200-pounder who stands six-foot-one, Esposito is a marvel at moving into the slot in front of the goal and staying there while his teammates maneuver to get the puck to him. He is big enough to hold his place, strong enough to shake off the efforts of foes trying to dislodge him, and clever enough with

his stick to get his shot off in a split second.

Jean Beliveau of the Montreal Canadiens, who straddled two eras of hockey during a long career that ended with his retirement after the 1971 season, owed much of his brilliance as a center to his build. Six-foot-three and 205 pounds, Beliveau not only was a marvelous skater and stick-handler, but had the strength to withstand everything the defense threw at him when he was in the attacking zone.

PLAY OF THE WINGS

In today's game the wings have assignments that go beyond the job of wings in former years. Perhaps the most important job a wing has is the hardest to carry out—disciplining himself to stay on his own side of the ice while patrolling his lane. This problem is complicated by the fact that he must also know when to leave his own territory and pick up the slack of a teammate who has failed to fulfill an assignment.

The common saying that hockey is a game of mistakes probably applies more to wings than to anybody, because it is usually a wing who loses the puck on an offensive rush, and it is usually a wing who gets caught up the ice when the opposition has gained control and is moving toward his own net.

Any time a goal is scored it is partly the result of the scorer's own alertness, but it is mostly the result of someone on the defensive team having made a mistake. When a goal is analyzed, the first inclination is to blame the goalie. But then it is remembered that somebody—

probably a defenseman—failed to give the goalie the protection he should have had. It is then further remembered that the defenseman would not have had to provide that protection if a forward had not lost the puck. And in most cases, the puck is lost by a wing deep in the territory of the other team.

This is not to say that the wing can be blamed for the loss of the puck. After all, he was down in the opposing zone trying to score or set up a goal. Nobody is ever perfect. In hockey, this is particularly true. Everyone, from the top pros to the rawest kids, will make mistakes. These mistakes usually come in chains —from the forwards to the defensemen to the goalie. Sometimes all of them have missed their assignments. If one, two, or all are guilty, the thing the wing must keep in mind is that the chain of errors is most likely to start with him. Even when it does, the goal that could result is not his fault alone. A teammate also erred. That is the wing's consolation; and that is why hockey is a game of mistakes.

The wing should be an outstanding skater, with speed being the essence of his game. He should be master of both skating and shooting techniques. He should have the ability to forecheck properly when the situation demands, the tenacity to dig the puck out of corners, the cleverness to get it away from an opponent, the knack of feeding it to a teammate, and the ability to shoot when the opportunity presents itself.

He should be very careful not to get caught out of position, yet he must know when to forecheck in backing up his center. He should have split-second judgment, for he might often be forced to choose between going in to forecheck someone else's man or hanging back to

check his own wing. If he leaves his own wing, it means he is gambling, and only he can tell whether or not the gamble is worth taking. If he goes in to score or help someone else score, the chance *is* worth taking. But if no score results, either directly or indirectly, from his move, his gamble has failed to pay off. He can too easily be caught out of position and find himself trailing a play that may have already moved so far ahead that it is almost out of sight.

Although it is usually the center's job to lead the way into the offensive zone, the wing must know when to break across the blue line ahead of the center. An offside, calling for a faceoff outside the offensive zone, will be called if a man is in the offensive zone ahead of the puck carrier. Ordinarily, the center will go in first, carrying the puck, and the wings will follow him. However, it is sometimes better for a wing to carry the puck in, with the center and the other wing trailing him. The decision to go in with the puck is often the wing's, and when it is, it must be made on the spur of the moment. He may take a pass on top of the blue line, with no time to return the pass to the center. He may steal it while the rest of the line is backchecking. He may carry it so close to the line that he would lose too much time if he passed it before going over. He may be the nearest forward to the puck when it is shot into the offensive zone by someone else. There are, in short, dozens of possible situations justifying the wing's taking the puck into the offensive zone. He must be able to think quickly enough to take advantage of any of them.

While efforts of an opponent are being made to check him, the wing should constantly be looking for open ice into which he can move quickly to take a pass from a linemate. He should be ready to break to center ice but have the patience to wait until the center, in the quick movement of the action, has had time to move in on one wing or the other. The perfect wing should know exactly when to make this break, for he can be neither too soon nor too late.

This is what really makes the wing's job so hard—if he breaks out of his zone too soon he might skate himself out of the play; if he does it too late, the play may have gone by him before he reaches the center zone. He is, in fact, more likely to break too soon, a common failing of any wing. A good wing should think with his center, know his center's moves, and anticipate his center's direction. The center is the leader of the play and what the wing does depends entirely on what the center does. Timing is the answer.

A good wing should develop an effective scoring technique. He should be able to shoot coming in on the goalie from his wing, developing both slap and wrist shots primarily for this purpose. He should also be able to "deke" (fake) the goalie from up close. Every skater must know how to "deke," for it is a common maneuver designed to draw an opponent out of position in order to get by him with the puck. "Deking" a goalie, of course, is the ultimate, for, when successful, it gives the puck carrier a clear shot at an open net.

In tight situations in the offensive zone, the wing should be prepared to move the puck back to the points (defensemen) who, in today's offensive-minded game, will be guarding the two sides of the offensive blue line. When the wing is caught with the puck and has no place to take it, a pass back to

one of the points is often the only way he can keep his team in possession. This also can give his team an entire new pattern of offensive play, for both defensemen have a good panoramic view of the action. They know who is clear and who is not. If no forward is clear, one or the other can take the puck in himself, a job at which a good defenseman can be effective. If a defenseman breaks into the offensive zone, a wing or the center should come out to the point and take his place.

Defensively, a wing should never be caught out of position. He should sense when the puck is changing hands, when the play is changing direction, and when he no longer has a good offensive opportunity. At that point, he should be turning, looking for the man he must check, and getting into position to cover his opponent all the way back to his own defensive zone and past his own goalie into one of the corners.

A common weakness of a wing is to carry out his assignment in covering his opponent only up to his own blue line, and then depending on the defensemen to pick the man up from there. This might happen, of course, but the wing has no guarantee that it will. He must stay with his man as long as possible. In any event, his coach may have certain defensive assignments for him, designed to get maximum results when the team is on the defensive.

A good wing should develop the habit of stopping dead and turning immediately in a new direction rather than making wide turns. Slower turns, like crossovers, are preferable only when there is no time factor. But a wing rarely has that much time. Speed is too important and crossovers are not for him.

The wing should be constantly alert

for possible careless play that might result in loss of the puck, which in turn puts added responsibilities on the shoulders of the defensemen. The play of the wing will dictate the play of the defense. If the wing cannot handle his assignments properly, the defense is forced into situations that put the whole team at a disadvantage.

One of a wing's most important defensive jobs is to be able to check close and tough. This brings out four fundamentals in wing play that must be borne in mind:

1. He should always be in position;

2. When checking an opponent, he should be sure the opponent does not go in behind him and head for his cage;

3. He should stay half a stride ahead of his check (opponent), keeping to the inside to be prepared for any burst of speed the check may try to use to break free of him; and

4. He should concentrate on the man —not the puck.

If a wing's check does not have possession of the puck but is trying to get into position to receive a pass from a teammate, the wing must watch him closely. Usually, the check's actions will tell the wing if the puck is being passed to him. Because he is trying to score (as are his linemates if the opportunity arises), he may resort to a change of pace, especially in from the blue line. That is why it is essential that the wing stay with him all the way to a spot parallel to the cage, or until he has skated himself away from a scoring angle.

A wing's common mistake is to chase the puck carrier when backchecking. If the wing's own opponent has broken away, he should let a defenseman handle his check while he looks for someone else to cover. This is the only way the wing can contribute defensive help to his own team once his man has succeeded in getting him off his back. Sometimes when this situation develops, the defensive wing cannot find an opposing wing to check. In that case, he should skate to the outside of the puck carrier, forcing the carrier to the defensemen, thus setting up an easier assignment for them, such as a possible bodycheck. Another method is to have the checking wing come in behind his defenseman and cover an opponent in the slot. This helps prevent bunching up in the offensive zone.

When the wing is the last man in a checking assignment, he should look for the trailer on his side—the opposing forward following the puck carrier. If the carrier has no chance to score, he might leave a drop pass for the trailer to pick up. This is most likely when the trailer, as is often the case, is the opposing team's most dangerous scorer. It may not be possible for the defensive wing to pick up the drop, but by properly backchecking he might succeed in forcing the trailer offside and thus prevent him from taking a legal shot on goal. In the 1972 Canadian-Russian series the drop pass was used very successfully by the Russians.

All three forwards must know each other's assignments, for hockey is so fast that conditions are always changing. The center must know how to play either wing, both wings must know how to play center or each other's wing position, and all three must be trained to handle any situation that arises.

Because of its speed and fluidity, it is

not possible to set specific rules for each forward position. The best a coach can do is set *general* rules, but these can only be followed when conditions are applicable. It is constantly necessary to consider alternative contingencies. The forwards must know these as well as the general rules, for they come up often.

Obviously, instruction on wing play sounds much like instruction on center play. The reason is that the potential for interchangeability among the three members of a forward line is always present. If the best skaters are the centers (there should be three, for it is now essential both in college and professional play to have three lines), the next best must be the wings. On any line it is also essential that *any* forward—center or wings —must really be able to play any other forward's position. There will be times when the center will play one wing or the other, times when either wing might become the center, even times when the wings may have occasion to swap places. These changes will never be permanent, but they may last as long as a play lasts.

PLAY OF THE DEFENSE

Perhaps the greatest change in hockey during the recent past has been in the duties of the defensemen. In earlier years, defensemen were almost always the biggest, strongest, roughest, most durable players on the team. They were often awkward stick-handlers and mediocre skaters, for their primary job was to hit an on-coming wingman and knock

him out of the play by sheer force. An occasional superstar like Eddie Shore of the Boston Bruins, who was neither an awkward stick-handler nor a mediocre skater, came along as an exception to the general rule, but Shore was one of the very few defensemen of the past capable of carrying the puck the length of the ice, getting through the opposing defense, and slamming it home past the opposing goalie.

All this has now changed. Coaches are no longer settling for defensemen whose sole attribute is strength. No longer are they interested in the defenseman with little to offer but muscle. No longer do they want defensemen unable to skate well or carry the puck only when the occasion demands.

Today's coaches look for the same degree of skating, passing, and playmaking ability in defensemen as they expect in forwards. Although strength is an asset, it is not an absolute essential any more. Bobby Orr of the Boston Bruins is an example of the modern defenseman —smart, graceful, an outstanding skater and stick-handler, a great shot, and possessor of the kind of hockey sense that helps him diagnose a play as opposing puck carriers approach him in his own defensive zone.

The new breed of defensemen is part of a five-man attack. The old breed was part of a two-man defense. And that is the real difference between hockey as it used to be played and hockey as it is played now. With two defensemen capable of doing everything a forward can do, the emphasis on attack means more goals, higher scores, and a generally more interesting game.

A modern defenseman must be aware of four fundamentals:

1. He should be capable of sizing up the opponents' attacking play immediately;
2. He should always know the speed and tempo of the game, which are never the same for longer than a few moments at a time;
3. He should be prepared to react quickly to whatever game situation presents itself; and
4. He should immediately recognize the probabilities as a play moves in on him. This means he must see what the opposition is doing, what he and his own teammates can do to cope with it, which teammates are available, where his own forwards are, how many men he and his partner must face, if the situation is (a) one-man-on-one, (b) two-on-one, (c) two-on-two, (d) three-on-two, or whatever. The moment he diagnoses the situation, he should call it out to his partner so that he, too, is aware of the exigencies of the moment.

The defenseman's ability to determine whether or not he will get help from backchecking forwards will help him decide immediately how to function in a given situation. There will be times when he may be the only man between himself and the goalie. More often, his defense partner will be on the other side of the rink, covering opposing forecheckers.

Perhaps least often of all, there *will* be backchecking teammates in position to help. The more men at his own end of the ice, the more flexibility the defenseman will have. If he is alone, he *must* do everything he can to keep a possible scorer from getting a shot on goal. Even an illegal check, which, if detected by the referee will mean a penalty, is better than giving a potential shooter a clear shot.

If the defenseman's partner is in proper position (which he should be unless he has carried the puck into the opponent's zone and is caught up the ice following the play back), the situation will not be desperate enough for possible illegal measures; and if backchecking forwards have come down to cover the attacking team, the defenseman will not normally have to worry about anyone or anything except his own man.

Whatever the situation, the defenseman must never forget his primary role as protector of his goalie, a traditional condition in hockey. In carrying out this role, he must bear in mind certain techniques and how to use them.

He should be carrying his stick directly in front of him, not to the side. In this way, he is forcing the play into a corner, well out of range of his own goal. If he carries his stick to the side instead of in front, he is opening many different alleys for a clever puck carrier coming in on him. By carrying the stick in front, the defenseman is forcing the puck carrier to make his move. Everywhere on the ice the battle is fundamentally dependent on who makes the first move—who makes the first commitment. Obviously, the burden is on the puck carrier. A good one knows what to expect from an equally good defenseman, and one thing the defenseman must make him expect is the necessity of making this first move.

If the defenseman commits himself first, the puck carrier gains a bonus advantage. Therefore, it is essential that the defenseman *force* the puck carrier into that first move—and the sooner the better. As soon as the carrier makes his move, the defenseman can make *his*. The defenseman's counter-move can be the difference between scoring or not scoring on the part of the offense.

The defenseman should develop the technique of holding his stick back five or six inches. He can do this by holding his elbows close to his side, and when the situation presents itself, he can jab the stick ahead in poke checking fashion.

He should know the absolute necessity of not committing himself too soon, for once he does, he might be lost. A clever puck carrier will "deke" him and he will be faked out of a play at a point too close to his own net for comfort. If in doubt about committing himself, he is always better off giving room and sliding back. He cannot move too fast to the outside because that will allow the on-coming forward an inside angle. By keeping his man on the outside, the defenseman can drive the carrier into a corner.

There is a tendency on the part of some young defensemen, especially at the amateur or college level, to look at a faceoff as if it were a penalty and try to avoid one in their own zone. This is understandable, since the situation will be dangerous for the defending team if the offense wins the draw (faceoff). Obviously, a faceoff to the right or left of the net is not an ideal situation for the defensive team. However, there are times when the alternative is virtually to *give* the puck to the opposition. Anything, including a faceoff wherein the defense has as good a chance of winning the draw as the offense, is better than that.

When moving to a corner to go after a puck carrier, the defenseman should play the man, not the puck. He should never go in with the intention of trying to steal the puck. In a corner at his own end of the ice, the defenseman must have one thought in mind—the man may go *by* him, but never get *around* him. The defenseman's responsibility is to keep the puck carrier out of the play. By getting him into a corner, the defenseman is giving the carrier nowhere to go.

In using body or shoulder checks, the defenseman should make sure his partner is close enough to cover him. These checks are best used when the puck carrier is at a disadvantage, but they can backfire. They usually take the checking man out of the play. They *might* take the puck carrier out of the play, in which case there will be little or no problem if the checking man's partner is backing him up. If he is not, however, the puck will be loose and there are few things more dangerous for a team than a loose puck in its own zone.

A much more useful check is a play-through or safety check, the type which permits the checking man to keep his balance and maintain control of his body. The perfect safety check finds the defenseman still in the play and the puck carrier out of it. If it can be used, it should be. The body or shoulder check, which often forces the defenseman to leave his feet and surely forces him to lose his balance, is not recommended except when there is no alternative to stopping the puck carrier.

One of a defenseman's prime jobs is to block shots. Every shot a defenseman blocks is a shot saved from the goalie. Obviously, the goalie cannot depend on his defense to take *all* the shots, but the good defenseman blocks as many as he can.

There are two styles of blocking shots for defensemen. One is by dropping to the knee, the other by sliding into the shot. When dropping to the knee, keep arms at the side and do not move until the last split second. The shot can be taken anywhere, but the stomach area is the best and the safest. You use this technique when the carrier is in a shooting position and unable to "deke" you out of position. When skidding into the shot, the defenseman moves sideways, usually taking both the puck and the opponent with him. In addition to the above, below are Milt Schmidt's observations on the play of defensemen.

One defenseman must always be in front of the net when the opposition is attacking. Defense partners must communicate with one another on the ice because it is essential that each know what the other is doing, whom he is taking, and where he intends to go.

A left defenseman should never be on the right side of the net unless forced to be because his partner has been caught up the ice after an offensive maneuver. By the same token, a right defenseman should never be on the left side of the net except when forced to by the same circumstances.

Most important of all is for a defenseman to keep himself between the puck carrier and the goal. He should move the carrier off to one side, where he will have less chance of getting off an accurate shot on goal.

Although it is wrong, left-handed forwards have a tendency to go to their right and right-handed men to their left. There they put themselves on their own backhands and make things harder for

themselves in trying to score. The defense should take full advantage of this tendency. When a shooter moves to his backhand side, the defenseman should do everything possible to keep him there.

A defenseman should always have at least one man covered in front of his own net. This does not mean standing face to face with the attacker because then there is danger of the play slipping in behind him and giving someone a close-up shot at his net. So while keeping his man covered, the defenseman must also know where the puck is. To do both means that the defenseman must have physical contact with the man he is covering. Although almost impossible to do this legally, infractions in a tight scramble in front of the net are seldom called by the referee. In working near his own goal, the defenseman has no choice but to touch his man somewhere either with his stick or some part of his body, which is illegal. If the referee called every illegal maneuver that took place when three or four men fought for the puck in front of somebody's net, hockey would become a game of whistles.

The offensive jobs of defensemen have become almost as important as the defensive. Although there are times when a defenseman will pass the puck to a forward, then move up with the play until he is guarding the opposing blue line after the puck is in it, there are also times when he is part of the actual moving of the puck.

A good defenseman must be capable of moving in for a wing or even a center on an offensive charge. This may not happen often, but the defensemen on any team should be prepared for it.

Suppose, for example, a defenseman

finds himself with the puck halfway between his net and his blue line, with open ice in front of him. He should be able to move it himself, picking up forwards along the way. When this happens, someone else will cover for him while he goes into the attacking zone. During that period, the defenseman is actually a forward and must play like one. It might not happen more than once or twice a game to the average defenseman, but all defensemen must be ready for it, although this is not the defenseman's primary job when his team is attacking—he must guard the offensive blue line. The classic situation will find the three forwards moving the puck among them, while bearing down on the opposing goal, while the two defensemen are stationed just inside the blue line. Their jobs are to *keep the puck in the attacking* zone.

Obviously, two defensemen cannot cover the entire width of the ice, but they can anticipate moves, since they have a panoramic view of the action. If their teammates lose the puck or are forced into a faceoff, the defensemen must decide immediately what to do. They have two basic alternatives. The best is to stop the puck from crossing the blue line into the center zone. Failing to do that, but getting possession of the puck, they must stall in the center zone until their forwards can get back into it to keep from being offside. When everyone is onside, the defenseman who has the puck either leads the way in himself, dumps the puck in, or passes it to a forward to take it in.

If the puck goes out of the attacking zone and neither defenseman can get it, the only hope is an icing call, which will come only if the puck goes all the way down to and beyond their own goalie's

crease. This will bring the puck back into the attacking zone for a faceoff.

The other alternative for defensemen guarding the attacking blue line is to backcheck if the other team gets the puck and obviously starts up the ice with it. Bad as it may be for two or three forwards to be caught deep in one zone while the puck is being carried into the other, it is worse for the defenseman to be caught unless he has carried the puck in himself or has been a part of the attacking unit. However, there is no excuse for a defenseman guarding the blue line to be caught. He must backcheck fast enough to be in position to stop the play when it reaches his own zone.

Offensively, the defenseman must also be ready to cover behind an attacking teammate carrying the puck out of his defensive zone in order to pick him up if he makes a slip and loses the puck. This may not always be an offensive maneuver. In one sense, it is a defensive move, for if the defenseman does not

Figure 3-2.   *Good moves by the goalie.*

cover his teammate closely enough, an opponent may swoop in and pick up the puck when the forward loses it. This is why the defenseman must cover his teammate closely enough to rescue the puck when it is lost. Many a goal has been scored and many a game lost because a defenseman who could have kept his team in possession of the puck failed by *not trailing* his own puck carrying teammate closely enough. A common rule to observe is: The first defenseman back is the point man on the opposite side from where the puck is coming out.

PLAY OF THE GOALIE

Goalies are a breed apart. In recent years much has been written about them from the point of view of their distinctive problems. There is no question that their problems are quite different from those of the rest of the team, yet in common with their mates, they are hockey players first and goalies second.

Few people—even close observers—can agree on much about goalies. There is even some doubt as to what to call them. They are "goal-tenders" in the rule book, "goalers" in Canada, and "goalies" in the United States.

There are several theories on how goalies should play—almost as many as there are successful goalies. The job is not easy, the pressure is terrific, and the possibilities of getting rather badly hurt are always present, yet many boys enjoy it and some are good enough at it to go all the way to professional ranks.

As hockey spreads, so does good goal-tending. There are more promising young

goalies today than ever, and there will be still more in the years to come. In the old days, both amateurs and professionals felt that one goalie to a team was enough. This has changed radically since the surge of hockey into the status of a major spectator sport.

The game is too fast, the pressures too great, and the duties too complicated for all the goal-tending responsibilities to rest on the shoulders of one man. Every team has at least two "regular" goalies, some three. Even the most durable goalie needs rest to stay at his competitive and emotional peak. This applies as well to big, strong National Leaguers like Cesare Maniago, who stands six-foot-three inches, as to small professionals like Charlie Hodge, a pocket-sized five-foot-six.

Contrary to one popular misconception, that goalies do not have to be outstanding skaters, skating is as essential to their job as to everyone else on the team. Goalies *must* be fine skaters. There was a time when a good one needed only to stand in front of his cage and stop shots, but that day is gone forever. The modern goalie must be prepared to skate out of his net, sometimes several feet, to meet on-coming puck carriers. There he can cut down the shooter's angle and smother his shot before it is on its way.

The so-called "wandering" goalie—a man who likes to drift out all the time—is no longer uncommon, although it once was. Some good goalies rarely stay put because they find it more expedient to meet the man coming in than to let him get off his shot. A "wanderer" will get fooled occasionally (which will probably cost him a goal), but this seldom happens to a good goalie. Too much wandering is not normally recommended. Since each goalie must find his own strengths by experience and experimentation, if wandering is his most effective style, then he should wander.

Broadly speaking, goalies come in two fundamental styles—the stand up kind who keeps on his feet whenever possible and plays the angles, and the kind who drops to the ice and spread-eagles his feet from a sitting position. Whether he does one or the other is immaterial, although some coaches demand their preference. It is, as are so many other things, pretty much up to the goalie himself. He knows which works best for him.

Nobody but a former goalie can really coach goalies, because only a former goalie can think like a goalie. Goalies would probably make good head coaches because they .often direct the play of the defense from their own vantage point, much as a catcher does in baseball. Busy as he is with his own job, the goalie is still the only man on the team who consistently gets a panoramic view of the action. He can see plays develop from both offensive and defensive standpoints. The best goalies are the best observers on the ice and, good or bad, they are the only players with momentary respites from the action.

The other five skaters are always moving. The goalie moves only when necessary. His basic position is in front of his net. He must be ready to take shots at all times. Even when the action is at the opposite end of the ice he must be on the lookout for a stray long shot that might trickle over his stick and into the cage.

The development of a goalie's ability should come when he first begins to play hockey. Most goalies have always wanted to play the position and started as youngsters. They sharpen as they grow older

and move through the younger ranks of amateur hockey. By the time a boy reaches high school, or Junior hockey in Canada, he knows that if he pursues a hockey career it will be as a goalie.

Right from the start, the goalie should go through the same skating drills that everyone else does. He should do some passing (although it is hardly necessary for him to receive passes), for he will often have occasion to pass to a teammate from his position in front of the net. But the important thing is that he skate with his mates.

Some goalies know this, but others will have to be supervised. Too many young goalies minimize the importance of skating. This is a skill that cannot be minimized. *Every man on a hockey team must be a good skater, and that includes the goalie.* He should be made to skate whether he likes it or not. It is a skill that he will need as long as he plays hockey.

He should be thoroughly adept at backward skating, especially if he is a wandering goalie. In skating backward, a goalie uses much the same technique as everyone else, moving in a semi-sitting position. He will probably find it easier to zigzag a bit more than the others on the team because of his heavy equipment. Skating straight backward will normally be clumsy, but many goalies prefer it. Whatever he finds most comfortable is best, as long as he can move fast and directly toward his net without looking back. A good goalie actually "feels" his goal, for he must always know where he is in relation to it, how far away, and in what direction he must go to get back to it.

In moving back, there is one thing a goalie must *never* do and that is turn around. Except when the puck is behind his net, his eyes are always in front or facing left or right, depending on where the action is. A skater watches his man. The goalie *always* watches the puck.

Once a goalie has developed his basic style—standing up or dropping to the ice—there is not very much a coach can or should do to change it. Obvious mistakes must be corrected, of course. A goalie must learn the angles, no matter what his style. He must know how to keep from getting faked out of position by a clever stick-handler; he must become accustomed to looking for the puck in a scramble, for the moment he loses sight of it he is in danger of being beaten by the opposition; and he must guard against the blindness of a screened shot —one that comes at him from behind an obstacle, usually another player. Sometimes he cannot help himself, in which case he must be ready for a quick save that he may make only when the puck comes back into his view.

Quick reflexes are a must for all goalies, just as for all the other players on a hockey team. The best goalies make some of their greatest stops at the last second. Often, their only weapon is instinct. They may not be able to see the puck until it is almost too late, but experience teaches them where to look for it, which, in turn, helps them find it after momentarily losing sight of it.

Although goalies are injury-prone because they are shot at by flying pucks, they are the best protected men on the ice. The mask, first consistently used by Jacques Plante but since picked up by amateurs everywhere and almost all professionals, is the newest and perhaps most effective device. Before Plante popularized the mask, facial injuries requiring multiple stitches were common-

place among goalies. Today's goalies rarely suffer stitches, although the mask has not prevented head injuries nor has it completely eliminated the kind of facial injuries that stun, even though they now rarely cut. Plante himself was knocked out in a Stanley Cup playoff game when hit squarely on the mask by a speeding puck. He later said the mask saved his life.

Long before masks were used, goalies wore chest protectors and thick leg pads that extended all the way to the thighs. Not only for protection, but for additional proficiency at doing their jobs, they also wear special mitts that enable many of them to develop unusually skillful abilities in catching the puck.

All this equipment, complete with an especially wide stick, gives the goalie certain advantages over his teammates. The goalie is the opponent's natural target, and anything that helps him become a better hockey player is good. He has one of the most important jobs on the ice. No matter how great everyone else is, if the goalie cannot do his part, the team will inevitably lose games that it would otherwise have won.

One of the best examples of a good dropping goalie is Tony Esposito. He goes down automatically, spreading his legs in eagle fashion from a sitting position. Because of his size—he is nearly six feet tall—he can cover virtually all the ice in front of the net. Because he goes down quickly, it is very hard to fake him. He can be beaten, of course— every goalie can be beaten somehow— but it takes a great shot and a very quick one to do it.

Glenn Hall, a goal-tending immortal who spent nearly twenty years in the National Hockey League, and Roger Crozier are other typical examples of good goalies who often leave their feet. Like Esposito, both play angles but constantly move back into the cage, going down as they move if they have not already dropped. They can do as well on their knees as on their skates. Esposito and Hall are big enough to cover the cage on their knees. Crozier, who goes from side to side as quickly as anyone in hockey, is just as effective because of his agility.

Plante, besides introducing the goalie's mask, was an innovator in wandering, the first to move consistently out to meet an on-coming skater. Gerry Cheevers is particularly good at this style of play, since he is a fine skater and perhaps the best stick-handler among all the pro-

Figure 3-3.   *Ken Dryden.*

fessional goalies. Some goalies use the stick almost as a crutch, others resort to it occasionally, but few, if any, use it as a defensive weapon as effectively as Cheevers. He considers the stick an important facet of his game. Although no count has ever been taken of such a statistic, it is probable that Cheevers stops more shots with his stick than anyone else in hockey.

Ken Dryden (Figure 3-3) was one of the best goalies ever to play for an American college hockey team. He was All-American for his three varsity years at Cornell, where he played his position as it has never been played before in college hockey. A six-foot-four inch stand up goalie who, because of his great size, could easily span the nets with his arms, he was great in all departments of goaltending.

Dryden, when he starred for the Montreal Canadiens, played essentially the same game as a professional as he did as an amateur. His quick reflexes permitted him to roam around almost at will. He played angles and split into the corners as fast and as effectively as anyone who ever played the game. He was also great with his glove, stopping many hard shots by catching them.

A good stand up goalie rarely leaves his feet, and Dryden was no exception. He went down only when there was no other way to stop the puck, and could scramble back to his feet as fast as a smaller man. Dryden, who may have been the best goalie in pro ranks, as he was college hockey's best while at Cornell, was probably on his feet more than any other goalie in the business. His only reason for going down was to make a stop or to smother the puck so he could force a faceoff.

Although it is virtually impossible to have two goalies of exactly equal abilities, it is essential that every team have a substitute to play half, or nearly half, the team's games. This is a comparatively new development. Until recent years, one goalie could handle the job, with his backup man usually in street clothes, prepared to take over only in the event the regular goalie was hurt.

Just how the two (or three) goalies in uniform are used is up to the coach. Some goalies are at their best playing two or three games in a row, then resting. Others are at their peak when playing alternate games. In professional hockey, some goalies do better than their partners against certain teams. In college ranks, the purpose of backup goalies is to give the first-string man a rest.

Some coaches split their goalie up in the same game—having Goalie A play the first and third periods, with Goalie B playing the second and vice versa, reversing the procedure in successive games, continuing this arrangement throughout the season. There should be no hard and fast rule about this. Changing goalies just for the sake of changing them does not necessarily make sense. The good coach experiments until he finds the best way to use his goalies. This might take part, half, or even all of a season. The temperament of the goalie himself might be a factor. Some goalies do better when they know in advance they are going to play. Others, inclined to fret, are better off given the game assignment at the last minute.

Temperament and personality are usually more important when dealing with goalies than with any other members of a hockey team. Goalies bear the heaviest burden, and if they do not know it by the time they reach college or high Junior status, they learn when they get there. Some goalies must be handled as carefully as stage stars because they are inclined to be prima donnas. Others take life as it comes and can be handled like any other hockey player.

One of the keys to Dryden's greatness was his calm refusal to let his job get him down. As a result, he had few bad nights. But brooding is an occupational disease among goalies. One bad night can get them down for a week or more. Some blame themselves for any loss, which, although hardly ever justified in the case of a good goalie, is understandable. If the puck goes by the goalie it lands in the cage. The fact that the goalie may have had no chance whatever to stop it does not make him feel any better.

The handling of goalies is an art that every good coach must learn. How the amateur or college coach handles him may make the difference between the goalie's failing or succeeding. The coach can help him in his formative years, but the pro coach cannot do very much for him. By the time the goalie gets into professional ranks, his ways are as set as his style of play.

It is not possible to lump goalies together and say, "This is how to be a goalie." Every goalie is different—different in style of play, different in temperament, different in his weaknesses and strengths, and different in all other ways. Even two goalies on the same team are different from each other. Each does his thing in the way he finds most effective. The only similarity between professional goalies, the one thing they have in common, is that they all know their business. They may perform in different ways, but their results are pretty much the same. Their job is to stop the puck from going into the net. When they

reach the major-league hockey level, they are all good at it.

Unlike amateur hockey, in which teams usually see personnel new to them, the professional goalie depends heavily on knowledge of his opposition. He knows who plays how, who wants to be in close before shooting, who tries to "deke," who likes to shoot from farther out—and how far out, who can be faked into making the first move, who cannot, who has the hardest shots, who has the trickiest moves. The longer a goalie is in the business, the more he knows. This is why, as a general rule, the experienced goalies do better than the inexperienced ones. The rookies who do the job well the first time around are few and far between.

Even experienced goalies have weaknesses they never overcome, weaknesses the opposition quickly learns and quickly tries to use to its advantage. One of the best goalies in pro hockey history, the late Terry Sawchuk, who won the Vezina Trophy as the league's outstanding goalie four times, had a serious weakness that stayed with him to the day of his death. He could not handle a shot that was high on the short side.

Even if the goalie does not wander, every good one will move out slightly toward the puck carrier to cut down all angles for the shot. The deeper the goalie stays, the better the angles for the man with the puck. Obviously, the farther out the goalie moves, the poorer the angles but the more chance for the carrier to stick-handle around him and get a shot at an open net (see Figure 3-4). Each, of course, wants the other to make the first move because the man who does that is usually the loser. But the goalie has a big advantage. There is no one in his way, no one harassing him, no one

a   b

Figure 3-4.   *Goalie out and in series. (a) Out—note more net coverage when goalie is out. (b) In—note more open area for scoring.*

following him, and time is on his side. The carrier has only a split second to shoot. If the goalie does not telegraph his intentions, the skater *must* shoot while still in a scoring position. Failure to do that will cost him the chance because he is going so fast he will skate himself out of position if he does not shoot in time.

When the skater comes at the goalie from the left, the goalie will fall away from the right post, and vice versa. The skater then shoots up high on the short side because that is where the opening is. If, for example, the goalie falls away from the right side, that will be the short side and the skater's best chance to score is to shoot high on the right.

Screened shots are among the tough-

est to stop. The biggest mistake goalies make on screened shots is trying to look over the players in front. A goalie should be looking down. The puck is almost always somewhere on the ice, not above it. In a scramble in front of the net, *down* is where to look for it. Sawchuk was so good at this that he rarely got beaten on a screened shot. He was one of the few goalies who knew how to handle it.

Equipment has become a more and more important factor for all professional goalies. Years ago, they wore the same gloves as other members of the team. Now they wear a different type of glove on each hand. Their free-hand glove (the side with which they do not handle the stick) is an almost exact replica of a baseball player's first baseman's mitt, with heavier padding than any other fielder wears, but not as heavy as a catcher's. The only difference is that goalies' mitts have additional padding around the wrist area. Broken wrists used to be fairly common goalie injuries, but now they are rare.

On the stick side, the goalie's glove is loose fingered, with fiber on the back and padding around the knuckle and, of course, the wrist area. It is loose fingered for freedom in holding the stick. The padding and fiber on the back is to stop shots, since a goalie will stop as many shots with the back of his glove as with the front.

The goalie's stick is also quite different from the skater's. In the major hockey leagues, all goalies do not use the same type of stick. Some are light, some are heavy. The stick's blade, much wider than any other stick, varies in width and handle, depending on the goalie's personal preference. The rules permit the stick to be up to three and a half inches in width going up twenty-four inches of the handle. The rest of the handle is the same width as any other stick. Some goalies do not want as much as three and a half inches in width, nor do all like the stick that thick up to twenty-four inches.

Most big-league goalies use a straight lie—around a 12 or 13—since they want the whole blade from toe to heel flat on the ice. It does not make any difference what type of goalie he is, whether he stays on his feet or goes down, whether he wanders or sticks pretty close to his net. He makes a good many stops with his stick, and he cannot afford to leave an opening between any part of it and the ice. The puck may go into the net over the stick, but never under

it if the goalie has the right stick and is holding it properly.

From the standpoint of efficiency, taping the goalie's stick is almost meaningless. The principal reason goalies use tape is to save wear and tear on the stick. However, tape causes friction, giving the goalie better control when passing the puck out to a teammate. A good goalie knows how to pass. In the major hockey leagues, just getting the puck out of the way is not always enough. The goalie should know which man is in the best position to go up the ice, and he should also know where to put the pass to help that man get off to a fast start.

Assists are credited to the man, or men, who handle the puck leading up to the actual scoring of a goal. In order for a goalie to get an assist, the man he passes to or the next teammate passed to must score without anyone on the opposing team breaking the sequence by gaining possession of the puck.

Among today's goalies, one of the best at getting the puck up to his forwards is Gerry Cheevers, who is a particularly good stick-handler. Although the stick looks big and clumsy, some goalies handle it as cleverly as other members of the team. A goalie should poke check the puck away from a skater bearing down on him, particularly from the side. A poke check is a surprise check. The player's stick comes out from nowhere like a snake's tongue to knock the puck off an opposing skater's stick.

Leg pads are very important to a goalie because they must be exactly right, not so low they leave him unprotected nor so high they interfere with his maneuverability. Professional goalies often spend hours selecting leg pads. An amateur

a   b   c

Figure 3-5. *Goalie without stick series. (a) Good position in net, although some coaches feel the goalie should be out farther. (b) Moving right skate for widest coverage; note bent knees. (c) Puck has been stopped, left knee is down on ice to prevent rebound score.*

who needs them would be well-advised to take an experienced or retired goalie with him to help pick them out. All goalies' pads are the same width—ten inches. The only variation is length.

Although other players wear tube skates, the goalie's skates are similar to a figure skater's, closed in front and back. Between the heel and toe are additional steel posts connecting the blade to the boot to keep the puck from slipping through openings. As with everything else he wears, a goalie's skates are used as defensive weapons, which is why they are longer than his teammates' skates—they are twelve or thirteen inches. This permits the goalie to kick out with his skates when necessary without worrying about the puck slipping around them. It also gives the goalie another little edge because his skates, like his stick, sit flat on the ice.

Except that the padding is a bit heavier, a goalie's chest protector is almost

exactly like a baseball catcher's. Goalies also wear arm protectors, made of felt, which run from the wrist to the shoulder with a break at the elbow for full freedom of arm and hand movements. Masks, although comparatively new, are essential for safety because most hockey play today is in the offensive zone, there are many more shots on goal than there used to be, and the puck travels faster than in past years. Today, with the curved stick and the slap shot, almost any forward can shoot at great speed. Several men have had shots clocked at 100 miles an hour and a few can shoot 120.

Along with skating, a goalie must practice falling on the ice and getting up and moving quickly from one side to the other. One good method of training is for a skater to stand in front of the nets, moving one foot or the other as the goalie gets up. If the skater moves his left foot, the goalie moves his right, and vice versa. Skaters can also make other moves to train the goalie in quick reactions.

Some goalies must be handled very carefully because, unless they have a sense of humor like Cheevers or are able to leave their game on the ice like Ken Dryden, they are apt to be moody, especially after letting an easy shot trickle through.

A goalie belongs in the area of his own crease. There is no question that he must move up a little to cut down the angles, but never more than a few feet. A young goalie who tries to move out as far as the rules permit (the red line at the center ice in professional hockey), is usually asking for trouble. If some-one poke checks the puck away from him, he will be stranded far from his goal and the man who takes the puck away from him has an empty net at which to shoot.

Even if a defenseman or forward can get back to the net ahead of the opposition, the odds are all against the wandering goalie's team. Trained goalies have their hands full doing their job. Any other player moving into an unprotected net to cover for a goalie who has wandered too far away from it almost takes his life in his hands. No one else is equipped to take the beating a goalie must take and no one else should be asked to do so.

The wandering goalie not only fails to do his job but risks the good health of one of his teammates if the other team steals the puck. Wandering is not recommended for any aspiring goalie. His job is near his net, and that is where he should stay.

4

Common Penalties and Violations

PENALTIES

Hooking

This is jabbing or pulling with the stick around an opponent's arms, feet, or body from behind him. It calls for a two-minute penalty. This is a lazy man's penalty because a player only hooks when he cannot catch up with the man he is chasing, so he reaches out with his stick. It is much better to wait until the man has had to slow up or turn or do something that gives his pursuer time to catch up. Hooking is usually so wide open that the officials are almost sure to catch it and anyone hooking should know he is almost surely asking for a penalty. Although illegal to hook a man's body, it is perfectly legal to hook his stick. When the hooking is wood to wood there is no penalty—only when it is wood to body. Most people do not know this and wrongly demand that a penalty be called when it happens. In poke checking, which is legal, a player might hook his opponent's stick.

Slashing

This is a totally unnecessary, indeed a ridiculous way, to pick up a two-minute penalty. Slashing is grabbing the stick with both hands and hitting an opponent's pads, arms, or any part of his body. Easily spotted and quickly called, it is nearly always the result of a momentary loss of temper. A cool head is the best way to avoid a slashing penalty.

Elbowing

Although not always done purposely, since a player's elbow might come up involuntarily while he is making a legal bodycheck, it can be dangerous and calls for at least a two-minute penalty. It is seldom called unless the player brings his elbow up high enough to hit an opponent in the face. If he draws blood, he will get a five-minute penalty, as he will when drawing blood on any illegal maneuver. However, if a player draws blood while making a legal check, there is no penalty. The best way to avoid an elbowing penalty is to be careful not to bring an elbow up too high while making a legal check.

Interference

There is a thin line between interference and a legal check. If, for example, a player is coming out of his zone in possession of the puck and one of his teammates moves in front of an opposing player coming in to forecheck the player with the puck, the teammate is guilty of interference. There is no penalty if he blocks out a man who has no chance to check the puck carrier—it must be the one who might forecheck the player if he had a clear shot at him. Another form of interference is to take a man out of the play who is not in possession of the puck. This is an even more difficult call to make unless the offending player touches an opponent not in possession. In that case, it is clearly interference, calling for a two-minute penalty. The best way to avoid an interference penalty is to keep hands, stick, and everything else off a man without the puck or to be sure the would-be forechecker of a teammate with the puck is left alone.

High Sticking

This often covers a multitude of sins, including fighting. Fighting is a major penalty, calling for five minutes, and professional-league officials do not like to call it unless one man clearly started

the fight or unless both keep trying to commit mayhem on each other while cooler heads are attempting to part them. Usually, what appears to be fighting is called high sticking, especially if nobody gets too violent or tries to continue a fight after it has been broken up. Otherwise, high sticking is called if, in making a check, one player or the other brings his stick up over his shoulders, threatening the danger area around the head or face with the stick. Obviously, the easiest way to avoid a high sticking penalty is to keep the stick below the shoulders at all times.

Holding

Another minor infraction calling for a two-minute penalty, holding is grabbing another player with the arms or locking an elbow on an opponent's arm to keep him from moving. It is most commonly done in the corners against a strong man trying to get out. Not always easy to see, it is an infraction often missed by officials, especially in a crowded situation during which several men are battling for the puck. Holding is sometimes unavoidable, and often not committed purposely.

Boarding

This is running at a man and crashing him into the boards, a dangerous maneuver since it might draw blood. If it does not, it is a minor infraction, carrying a two-minute penalty. If it does, it is treated like any illegal check drawing blood and calls for a major five-minute penalty. It is not an easy infraction to hide. It could be put in somewhat the same class as slashing, often the result of a loss of temper, and never very smart. It is, of course, completely avoidable and inexcusable, really asking for at least a minor penalty and risking a major.

Tripping

When deliberate, this is obvious and easy for everyone, on the ice or in the stands, to spot. It is usually done with the stick, an overt attempt to take an opponent's feet out from under him. If he goes down because of a flagrant, open trip on the offender's part, it calls for two minutes. However, if a man trips an opponent by accident while trying to take the puck away, there is no penalty. Whether or not it *is* an accident is usually up to the official's discretion. If he thinks it was done on purpose he will impose the penalty. There is no way to avoid an accidental trip, but a deliberate one is sheer stupidity.

Charging

This is another minor offense that may or may not be a judgment call on the part of the referee. Ordinarily, it is easy to spot because it is usually done from several feet away. The offender runs at a player, gathering speed as he moves. After he takes more than two steps, charging will be called if it is at a player in possession of the puck. If the man hit does not have the puck, it is interference. Charging is occasionally a deliberate, desperate maneuver which may be designed to help the team. If, for example, a man is free and headed for a possible score, charging him is one way to keep him from getting a shot off. In that case, a defensive player would be justified in taking the penalty purposely. This is the only circumstance in which deliberate charging makes sense. Otherwise, it is just asking for an unnecessary penalty.

Cross Checking

This is an illegal stick maneuver. The offending player holds the stick in both hands and pushes at an opponent, usually aiming for his arms where there is no padding. The result is often a painful, but not serious, bruise-type injury. Cross checking is deliberate and usually perpetrated by somebody who has momentarily lost his temper. It calls for a two-minute penalty and, of course, is easily avoided.

Spearing

Actually, this is one of the dirtiest tricks in hockey because either end of the stick is aimed at the stomach area, where there is no padding and where dangerous injury to the spleen, ribs, or stomach can be caused. An attempt to spear without hitting the man calls for a two-minute penalty. Whether or not it is a major five-minute penalty depends on how badly the victim may be hurt after he is hit. In any event, spearing can set off a fight, sometimes a free-for-all. An inexcusable infraction, it is nearly always the aftermath of bad blood between two players causing loss of temper, often on the part of both.

Misconduct

This is a personal penalty of varying degrees, depending upon the circumstances. The most common penalty is for reacting hastily or talking profanely to an official, usually in protest of a decision, or for gross insubordination toward an official. Normally, a misconduct, which can be imposed on a man on the bench as well as somebody on the ice, calls for ten minutes in the penalty box. In the professional leagues it includes an automatic fine of fifty dollars. Whether the penalized player is in the game or on the bench, the team does not have to play short-handed. Much more serious than an ordinary misconduct penalty is either a game or a match misconduct. This is for aggravated behavior on the part of a player or someone on the bench toward an official. It would include persistent abuse, a physical attack on the official, or an overt attack on another player with the obvious intention of causing serious injury. A game or match misconduct requires a full report to the league president, who then imposes whatever penalty he may see fit. It is a rare penalty, because few players, even when they lose their tempers, carry their abuse to such extremes. On their part, officials will call it only when the infraction is so grossly apparent that they have no other choice.

A word about fights: until the 1971–

72 season, when stiff punishment was meted out to any third player who injected himself into a two-man fight, gang battles were fairly common in the National Hockey League. This was the first time really effective legislation against fights was devised by the league's governors. Up to then, the only rule designed to curb fights was a heavy fine imposed on a man leaving the bench to join in a free-for-all, and although this move cut down the magnitude of the fights, it did not stop team fighting altogether. The third-man-in rule, on the other hand, did much more to cut down the wild melees which not only stopped game action but increased the chances of injury.

Fights usually develop from high sticking duels between two players. There is no way individual tempers can be curbed, especially when one man is sure another deliberately fouled or tried to hurt him. Alert officials can stop even two-man fights from developing by quickly imposing high sticking penalties. Their power to stop gang fights is much greater with the third-man rule.

Penalties are as much a part of hockey as they are a part of basketball. Although they put extra power into the hands of officials, there is no question that they are a necessity to keep the game under control. Hockey is a fast, exciting, perpetual motion sport and, as is common with most other sports, a potentially dangerous one. The chance of injury is always present even in the natural course of events. That chance is increased many times when a fight develops. When fights are cut to an irreducible minimum, so may injuries be.

This is why the rules include penalties. Too often, infractions can cause injury.

84

Since they do not have eyes in the backs of their heads, officials cannot catch every infraction.

PENALTY SHOTS

Now also rare, a penalty shot is awarded when a player commits a foul against an opposing man who is bearing down alone on a goalie and apparently is headed for a clear shot at him. The offending player must obviously be fouling his man with the express purpose of preventing him from getting off a shot on goal. If, despite the infraction, the attacking player succeeds in scoring, there is no penalty. When a penalty shot is called, play stops while a member of the attacking team takes a clear shot at the goalie. Even if a penalty shot is almost sure to be called, this is one rule infraction which sometimes makes sense. The infraction itself might prevent the skater from taking the shot. The penalty shot that might result is not a sure goal, but it does put the goalie at a disadvantage because, with no protection in front of him, he must do everything himself. No rule infraction is recommended, but this one is easier to justify than any other.

VIOLATIONS

Icing

This is determined by a linesman instead of the referee and is never called against a short-handed team. If a defending player shoots the puck from his side of the red line (the defensive blue line in college hockey) all the way down to the opponents' crease, with the two teams at equal strength, it is probably, although not always, icing as soon as anyone on the defending team touches it beyond the crease. However, if the linesman feels that someone on that team could have touched the puck before it reached the crease and purposely stayed away from it when he could have prevented it from crossing the crease, the official may not call it icing and play will continue at that end of the ring. If icing is called, the faceoff goes back to the offending club's zone.

Offside

This is called against a team when one or more of its players crosses the other team's blue line ahead of the puck. It calls for a faceoff on the offending team's side of mid-ice. It is a frequent infraction because when a team in possession skates toward the opponents' zone everyone is going so fast it is hard to stop at the blue line before the puck carrier gets over it.

Delayed Call

This comes when someone on the team not in possession of the puck commits a foul. If play is stopped at that point it would, in effect, penalize the nonoffending team. The referee holds his hand in the air to show that he will call a penalty as soon as the puck changes hands, but not until it does. In the meantime, the attacking team is not interrupted while on its way to what might be a score. An alert goalie will skate off the ice to make room for another skater when a delayed penalty is called against the opposition. Since play will be stopped as soon as that team gets possession, there is no way it can score, and a sixth skater will add pressure when the goalie's own team is trying to score. The moment a delayed penalty is called, the goalie is not doing his job if he does not skate right to his own bench. His doing so gives his team everything to gain and nothing to lose. He is not needed in the nets because the other team cannot score anyhow.

Players can and should cooperate with officials. Through knowledge of the rules and willingness to try to live up to them, there will be a better, cleaner game.

III

Team Play

5

Zone Play

DEFENSIVE ZONE

Coaches usually find it harder to teach defensive hockey than offensive hockey. Any youngster is offensive-minded, because that is where the glamor is—in scoring goals. This is a common weakness among all players. If they would spend more time on defense, they would be better all-round hockey players.

Faceoffs

There are variations in defensive zone faceoff patterns, depending on several factors—the talent available, the coach's preference, the immediate game conditions, and individual strengths and weaknesses. In any faceoff situation, the most important factor is the center's talents— specifically, his strengths and weaknesses.

By the time a team gets into the regular season, the coach should have given drills in the alignment of the team in a defensive faceoff. In discussing defensive faceoffs, offensive faceoff alignments must be touched on, too. Offensive faceoff drills will be considered in detail later in the text. Reference to the offensive faceoff arrangement in this section is only with relation to the defensive faceoff situation. In other words, the defensive faceoff alignment will depend on what the offense is doing.

This is particularly true when meeting a familiar opponent, a team that has been faced before fairly often. Although this is more likely in professional hockey, which has set teams playing regular season schedules, it is often also true in amateur hockey. School, college, and amateur coaches, and often team personnel as well, learn what to expect from certain opponents. They also know, either from scouting or playing against a team before, which men are more proficient at doing what.

In a defensive faceoff situation, the most important man is the center. Normally, he is the one fighting the offensive center for the *draw*—the advantage in the faceoff. When the referee drops the

91

puck for a faceoff, one or the other of the centers (who usually are facing off against each other) will get control of the puck.

It is most important for the defensive team to know what the offensive center is most likely to do with the puck if he gets control of it on the faceoff. This is why the offensive alignment must be considered when discussing the defensive alignment in faceoffs in the defensive zone.

One team's defensive zone is the other team's offensive zone. Therefore, the actual location of the defensive or offensive zone is the same. The only difference is in the point of view. If that zone is one team's defensive zone, it is that team's job to get the puck out as quickly as possible. By the same token, if it is a team's offensive zone, its objective is to get the puck and score.

At each end of the ice, there are two circles, one on each side of the ice. Each circle is drawn around its center (where the opposing centers will face each other on a faceoff) which is fifteen feet in front of the *crease*. The crease is that part of the red line drawn across the ice which is in front of the net.

There is no line to designate the face-off circle—only the circle itself. Therefore, an imaginary line must be drawn through the center of the circle (and its mate on the other side of the ice). Although fifteen feet in front of the net and well off to the side, it is a dangerous position for the defensive team. The center of these two circles must be at least ten feet from the boards. This still leaves the circles too far to the right or left of the crease to make a direct shot at the goal practical. It is possible to score from there, but highly unlikely. The offensive center will therefore not

find it to his advantage to try to keep the puck if he wins the draw. His job is to pass it to someone, preferably a wing who is in a better position to score than he is.

The defensive center tries to prevent the offensive center from gaining possession of the puck. There is little point in *his* trying to keep the puck either. He has to concentrate on winning the draw. If he does that, he must then pass the puck to a man who can be the next link in the chain the defensive team forges in trying to get the puck out of the zone.

The offensive center wants most to get the puck to a man who is in or close to the *slot* (see Diagram 1). This is the scoring zone, a point formed by imaginary lines diagonally out from the net. The slot is actually a triangle, with the net the point, the diagonal lines the sides, and the long side thirty or forty or more feet in front of the net.

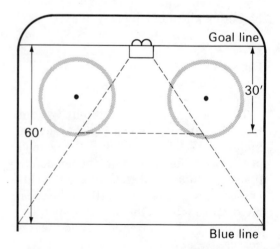

Diagram 1.   *The Slot. At least one offensive player (no team penalty) should be in the slot most of the time.*

In the age of the slap shot, the slot is bigger than it used to be. Before the slap shot, which can enable a man to score from the blue line, the long side of the slot's triangle was fairly close to the net. Today, it may be the blue line itself.

Wherever it is, the scoring zone is any area in front of the net where the angle makes it possible for the offensive team to get a shot on goal. (See Diagram 2 and Figure 5-1.)

The defensive center in a faceoff tries first to keep the puck out of the slot. If he is to attain his objective of getting the puck out of that zone, he wants to pass the puck to a man as far away from the slot as possible. He will not always succeed, of course, any more than it will necessarily be disastrous if he does not succeed. After all, other men on the defensive team are in the slot whose job it is to keep the offensive team from

scoring. But in hockey, the best defense is that which makes the immediate area safest for the goalie. He is there to stop the puck, but the fewer shots the opposing team gets at him, the less chance it has to score.

The most common faceoff is called the *special spot faceoff.* The special spot is one of the circles in front of and to the right or left of the net. Which circle is used is up to the referee. Usually, this is the circle closest to the point where play has been stopped. It is an advantageous position for the offensive team, a risky one for the defensive team.

On a special spot faceoff in the defensive zone, the only men permitted inside the circle are the two centers who are actually facing off. None of the other four skaters on the offensive team may be between the imaginary line across the center of the two circles. The only player always there is the goalie. Players of the defensive team are all on or behind the imaginary line and may have one skater at or near the red line.

Assuming that the faceoff is at the circle to the right of the goalie, the most

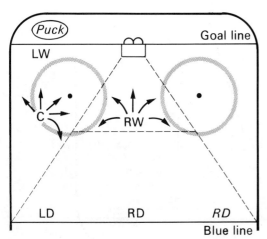

Note the defense may be spread to both points.

Diagram 2.   *Slot Variation. RW should move in and out, always looking at the puck.*

Figure 5-1.   *Properly stationed. Number 14 is in the slot.*

common defensive alignment is as follows:

1. The center in the circle for the faceoff.
2. The right defenseman at the red
   line to the right of the net.
3. The right wing on the imaginary
   line running through the center of
   the two circles, slightly to the right
   of the net.
4. The left defenseman immediately
   to the left of the right wing, also on
   the imaginary line, about fifteen
   feet from the left post of the net.
5. The left wing slightly to the left of
   the net and on the imaginary line.

6. The goalie in the right corner and
   about two feet from the net. (See
   Diagram 3.)

A typical offensive alignment under
the same conditions would be as follows:

1. The center in the circle for the faceoff.
2. The right wing either near the
   boards to the right of the center or
   in front of the net, to his left. In
   either case he is on the imaginary
   line.
3. The left wing just outside the circle
   at a point between the center and
   the blue line.

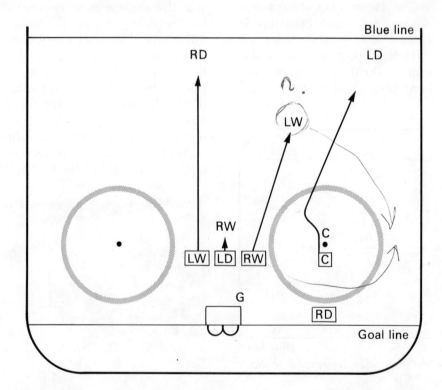

Diagram 3.   *Special Spot Faceoff. Man-to-man assignments: RD
plays offensive center; C plays offensive center, then to offensive
left defenseman or left point; RW plays offensive left wing; CD
plays offensive right wing.*

4. The two defensemen at the blue line, one near the boards, the other about on a direct line with the right wing.

Three members of the defensive team are to the net, with the two wings flanking the left defenseman in front of the crease. The right wing, however, is prepared to skate for the opposing left wing if the opposing center wins the draw and passes the puck to him. In this case, the offensive left wing is the most dangerous man, since he will be in position for a direct shot on goal, a pass to his right wing in front of the net, or a pass or back to his center if the latter is in a scoring position.

The defensive left defenseman must be prepared to intercept a pass from the offensive left wing to an offensive forward. If he fails, he must keep himself between the opposing forwards and his own goal. In any case, if the offensive center wins the draw, the defensive team is in trouble because the opposition will be deep in its zone and in possession of the puck.

One of the key men on the defensive team is the right defenseman. He is stationed on the red line to the goalie's right. If the defensive center wins the draw, his safest move would be to pass to the right defenseman, who will then be in a position to skate around the back of the net or, if there is an open teammate, pass to him.

Changes in these typical alignments are fairly common because of the differences in the center's preference or the manner in which the coach prefers to station his men. The center's forte is perhaps most important of all. He knows that strength better than anyone else, and will station his men accordingly. In

every case, it will be where he finds it easiest to pass to them. (See Diagram 4.)

The offensive center will usually want the best shooter other than himself nearest the faceoff circle. Assuming this is the left wing and the center is stronger getting the puck to his right than to his left, the left wing would be placed either behind the center or to his right—not near the boards. Since the defensive right wing must cover this man, the defense will depend heaviest on that right wing if the opposing center's strength on the draw is passing to the right.

Since the offensive defensemen must be on the points in this case near the blue line (if the puck crosses it, everyone on the offensive team is automatically offside), the defensive team must be prepared to cover them. If one gets the puck, he will have a shot on goal from a good angle, although it will be a long one.

Some coaches want these offensive defensemen on the blue line. Others prefer that they play two or three feet in front of it. Although this brings them that much nearer the goal, it also cuts their angle and can nullify whatever advantage the offensive team has if, after winning the draw, the offensive center fails to place the puck on the stick of one or the other. Because the puck will then pass the blue line it is the worst thing that could happen to the offensive team on a faceoff.

The defensive team must always bear in mind that in the cat-and-mouse game that is essential to hockey, anyone on the offensive team will try to deke (fake) it out of position. The defensive left wing, who is playing almost opposite the offensive right wing and beside his own left defenseman on a faceoff, is

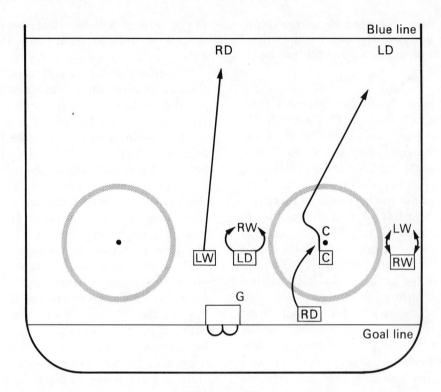

Diagram 4.   *Pro-Type Faceoff. Man-to-man assignments: Note change of position by offensive LW and defensive RW. Defensive C holds up offensive C until RD takes him.*

particularly vulnerable. This is why he continues to crowd the imaginary line and why the referee often must hold up play to push him back. The objective is to get the puck if it is passed to the opposing right wing either directly from the offensive center or indirectly from the offensive left wing, the man to whom the center is most likely to try to pass the puck.

Both defensive wings, who are on the imaginary line, as well as the defensive left defenseman, who is also on that line and between his two wings, must guard against obscuring the goalie's vision. The latter has trouble enough from the offensive team, which is trying to set up

a screen, without having to worry about his own teammates getting in his way.

The position of the offensive right wing will determine how far apart the defensive wings and defensive left defensemen are on the imaginary line. They can be packed solidly—almost touching each other—or they can be as much as a couple of feet apart. Their opponent— the offensive right wing—will provide the key. In any case, that offensive right wing is in the slot and only about fifteen feet from the crease, a good position to take a shot or snap in a rebound. The defensive team will try hard not to let him do either.

Another thing to be borne in mind on

the defensive team alignment in a face-off is that everyone must be prepared for almost any conceivable type of change. Hockey is a fast, fluid game. The alignments are to take care of the things that are most likely to happen, but there is no guarantee any of them will.

Hockey is, as has often been pointed out, a game of mistakes. The puck moves fast, the players move fast, and conditions change fast. It is impossible to predict, for example, who will win a draw. Some centers are much better at this skill than others, and some are so inept at this particular phase of play that they may not be used at center in faceoffs at all. Some centers are excellent at all other normal duties of a center, but unable to win the draw. There is no purpose in putting one at a wing if he is better at center when his only major weakness is in faceoffs. Many teams will use a wing instead of the center for the purpose and in these cases, the center will position himself where the wing would normally be on the faceoff. In effect, he is a wing, just as, in effect, the wing facing off is the center.

This is one of the factors for the interchanging among wings and centers. All three must be able to perform the jobs of the other two. If one of these jobs happens to be facing off, the men will swap places accordingly.

Sometimes, the referee will force a man other than the center to move into the circle. This is a pressure job. Each opposing center knows the importance of winning the draw. Either or both may jump the gun—start moving their sticks before the referee drops the puck. If it happens too often, the referee will wave a man out of the circle and a wing will have to move in.

Every offensive man is important in a faceoff, which is why the defense cannot leave anyone uncovered. The offensive right wing, stationed so near the net—within fifteen feet and practically in front of it—has to be closely watched by the defensive left defenseman, because the wing is in position to do almost anything.

He can take a pass and shoot. He can pick up a rebound, one of several types popularly known as a *garbage goal*. This may be scored from out of a tangle of players in front of the net. It may come on a screen shot. However, if it does come, the offensive right wing is in the best spot to execute and score. It will not be easy. That wing is blocked by at least two men—the defensive left wing and the left defenseman—and the defensive right wing is not far away. More than one goal has been scored and more than one game lost because of faulty work by one of these defensive players in a defensive zone faceoff.

One of the big changes in hockey during the past few years is the emergence of the slap shot as a strong offensive weapon. The importance of watching the offensive points—the defensemen—out near the blue line in a faceoff situation cannot be overemphasized.

Defensemen used to be big, strong, rough men, expert at dumping an oncoming wing, but today any good defenseman must also have an effective slap shot. In a faceoff, this may be the weapon that scores the goal the offensive team seeks. Both in amateur and professional hockey, more and more goals are being scored on slap shots from well out. Bobby Orr of the Bruins is a master at this. What a player has to do is develop a good slap shot. Among his best chances to use it will be as an offensive point (defenseman) in a faceoff situation.

When an offensive defenseman has a good slap shot, the defensive team must cover him as closely as possible in a faceoff in the defensive zone. The man who should do it in that situation is one of the defensive wings. They are flanking the offensive right wing at the imaginary line at the time of the actual faceoff. The defensive right wing will head for the offensive left wing if he gets the puck.

If one of the offensive defensemen—in a slap shot position near the blue line—gets the puck, the defensive wing should try to cover him on that side. One of the defensive defensemen must temporarily become a wing. He will be covering an opposing wing and may have to be ready to move up the ice as a wing if his team gets possession of the puck.

Here is a typical example of the fluidity of ice hockey. Wings and center are always interchangeable. Wings and defensemen must also be interchangeable at times. A muscle-bound defenseman who is all power and no finesse is not effective in modern hockey, any more than a muscle-bound guard is effective in modern football.

When the defensive left wing becomes the left defenseman, the defensive right wing will take the offensive left wing, who is between the faceoff circle and the blue line. This is his normal assignment. The defensive right defenseman, who is standing on the red line near the boards, may have to swoop down on a loose puck. His own center will try to pass him the puck if he (the center) wins the draw. If the defensive center fails to do that, he is better off shooting the puck down into the corner than passing it to one of his wings or to the left defense-

man. They are all too close to the net for comfort.

One of the hardest things in hockey is to get the puck out of the defensive zone legally. Only a short-handed team can shoot it to the other end of the rink without being called for icing. Assuming that the teams are at equal strength, the best way for the defensive team to get the puck out of its own zone on a faceoff is to get the defensive right defenseman loose and in possession of the puck. His best bet is to take the puck around behind the net, then pass it out to a teammate, either directly or by angling it off the boards.

Some people think scoring is the hardest thing to do, but most coaches know that scoring is a gift—usually something a man is born with. Getting the puck out of the defensive zone is no gift—it is hard work, something that can be accomplished only by intensive practice.

In reacting to a faceoff that finds the defensive team winning the draw, the offensive team must take the score or game condition into consideration. If the offensive team is leading by two or three goals, it can afford to backcheck. But if the game is close or the offensive team is behind, its players must forecheck—they have got to get that puck. Tenacious forechecking is their only hope to get back into the game.

On a faceoff in the defensive zone, there are two most likely situations the defensive team must watch for if the offensive team wins the draw:

1. The first choice of the offensive center is to pass the puck to his left wing, who is between the circle and the blue line.
2. The second choice of the offensive center is to pass the puck to his

right and on a diagonal behind him. This gets the puck to one of the offensive defensemen, putting that man in good position for a slap shot.

These are the popular (and logical) alternatives. In either case, the defensive right wing, who is in front of the crease to the right of the goalie, must go out to harass whoever gets the puck. This is the name of the game—knowing what to do in the defensive zone when the offensive team has the puck.

The goalie, who has the best view of the faceoff and thus knows best where the puck has gone, governs himself accordingly. He must move out to cut down the angle of the offensive team's shot—assuming one of its players can get off a clear shot. He can leave the left side of his net unprotected for the moment. The big danger will come from his right, where the entire offensive team (except its goalie) is packed.

The defensive goalie might have to move a bit over toward the middle of the net. This will be necessary if the offensive center, after winning the draw, has passed the puck to his right defenseman, who is at or near the blue line but almost directly in front of the net. This will put the defenseman perhaps fifty feet out, but he may be in a good position for a slap shot. If screened, as it could be, it will make a stop that much more difficult for the goalie.

A goalie should know where the puck is at all times. This is why he must watch the faceoff carefully. If his own center wins the draw, he has little to worry about, but if the offensive center wins it he must be on the alert for a shot from any angle from his right.

In this analysis of the faceoff in the defensive zone, it has been assumed that all the play is to the right of the goalie— that the special spot faceoff has been on the circle to his right.

If the special spot faceoff is at the circle to the goalie's left, everything is not necessarily reversed, as there will be some changes. Instead of the defensive right defenseman being stationed on the red line, the defensive left defenseman will play there in a faceoff situation. The right defenseman will be in front of the net, on the imaginary line bisecting the faceoff circles and between the two defensive wings. These wings will be in the same relative position.

However, the offensive right wing (who, with the faceoff on the left side of the ice, was stationed in front of the net on the imaginary line) will now probably be between the center and the blue line. The offensive left wing will be the one closest to the crease.

Thus, instead of the defensive right wing skating out to cover the offensive left wing, it will be the defensive left wing skating out to cover the offensive right wing. The offensive defensemen will be near the blue line, but the left defenseman will be closest to the center of the crease and the right defenseman nearer the boards, which now are to the goalie's left instead of to his right.

The goalie himself will be guarding the other side (the left side) near the post and his moves, although governed by the location of the puck after the faceoff, will be concentrated on his left side, rather than his right.

Whichever faceoff circle is used, the principle of the defending team's position will be the same. Everyone must do his job and cover the man designated to him, depending upon the conditions.

Everything in hockey is, in a sense, an

art. Every move is dictated by conditions. This includes faceoffs in the defensive zone. They are important to both teams, but are potentially more costly to the defensive team. If the players on the defensive team understand that and carry out their assignments, they have the best possible chance of staving off an attacking position that could result in a goal for the other team.

ZONE DEFENSE

The key to good zone defense is protection in the slot. The slot is a triangle with the long side anywhere from thirty to forty feet out from the crease to the blue line. The point of the triangle is the crease—the net. The slot is the scoring zone. The team that fails to protect it properly is the easiest team on which to score. It is essential in mapping out an effective zone defense that the slot be properly covered.

In covering the slot, the defensive team forms a *box*. This is exactly what it sounds like—a formation which roughly resembles a box around the slot and which best protects the net. In a box, the defensemen are normally in front of the net, with the forwards between them and the blue line. The right defenseman is to the goalie's right and the left defenseman to his left. The left wing is in front of the left defenseman and the right wing directly in front of the right defenseman. The center is nearest the blue line, ready to check the opposing center as the offensive team comes down in possession of the puck.

This is the way the play begins, but changes in the box are fast because of the movement of the puck. The purpose of the box is to keep the slot clear and, if possible, divert the puck to one side or the other (against the boards or into a corner), or to get control of it. If the offensive team carries into a corner or behind the net, the box breaks up as defensive players go to cover their men. But the offensive players will stay in the box as long as practical—until they either get possession of the puck, force the play into the corners away from the slot, or pin someone against the boards and force a faceoff.

The offensive left wing is coming in with the puck, ready to pass it to his center or right wing. The defensive right defenseman moves up to meet the offensive left wing. He will try to keep the left wing out of the slot. The defensive left defenseman must check the offensive right wing. He will protect the goalie's left flank while his right defenseman is either dumping the puck carrier, driving him outside, or trying to take the puck away.

The three attacking forwards will be passing the puck back and forth among them. The three defensive forwards will be trying to intercept, with each waiting for his own man. The attacking defensemen will be trailing the forwards and setting themselves up at either side of the blue line where they will try to keep the puck in the offensive zone.

The attacking defensemen cannot be ignored by the defensive team. They must be watched for a possible slap shot or for trying to move in the puck. One or the other would then become a forward with a teammate replacing him at the blue line. The attacking team is trying to break up the box, keep the puck, and score if possible. The defending team has only started in the box, but will not stay in it just for the sake of keeping it intact. The only purpose of the box is to set up a defense against an attacking team. It will probably not be possible to maintain the box formation indefinitely—the play moves too rapidly for that. It is strictly a defensive measure.

If the defensive team gets possession of the puck, the whole picture changes. The box breaks up because it has no further use. A team will not maintain a defensive formation like a box when, by gaining possession of the puck, it has become the offensive team.

The only time the box is maintained after a team gains possession of the puck in its own zone is when the defensive team is short-handed. This situation will be dealt with later. With a team at full strength, the box is only effective as a defensive measure.

In protecting the defensive zone, it must be borne in mind that basic maneuvers always apply. The defensemen in particular play the body, then the stick, then the puck—in that order. If a defenseman hits an attacking opponent in possession of the puck, he is doing his job only if he has succeeded in driving him away from the slot, shaking the puck loose, getting possession of it, or freezing the puck against the boards and forcing a faceoff.

Assume the attacking left wing, inside or approaching the defensive zone, has just received a pass. It is the defensive right defenseman's job to play him somehow, tie him up, stop his drive, or keep him from passing to a teammate. This right defenseman may *slide*. That is, he will go over a little to his left as he backchecks to force the approaching skater between himself and the boards.

The defenseman must know the possibilities. What alternatives does the puck carrier have when a defenseman is blocking a shot, a pass, or his progress? Forgetting for the moment what the wing should do, consider only what the defenseman should look for.

To begin with, the wing will have to slow up, turn, or come to a dead stop. Perhaps he will try to deke—fake the defenseman out of position to clear the way to get off a shot, get through, or pass to someone in a better position to shoot than he is. Possibly, he will come back to his right, but that will not be his preference. By doing that, he will have to shoot from his backhand. Few backhand shots are as effective as forehand shots, although some shooters have very good backhands. If the defenseman can force the wing to use his backhand, he is gaining something.

There is the possibility that the right defenseman will miss the man altogether, letting him get through. As the play develops, with everything concentrated to the goalie's right, both teams will have a tendency to swing over in that direction. If the right defenseman misses the puck carrier, the left defenseman should be in a position to stop him. In this case, the two defensemen will simply swap places. For the moment, the left defenseman is playing right defense and vice versa.

All skaters must realize the fairly constant need to cover another man's position. Once again, this is the essence of the game of hockey. The players must always be ready to pick up slack left by someone else's lapse. There will be lapses, for, as has been pointed out, hockey is a game of mistakes.

It is also essential to remember that even the goalie must sometimes be covered. If he comes out too far in making a stop and then fails to tie up the puck, the net will be open for a few seconds. In that case, it is best for a defenseman to cover for the goalie until he can get back, but if a defenseman is not in position, a forward must do the job. In any event, the net must never be left open when play is at that end of the ice.

Backchecking forwards, approaching their own defensive zones after losing the puck, should approach through the middle third of the ice—not on their own sides. The right wing and the left wing must both backcheck more toward the center than the sides because they will then end up in the slot, automatically protecting the scoring zone.

If they backcheck on the sides they may push their opponents into the slot. While the defensive defensemen are sliding toward the middle, the forwards can help them by being there already. Therefore, a good rule of thumb for a defensive forward is to stay away from the sides and concentrate on the middle. That is the danger zone—the scoring zone. For defensive purposes, it is better for the defensive team to be there —sometimes involuntarily forming a box.

Various factors will determine whether to backcheck directly or to rag the puck carrier after a team has lost the puck. One is the score. Another is familiarity or lack of it with the opposition. A third is the time of the game—early, middle, or late.

If it is the first time facing the other team and it is too early in the game to pick up peculiarities or habits of its individual performers, it is best to play with extreme caution. Normally a certain amount of caution will be exercised in the early stages anyhow. After losing the puck, a player should not lose sight

of it. The carrier might be deked, over-skate, not pass well—in other words do almost anything that could cost him the puck.

On the other hand, if he gets the puck into the defensive zone, then a player acts on defense against him as against any team. He does the things that should be done with the same objectives—stopping the other team from scoring and trying to regain possession of the puck.

If it is late in the game and a team is trailing by one or two goals, it does not pay to backcheck too fast, since there just is not enough time. It is necessary to forecheck, battle for the puck, taking the chance that the man will get away. If he does, the trailing team must backcheck, but its prime purpose is to get the puck. It cannot score without it, and late in the game in a trailing situation, scoring quickly is the only hope.

There are variations in setting up the zone defense in the defensive zone. Assume again that the left wing is carrying the puck in, approaching the defensive right defenseman. (In any of these examples, defensive zone play is the opposite if it is the right wing coming down, or the center on the right side, and the left defenseman waiting to meet one or the other.) The right defenseman is playing the left wing. The left defenseman is playing off the left post of the goal ready to play the offensive right wing. The right wing—under these conditions called the *hanger*—is trying to get in behind the goalie's back in hopes of shooting in a rebound or scoring a garbage goal in some other way. The offensive center will be following the left wing going in. In this way, he might pick up a pass or a drop pass or grab a loose puck if the left wing has lost it.

As the wing gets into the defensive

zone, the center will gradually start bending toward the net to be in a position to score if the puck is laid on his stick. In a scramble in front of the net, the center is usually the key man—the one to whom the puck should be passed if an offensive forward gets it but cannot shoot it. Sometimes the center might head directly for that spot. But if he is trailing a wing, he will watch for some sort of pass from that wing. He should be covered by one of the defensive forwards for that reason alone. It might be possible to intercept a pass, steal a drop, or do anything that will change the situation from a defensive to an offensive one.

Since the ideal move is to pass to the center bending in toward the net, the defense must try to keep that from happening. A smart offensive left wing might pass the puck *back,* either directly or by caroming it off the boards, to his own left defenseman if he finds it impossible to get past the defending right defenseman. If he does that, the defending right defenseman must not, under any circumstances, go back after the offensive left defenseman. He must stay with the offensive left wing. If he does not, it will leave the offensive team with an open shooter. If the offensive left defenseman cannot get a slap shot off, he must find an open man. His unprotected left wing—the man who originally brought the puck down or had it passed to him by another forward—might be just the one he is looking for.

Obviously, the offensive left defenseman should not be left unprotected either. In the event of a backward pass to him from the offensive left wing, the defensive right wing, who has been backchecking, should circle and head back through the middle to cover. It will

take him only a second or so to get there, but, once covered, the offensive left defenseman no longer has a clear shot at either the goal or a teammate.

Let us assume that by the time the defensive right wing has reached the offensive left defenseman, he has already passed across to his own right defenseman. That puts the puck on the other side of the rink from where it originally crossed the blue line. The worst thing the defensive right wing can do is chase the puck. Once on top of the offensive left defenseman, he should stay there. For the moment, that is his man.

It takes longer to describe these situations than for them to happen. Actually, every move is being made in split seconds. Everyone must think fast, act fast, and pick up men fast. At the outset, each man on each team—except the goalies, of course—has a specific man to cover, but only when conditions warrant it. Every hockey player will sometimes find himself in a position to cover someone else's man. In a potential scoring situation, it is necessary to cover the nearest man or the man who needs special coverage, such as the offensive left defenseman when taking a backward pass from his left wing.

Since the center is usually the best skater and best shooter, it is best for the defensive center to try to cover the offensive center in the defensive zone. This may not always be possible, but it is usually desirable. The offensive center should be in front of the net, ready to snap the puck in if it is laid on his stick. The defensive center should be right with him. Only if he has had to pick up another man—in which case a wing should move in so that the offensive center will not be uncovered—is there any excuse for him not to cover the opposing center when a shot on goal by him is imminent.

Many coaches have consistent success in *overloading*—packing the entire team on one side of the ice. This has a tendency to draw the defensive team over. The goalie, too, is faced in that direction. The effect is a lopsided game—everyone is on one side—and when that happens, the advantage is with the offensive team. It can smother the goalie with shots, set up screens, grab rebounds, and shake a man loose on the opposite side, leaving him virtually an open net if the puck is passed to him.

To try to cope with an overloaded offense by overloading the defense on the same side is a common mistake beginning coaches make. This is exactly what the offensive team wants. Therefore, it is the last thing the defensive team should do.

The simplest and probably most effective way to fight off an overload is not to fight it. Do not pack that side of the ice with defenders. Go right into a box. That will protect the slot and keep the defense from making a costly mistake. The offense will have to change its tactics, get back into a normal formation or some semblance of one, and play the defensive team's game rather than its own.

This, among other things, keeps the offensive team from shaking loose a shooter who can work from the goalie's blind side. By keeping the defensive team in a box, the goalie will not have a blind side. Furthermore, the stage is then set for the defensive team to cover everyone and there is less chance of an opposing skater getting clear. The whole purpose of overloading is thereby defeated, and the offensive team loses the advantage it has gained by overloading.

It will always take a disciplined defense to force a disciplined offense. By adequately defending its zone, the defensive team will minimize the easy shots—the garbage goals, goals from the blind side of the goalie, and hangers who get inside the defense for clear, close shots at the net.

A properly disciplined defense will force the offense into making long shots — from forty feet out or more. Even slap shots from that distance are stoppable. A good goalie can handle a long unscreened shot. There are goalies who will settle for dozens of them if it means no short, screened shots. They are the most common goals, the goals that often mean the difference between victory and defeat.

MAN-TO-MAN DEFENSE

Man-to-man defense in the defensive zone has changed during the past years. Prior to the change, forwards did not try to *shake their cover*. (The cover is the man assigned to take the forward coming toward the defensive zone with the puck.) In former days a puck carrier would often try to bull his way through the defensemen. The two defensemen used to work together, trying to squeeze the puck carrier as they dumped him. There was no real finesse to this maneuver. It was sheer power all the way—the power and nerve of the puck carrier against the strength of the defensemen. This type of defense made for the thrills once given professional hockey fans by Eddie Shore of the Bruins. He would take the puck, swing around the back of his own net (unmolested, since the offensive team backchecked to the blue line if it lost the puck in the other team's zone), pick up speed, fight his way through the forwards at center ice, then try to go between the defensemen. If he succeeded in splitting the defense—getting through on his own power in possession of the puck—he had only the goalie to beat.

This type of rush is more difficult today. When a team loses the puck in the opponents' zone, it can stay there, forechecking the puck carrier and covering teammates. One man seldom can get through that maze of opposing players, and, in fact, should not try. Hockey is not a one-man game, but a team game played much more scientifically than in Shore's time.

When a team loses the puck everyone usually backchecks (except under special circumstances, such as when a team is down one or two goals near the end of the game). The defensemen, if they are guarding the blue line in an offensive situation as they normally would be, should be the first into their own defensive zone because they are closer than anyone else. As they backcheck, they will be waiting for the men they are assigned to—the offensive left wing for the defensive right defenseman, the offensive right wing for the defensive left defenseman, etc. Each man has a man. The member of the defensive team covering a man is thus called that man's cover. Shaking the cover is what the offensive man is trying to do. If he succeeds he will get through, have a shot on goal, be free to pass to an open teammate, control the puck, or do anything else that seems feasible at the moment.

When the defensive man tries to stop the offensive puck carrier, he may hit him legally as long as he takes no more than two steps to reach him—otherwise

he is charging and is subject to a two-minute penalty. This is why a defensive left or right defenseman should wait for the puck carrier to reach him rather than *move up* to meet him.

When hitting, it should be body to body. The defenseman should have good balance—complete control of his skates, legs, stick, and body. He should tie up the offensive player's stick to prevent a shot of any kind, either on goal or a pass to a teammate. He should, in short, cover his man using everything legally at his command. This takes tenacity as well as skill. The closer the cover, the harder for the offensive player to shake him. The ideal cover is unshakable.

Although the defensive player stays in his zone unless he has a good reason for leaving it, his man-to-man coverage is well defined. He is responsible for any man who comes within the periphery of his zone. Whomever he hits or whomever he takes, the method of coverage is the same.

Special maneuvers sometimes make man-to-man coverage especially difficult. One of the most interesting and, if not handled properly, the hardest to stop, is the Russian crossover. It is a set offense used sometimes slavishly and not always to any good purpose by the best Russian teams.

In the crossover, a mandatory attack by Russian hockey teams (individuals who fail to conform are benched or penalized in some other way), the wings keep moving back and forth while the center stays at the apex between them when the line is attacking. Although this eliminates a certain amount of passing, it necessitates much more skating.

As a rule, the center carries the puck into the opponents' defensive zone. He is in front and would be offside if one of the wings carried it in. However, in the crossover maneuvers, there are times when the center may move to his right or left, to be replaced by the wing whose zone he is assuming. In that case, the wing, now in front, would bring in the puck.

The Russians seldom "dump" the puck into their attacking zone—that is, just shoot it across the blue line, with everyone following it in. Their crossover system makes this inadvisable because it might place their forwards out of position.

The attack is dangerous only after the forwards get inside the blue line. At that point, they begin to screen the goalie's vision, which becomes even worse when his own teammates start moving around to cope with the crossover. Once into the attacking zone, the center takes up a position in front of the net, much as he would in a conventional attack maneuver, while the wings continue to cross from side to side.

The Russian crossover is a standard formation from which the forwards rarely deviate. The trick is *not to follow* the skaters, but to *remain in the assigned zone*. Although in a sense this is zone defense, it is actually man-to-man. The difference is that the cover must constantly change. For example, he might be covering first the right wing, then the left, or on occasion the center.

The maneuver is successful only if the defending team tries to play the puck instead of the man. When that happens, there is a double screen in front of the goalie—the offense and the defense—and the goalie has that much more trouble seeing the puck. Since he must watch it constantly, he might be vulnerable to a score with so many skaters in his way. He has trouble enough when

the attacking team screens. When both do, he is always peering around trying to find the puck. Too often, in cases like that, it ends up in the net behind him.

Before playing a Russian team, it is essential that the coach put his team through a constant series of defensive maneuvers. Each man must know his exact assignment. If he fails, he will find the whole crossover so confusing that he will not know how to cope with it. There is no element of surprise, of course. This simply happens to be the way the Russians attack. Everyone knows it, and should understand the best methods of defensing against it. Hockey has been played this way for years.

In any hockey game, players working together must be ready to call out to their partners what to watch for. They should do this in practice so that it comes as second nature to them in a game. For example, if a defenseman sees he is going to lose his man, he should yell for help from the other defenseman. The goalie, in the best position to see everything, should also be yelling emergency instructions—"Watch your man . . . watch the center . . . watch the hanger. . . ."

In the Russian crossover, the wings and center should be constantly calling out who they will take on defense. In this way, the defensive right wing, for example, can yell that he is taking the opposing right wing as he approaches in the crossover. Then the defensive left wing will know—and call out that fact —that he is shifting from the offensive right wing, whom he had been covering, to the offensive left wing, whom he now will cover. Thus, while the Russian team continues to try to screen the goalie by crossing back and forth in front of him, the defensive team will be remaining on one side or the other, shifting men instead of zones.

This all sounds more confusing than it is. The proper shifts can be worked out in practice sessions, which is where the mistakes should be made. Once these are squared away, the Russian crossover is no longer confusing and may be somewhat easier to handle.

In explaining how to defense against a successful pass, including a drop pass wherein a man leaves the puck for his trailer to pick up, it is necessary to carry the play through to its offensive climax—the possible shot on goal.

A three-man line is coming down in possession of the puck against two defensemen. Behind these men are the defensive team's backchecking forwards. They have just lost the puck, which is why they are behind the play but not yet on it. The offensive center passes off to his left wing. This should be a *lead pass,* just a bit ahead of the wing so the latter will not have to slow up to get it. A lateral pass will kill his burst of speed and give those backchecking defensive forwards time to catch up with the play.

The offensive left wing gains possession by taking the pass and is fighting the defensive right defenseman, who is trying to squeeze him toward the boards. The left wing, realizing he cannot get through, has to get rid of the puck without losing it to the other team. The center, having passed the puck to the left wing in the first place, should be trailing him (by about ten feet) and *calling out that he is there.* This gives the left wing a good alternative to battle the defensive right defenseman or, hearing the center's voice, he knows the center is right behind him. He can *drop pass* (leave the puck on the ice) for his center to pick up. He knows it is a safe maneuver be-

cause the center will pick up the puck in a fraction of a second.

What does the right defenseman do? The nearest man on his own team to the play, he sees that the man he is covering no longer has the puck. Should he stick with that man—the offensive left wing—or should he go after the center, who has taken the drop pass and has possession of the puck? *He stays with the left wing.* This is very important. The left wing has become his man and he *must* continue to be the left wing's cover. The center is gone the minute he picks up that drop pass. The right defenseman cannot hope to catch up with him. If he tries, he not only will be trailing the play deep in his own defensive zone, but will be leaving an offensive forward open. With his cover out of the way, the left wing can move in close and be in position to take a pass with a possible shot on goal. If the play has moved to the other side of the net, he might even get that shot on the goalie's blind side.

A goal under those conditions would primarily be the fault of the right defenseman. If he had continued to cover the left wing, he would have made it difficult or impossible for this offensive forward to take a pass. Whenever an offensive skater has the puck and cannot do anything with it, he must find an open man. It is the right defenseman's responsibility to see that that open man is not the left wing.

In the meantime, the center who has taken the drop pass from the left wing must be covered by the *defensive left defenseman.* He will be drifting from his side of the defensive zone to keep the right wing covered. He must switch—on a man-to-man coverage basis—to the man with the puck, the center. By this time, the defensive forwards, who have been backchecking, should have arrived in their own defensive zone. The first one in should take the offensive right wing as soon as the defensive left defenseman has moved away from him to take the offensive center.

These are the ideal assignments for the defense. If they are properly carried out, the offensive team will not get a clear shot on goal. But they may not be carried out. Somewhere along the line, something may happen that will make it impossible to defense the situation properly. The puck carrier may be unusually fast and unusually clever. A man may have missed an assignment because he simply was not fast enough to handle it.

What happens when one free man with the puck in his possession gets inside for a shot on goal? To save the score, only one thing can happen. The goalie must make the stop. This is his primary assignment.

However, it does not necessarily have to be his *only* assignment. He should be able to help himself and his team by intercepting passes close to the net, smothering the puck before an offensive skater can shoot, or actually covering an uncovered man by going a step out to meet him. He cannot afford to go out farther.

If he must make a stop, he then should try to smother the puck to prevent a rebound. Rebounds are among the hardest to defense. Perhaps half the goals scored in hockey come on rebounds. The goalie has made a good stop, but cannot keep control of the puck. It caroms out, somebody pounces on it, and a goal results.

These are common problems to a goalie—the problems with which he constantly copes. However, he should always bear in mind that stopping the puck is only his *primary* job. It is not his

only job if he is alert, fast, and has good stick control.

Presume, for example, that the offensive left wing, caught in a box by the defensive right defenseman, cannot execute a drop pass. Instead of leaving the puck for the trailing center to pick up, he passes laterally to his own right wing, who is breaking toward the net as he tries to fight off his cover—the defensive left defenseman.

If the play is close enough in, this is a typical example of how the goalie can help himself without stopping a shot. His stick is on the ice—in fact, everyone's stick should be on the ice. This includes the potential receiver of the pass (the right wing) and his cover (the left defenseman). The goalie's role here can be as the intercept. If the play is close enough for him to reach the pass, he should try to stop it, then shoot it to a teammate, or in some way get it out of danger. In that way, he is, in effect, a sixth skater on the defensive team.

A good goalie will intercept perhaps half a dozen passes in the course of a game. This is not an extra job, but part of his regular duties. He cannot just stand in front of the net waiting to be shot at; he must help his teammates whenever he can.

If the goalie fails to intercept the shot, then it should be done by the left defenseman. He is the offensive right wing's cover, and stopping that wing from taking a pass from the opposite wing is part of his job. All players should know where the puck is at all times.

On an indirect pass, which caroms off the boards and usually is meant just to dump the puck into the defensive zone by the offense, it is a great temptation to go after the puck. Often a player on the defensive team can do this effectively, but most of the time the same old rule applies—play the man, not the puck.

This rule applies if the defensive player has less than a sixty percent chance of getting the puck. If it is fifty-fifty, he *must* play the man. If his chance is sixty percent, he uses his own judgment, always bearing in mind that if he fails, he is putting his team in a deep hole. Only if his chances of getting the puck are over sixty percent should he go after it when the offensive team has dumped it into the defensive zone.

Obviously, *somebody* on the defensive team must try to get possession. For safety's sake, it *must* be the man with the best chance to keep it or get it out of the zone. If the play has just returned to the defensive zone and the backchecking forwards have not yet arrived, it is up to the defensemen to tie up the offense until help comes.

On defense, however, it must always be remembered that possession of the puck by the opponents is not necessarily disastrous. Possession is useless if nobody in possession is able to shoot. That is what defensive hockey is all about. The best hope is to get the puck, of course. But the team that cannot get the puck can do just as well defensively by tying up the team that has it.

By playing the man (and his stick), a good defense can prevent shots on goal. An offensive skater pinned against the boards cannot score even if he has the puck. Neither can one whose stick is tied up, nor one who has an impossible angle for a shot. In other words, any offensive man properly covered usually cannot score.

With hockey a game of mistakes, the three defensive mistakes that are most common to young, inexperienced players are:

1. Breaking forward too soon in trying to cover an on-rushing skater. Anyone protecting a defensive zone must wait for the man to come to him. The individual battle between forward and defenseman will be won by the man who keeps his head and forces his rival to make the first move. The forward is already moving. He knows he has to get by the defenseman on his side or get rid of the puck. As he approaches that defenseman, the thing he wants most is to know what the defenseman will do. A premature move on the defenseman's part will give him the answer. Therefore, the defenseman *must* be patient. If he moves too soon, he commits himself. Once the defenseman commits himself, the rushing forward can move accordingly—angle away, deke, slide through—and the next thing the defenseman knows, his man is behind him with a possible shot on goal.

2. Not covering properly once the forward does reach him. The defenseman must hit his rival's *shoulder*. This is a legal check and a most effective one. Inexperienced defensemen sometimes try to stop a rusher in an easier way, reaching out with the stick, by bumping a man's hip, or by trying to play the puck. *There is no easier way than to hit him shoulder-to-shoulder.* This does not mean the outer part of the shoulder, because the puck carrier might simply bounce off and keep going. It must be the inner part, almost at the chest. There is more to covering than just hitting. A good defenseman will, once he has hit his man, smother him as much as legally possible. That means covering his body, blanketing him, blocking his view, and tying up his stick. By keeping constant pressure on the

offensive man's stick, it prevents him from getting into position for a shot.

3. Not controlling balance. Young skaters have a tendency to tense up on the approach of the offensive skater. The usual result is that their knees stiffen and, once that happens, they are standing straight up instead of crouching. The stick comes up off the ice automatically and all semblance of balance and control of the body is gone.

Although the above are the most common mistakes, there are others that young players are likely to make on defense. For example, they forget they should skate with short strides. A long stride while meeting an opponent throws a skater off-balance, makes him reach instead of hitting, and often carries him so far that the offensive skater will go right by him. Young skaters try to do the impossible—run through an opponent instead of tying him up. These are the moves the offensive skater is looking for in the defense; these are the weaknesses.

Young skaters, in their anxiety to hit, invite charging penalties by taking more than two strides in going after a man. They do not know how to ease themselves into a man rather than hitting him. This does not mean they should not hit hard. A good defenseman will wait until the last second before hitting, and when he does hit, he does not want to bounce off. By easing his body toward his opponent's, he can cover his man completely, tie him up, and prevent him from using his stick, all in one motion. This facility of movement can be acquired only through practice, dedication, and experience. No teacher expects a learn-

ing skater to know these things instinctively.

Another lapse often peculiar to young players—and sometimes to experienced ones as well—is failure to keep track of the puck. This is a must at all times, but particularly when playing defensive hockey. Obviously, it is impossible to prevent a shot if the puck is lost. Only in a wild scramble in front of the net, with half a dozen men struggling for possession, is there an excuse for losing sight of the puck. In that situation, everyone is looking for it, especially the goalie. But even in that situation, a few pairs of eyes should be trained on it. It is a potential scoring situation. In what amounts almost to a death struggle with one team trying to score and the other trying to keep it from scoring, anything can happen in front of the net, with no one man to blame if a goal results.

There can also be scrambles at other points on the ice. These almost always occur on the boards and usually near the corners. When several players are fighting either to free or freeze the puck, it is not always possible for everyone to keep it in view. However, that type of scramble is not imminently dangerous.

The most experienced hockey players have trouble seeing the puck under these special circumstances. But there is never an excuse for losing sight of it when movement is fluid, individuals are handling it, or two men are fighting for it. This is where young skaters have a tendency to fail. If a player remembers to watch the puck even if only out of the corner of his eye, he has a distinct advantage over the one who does not. To lose sight of the puck in a defensive situation can be a deadly error. Aside from the possible loss of a goal, it is essential to know where the puck is because of the speed in which a defensive team becomes an offensive team. The puck changes hands so quickly that failure to keep track of it can mean missing an important assignment that might arise in a split second.

For example, presume a team is fighting for the puck in its own zone. Everyone is playing defensive hockey. However, if a man steals the puck, intercepts a pass, or gets possession in some other way, the whole situation changes. The defensive team becomes the offensive team. Someone is carrying the puck down the ice, picking up mates on the way. The man who has no idea where the puck is can throw the whole offense off. If he happens to be a wing, he will chase a play of which he should be a part. If a defenseman does not cover for him, the forward line is crippled by the loss of a man. If a defenseman loses sight of the puck when it changes hands, he, too, is following the play to his assigned position. On offense, this must be on one side or the other of the offensive blue line. If he is late in getting there, an important point is left uncovered for the few seconds it takes for him to recover.

In hockey, scoring is the name of the game. A game is won or lost because of the number of goals it has accumulated. But, although scoring is the name of the game, one of its most important facets is defense. A good offense is the best defense in many games, but not in ice hockey. There, defense is an art in itself. The team with the best defense will win more games than the team with the best offense. The best offense cannot prevent the other team from scoring. Only the defense can do that.

OFFENSIVE ZONE

Faceoffs

There is a distinct difference between handling faceoffs in the defensive and the offensive zones. In the previous discussion about faceoffs, the emphasis has been on how the defensive team should react, and what it should do if its center wins the draw. Its objective is always to get the puck out of the zone. The offensive team's objective is just the opposite —to keep the puck in the zone and to score if possible.

The actual locations of the zones are the same; the difference is only the point of view. To the defending team it is the defensive zone. To the attacking team it is the offensive zone.

In faceoffs the offensive center must never go to the circle where the referee will drop the puck without first having placed his men. Assuming his team is at full strength, there will be four besides himself. Placing them is his responsibility, not that of the coach. In practice drills the coach can certainly help. In actual game situations, the center must do it himself.

The center knows his forte, and knows what the other skaters can do. In placing his men, he should try to take full advantage of his own ability and, remembering that his team's primary objective is to score, he must put all four skaters into potential scoring positions.

Assume that the faceoff is in the right circle on the imaginary line fifteen feet out from the crease and ten feet in from the boards. (Right and left is always designated as the way the goalie sees it. In other words, when we say "right circle" we mean the faceoff circle to the right of the goalie, and vice versa when we refer to the "left circle.") The two offensive defensemen will be near the blue line, about four feet inside the zone. The left defenseman should be nearest the boards. Although not essential, he has an advantage if he is a left shot. He can take the puck off the boards more easily, and, since he is so far from the nets, he can shoot at a pretty good angle more easily. A defenseman with a good slap shot can always get a shot on goal from that close to the blue line if he has a clear alley along which to shoot.

The right defenseman, also four feet inside the blue line, should be about even with the right post of the nets. Although this leaves the rest of the blue line uncovered, it gives both defensemen possible shots on goal, if the center passes back to one of them on winning the draw, and clear passes to teammates. Despite the open half of the blue line, the defensemen—for faceoff purposes—are in a good position to protect the blue line.

It is probable, however, that they will not receive the puck if their center wins the draw. He would prefer not to pass to them unless he is desperate for an open man. His wings are closer, and presumably are better shots. If he can get the puck to one of them, the chances for a score are obviously better than if he is forced to pass along the boards to his left defenseman or back to his right defenseman.

The left wing will be on a direct line behind the center, closer in but somewhere between the defensemen. The right wing will be on the imaginary line to the center's right, in the slot (scoring zone), the required fifteen feet from the crease. He will, usually, be well-covered by the defensive team, but the moment the puck is dropped, he will move, hoping to shake off his cover so that he can take a pass from a teammate, in the event the center wins the draw.

All the offensive players should be alert for the puck. The defensemen, even when very young, should have excellent split vision. They must know where their teammates are, how far from the net they themselves are, where the opposition is, and, knowing their center's forte, where the puck is most likely to go if he wins the draw. At the same time, they must realize the absolute necessity of keeping the puck in the offensive zone. If they fail, the minute the puck drifts out—over the blue line and into the neutral zone beyond—everyone on their team, including themselves, is offside.

Every hockey player has preferences in his style of play, and abilities that outweigh other abilities. When the center lines his team up for a faceoff in the offensive zone, he knows to which man he hopes he can pass the puck. He also knows which direction each man will go as soon as the puck is dropped. Normally he wants a wing to get it, and will try to pass it to one if he wins the draw.

If the center shoots left, he wants a wing to be ready to take the shot from that direction; if right, from the opposite direction. Some centers have especially good control with their backhands on faceoffs. In their cases, they will want their primary target to move to a spot where he can most easily pick up the backhand.

Some centers are too weak on faceoffs to control a pass if they win the draw. It is a common fault, and one that can be overcome. Faceoff drills must be designed to help a center learn to control the puck in this situation. It does little good to win the draw if the winner cannot do what he wants to do next. He must learn. Off-season practice is beneficial. If teaching does not help, then someone else on the team should be used for faceoffs, with the center taking his place.

A common error peculiar to young defensemen is to try to shoot through a body—an opposing skater between himself and the net. Everyone does it at one time or another, and it takes repeated warnings to correct this tendency.

If the man in the way of the shot fails to gain immediate control of the puck, it will ricochet off his shinguards. It will not go far, and therein lies the real danger. The man it hits will almost always be closest to it, which means he has the best chance of controlling it. The next thing the originally shooting defenseman knows, the opposition is on its way down the ice, no longer the defense, but now the attacking team.

This nullifies the advantage of winning the draw. Instead of descending on the opposition's goal, the team that just lost the puck is frantically trying to catch up with the play. The defensemen must turn, along with everyone else, and then chase a rival forward who may be faster than they.

This happens time and again in hockey games, even at the professional level. In split seconds, a forward line has been forced, or a teammate picks up the puck carrier. Only superior speed or mishandling of the puck on the part of the newly offensive team can save the goalie from having to defend alone against a clean shot, possibly with two men bearing down on him.

If a defenseman gets the puck after a faceoff but cannot get a clear shot on goal, then he must not take one. His only recourse is to pass directly to a teammate—possibly his defense partner—or, if that is not possible, to make an indirect pass. He can use the boards for that or, if that is not practical, shoot into a corner off the boards.

It is a truism in hockey that the home team's best friends are the boards. Boards are never the same—there are always some subtle differences. The players on the home team should know every carom, and a defenseman should be especially familiar with the action of the boards between the blue lines and the nets. This is one of the great advantages of playing on home ice.

Normally, the center's preference if he wins the draw is to get the puck to his own left wing. When the puck is dropped by the official, the left wing will come from behind the faceoff circle and be close to the perimeter, skating toward the net. If the center can put the puck on his stick, the left wing's momentum will carry him in and enable him to get a close-up shot on goal. He must be a great stick-handler and move fast, because in order to take that shot he must get by the defense that is packed in the slot. But a good left wing can do it. Many a goal has been scored in that manner.

The side of the rink where the faceoff occurs should often be the deciding factor as to whether the center or a wing should be in the circle. If, for example, the faceoff were to the goalie's left instead of his right and the center is a right shot and not good at bringing the puck to his left, the right wing might go into the circle. In that case, the center will take the right wing's place on the faceoff play.

There are rare times when a defenseman might be in the circle. This would happen only if he is exceptionally good at winning the draw. Some older defensemen, in the pros for example, are former forwards with years of experience in the circle. An occasional defenseman may be the best faceoff man on the team. If so, he should be used for that purpose.

Although it does not happen often, there are some faceoff men—usually centers—who are so clever with the stick that they can actually get a shot on goal direct from the faceoff. They do it with what is known as a *heavy stick*. In other words, when the puck drops, the center leans heavily on his stick and shoots in the same motion with which he wins the draw.

Not being at a good angle, his chances of scoring are not too good, although goals have been scored that way. Some goalies, either from inexperience or youth, are so surprised to see a shot coming directly from the faceoff circle that they fail to make the stop. Even if they do stop the shot from the circle they then have to watch out for the rebound. A well-integrated team should have scoring plays of this type. In cases where a center is able to take a shot on goal from the faceoff, both wings will know it and be down where one or the other can shoot a rebound past the goalie.

If the offensive center loses the draw, his team should quickly get one or two men on the puck to keep the defensive center from passing it back to the defenseman on the crease. This will be the right defenseman if the faceoff is in the right circle or the left defenseman if it is in the left circle. In any event, proper moves by the offensive team can prevent the other team from keeping the

puck even if its center wins the draw.

On any faceoff nobody except possibly the goalie stands still. Everyone should be moving somewhere (including the goalie, of course, if the play draws him away from the point he is guarding). It is up to the offensive center's teammates to cover for him if he loses the draw. The other center might be slow to pass it off, or may not be in position to, or may simply be inefficient at the job of getting rid of the puck after winning the draw.

On any faceoff the center must be sure the official dropping the puck is equidistant between the two centers. A good official will be there anyhow, but not all officials are that good. Some are so anxious to get out of the way and not get slapped by the sticks that they edge off to one side or the other. This gives one center the advantage of having a clear view of the official while the other might be blinded by him. All centers should watch for this. If the official moves away from a point equidistant between them, it is permissible to ask him to move back.

When a center "jumps the gun"—moves his stick in anticipation of the puck being dropped—the official will normally let him stay in the circle, especially in the early part of a game. But if he does it often, he will be told to leave the circle, to be replaced by a teammate. The man replacing him is designated by the coach in advance. Late in a tight game, where all skaters are inclined to be tense and anxious for play to begin, the official is likely to wave a center out of the faceoff circle more quickly—often after one false start. Since this is a matter of the official's judgment, such a call must be accepted without question.

Nine times out of ten, when one man is ordered out of the circle, his opponent stays in. However, if both have been repeatedly guilty of anticipatory moves, both may be waved out. There are also occasions when a coach prefers a different man to move into a circle when the opposing center is ordered out. Perhaps one player can handle a certain rival better than another inside the circle. This is more common in professional ranks, where the same teams meet frequently, than in amateur hockey.

If the offensive center in the circle sees that it is impossible either to shoot the puck himself or get it to a teammate, he then should try to shoot it behind the defensive team. This should usually be into a corner, if possible to a spot where the center himself can chase and freeze it. This will force another faceoff, giving the attacking team a second chance to control the puck in the offensive zone.

In the course of a hockey game, most if not all these options will come up time and again. *Faceoffs* are *important*. A good center can help his team. Derek Sanderson of the Bruins is a good faceoff man and is so clever on the draw that he actually anticipates the official accurately. In most cases, it does not pay to anticipate the official, but Sanderson seems to have a sixth sense that enables him to win the draw on a faceoff nearly every time he is in one.

Forechecking, Backchecking, and Breakouts

Forechecking. The best forecheckers are the best skaters. This highly important offensive maneuver takes all the skating skill a hockey player has. An effective forechecker must not only move fast, but turn fast. He must be able to turn left or right, quickly and with equal facility. Only occasionally may the stick be on one side or the other. Most of the time it should be in front of the man.

The forechecker is the hunter; the defensive man is the prey. It is the forechecker's primary job to get the puck if he can. If not, he must rag the puck carrier, cover him closely, and somehow make him give up the puck. Wherever the player with the puck is, the forechecker should be in front of him. He is trying to get the puck out of his zone. The forechecker is trying to keep it in. It all goes back to the basic situation— the forechecker is in his offensive zone and the defensive puck carrier is in his defensive zone. Geographically, the zones are identical.

The forechecker should never take his stick off the ice. If he lifts it, he is probably giving the puck carrier a chance to pass to a teammate, the last thing the forechecker wants to happen. Forechecking is harassment, preferably to distraction. A good forechecker can virtually force his man to make a bad pass or in some other way lose the puck in his own defensive zone.

There is no way a puck carrier can get out of the hole the forechecker puts him in unless the forechecker lets him. In forechecking, the strides are short, the harassment is complete, the defensive man's body is blanketed. The puck carrier will probably be able to get to the boards or into a corner, safely out of the slot, but eventually he will either shoot wild or find himself in a freeze necessitating a faceoff in his own zone.

This, too, is part of the forechecker's job—to force faceoffs by not permitting his man the freedom to get rid of the puck to a teammate. A faceoff is better for the attacking than for the defending team because that gives both teams an equal chance to get the puck, and an equal chance is better for the offensive team than for the defensive team to be in possession of it.

With the changes in rules that eliminate most of the differences between college and professional rules, a fore-checker may hit his opponent's body in the offensive zone. This does not necessarily mean that it is always best to hit the body. Sometimes it is just as effective to go in front of and across the body without touching the puck carrier. That obstructs his vision and keeps him pretty well-blocked. Actually, hitting the man legally is a matter of timing and expediency. The carrier may be able to get a pass off as he is being hit. By not hitting him, the forechecker can see where he is moving and move accordingly. But if it is best to hit, then hit. That is a matter of judgment in accordance with the situation.

It is not legal to forecheck anyone but the puck carrier. In a 2-on-1 situation (to be discussed later), the second man can make the check if the first man misses it—provided the second man arrives immediately. Even a split second can be enough time to allow the carrier to use one of his options—skate down the ice, pass to an open teammate, get the puck out of his zone, or anything else that will help his team. If he succeeds, there is no further point in forechecking because his has become the offensive team.

Backchecking. Opposing players who have been in their offensive zone must get quickly back to their defensive zone,

when someone on the opposing team is headed there in possession of the puck. This is where *backchecking* comes into play. Backchecking takes the same skating skill that forechecking does. The backchecker must be able to wheel quickly and head for his own zone while harassing his man as much as possible.

The other team has control of the puck. The man with it will not keep it if he can get rid of it to a teammate. The backchecker must harass him just as he would when forechecking. He must do anything he can to prevent the man—now on the offensive—from moving down the ice.

The best place for backchecking is in the middle third of the ice—between the two blue lines. (See Diagram 5.) For purposes of clarity, since the teams have changed places, let us continue to call the team that had the puck and lost it the offensive team. In backchecking, the offensive skaters should catch up with the puck carrier before he reaches the far blue line. In mid-ice, the backchecker should try to push the puck carrier into the boards, or at least prevent him from getting a pass away or dumping the puck into the scoring zone.

The backchecker should be able to catch the puck carrier even if the latter has had a good jump. It is easier to skate without the puck than with it. The man without the puck has nothing to worry about except getting to the man with it, which he does by backchecking. But the man with the puck has many things on his mind. Is the pattern of offense set up? Is he better off passing or taking the puck in himself? Shall he move to the left or the right? Who is calling to him—his own teammates or the opposition?

This is always a problem in hockey.

116

Everyone should learn to recognize the voices of his teammates and know if a voice is that of someone else. Everyone on the ice is yelling. A backchecker may

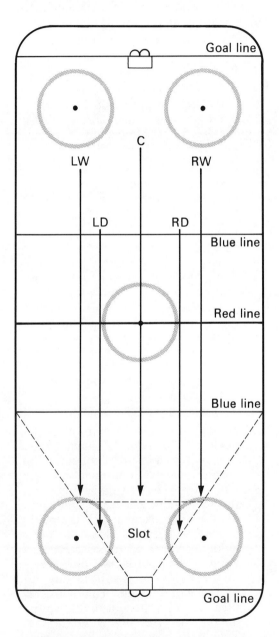

Diagram 5.   *Backchecking Drill.*

call for a drop pass—an old trick which inexperienced puck carriers often fall for. A call for a drop pass, or any pass behind or out of the sight of the puck carrier, might fake him into doing just that if he is not thoroughly familiar with the voices of his teammates.

A common failing of backcheckers is to reach for the puck with the stick instead of staying beside the carrier and skating with him, forcing him into the boards if he can. By reaching, he is losing all the advantage he gained by catching up with the carrier in the first place. The problem there is that when a backchecker starts reaching he stops, or drastically slows up, the speed of his skating.

When the carrier first starts up the ice he has several advantages. He has the puck. His opponent has to switch quickly from offense to defense. He gets a jump, a good start on his man, as he moves up ice. He probably will lose that advantage because he has the puck and has to worry about what to do with it. The backchecker can—and probably will—catch him. What good does it do the backchecker, however, if, instead of ragging the carrier with his body, he reaches for the puck with his stick?

From the backchecker's point of view, once he catches the carrier, he should get shoulder-to-shoulder with him before he begins using his stick. He can do this only when his heart is in it, for it takes courage, determination, and patience. It is a great temptation for the backchecker to reach for the puck when he thinks he is within range. But he is much better off pulling up even with the carrier, forming a screen to prevent him from passing the puck where he wants it to go, and playing the body.

First the body, then the stick, then the puck. This is a key that must be drilled and drilled until it becomes second nature to a hockey player. Reaching for the puck is reversing the procedure and asking for trouble. Almost every defensive move in hockey depends on working in the proper order—body, stick, puck. That is as important in backchecking as in other hockey skills.

When the defensive team becomes the offensive team, everyone who had been in the offensive zone must backcheck. The important backchecker is the man reaching the puck carrier, but the others must backcheck, too. The defensemen must get back to their positions protecting the goalie as fast as possible—therefore, they pay little attention to the man with the puck. The forwards must pick up their own men to prevent them from taking passes.

Backchecking is not a matter of one man going after the puck carrier. It is a team matter, a team necessity. Everyone now has a new job to do. Before, it was to try to score. Now it is to try to keep the other team from getting into the defensive zone, and, failing that, to keep it from scoring.

Forechecking is an offensive maneuver. Backchecking is a defensive one. But backchecking is just as important. Everyone but the goalie must learn to do it. Proper backchecking can help keep the puck out of the scoring zone. It can mean the difference between remaining on defense or quickly taking the offensive again.

Breakouts.   One of hockey's hardest jobs is the *breakout*—getting the puck out of the defensive zone after regaining possession of it. There should always be more than one breakout pattern, since

only one limits a team too much, providing only one option. An individual's carrying the puck out is a desperation maneuver when he leaves his defensive zone so far ahead of his teammates that they cannot catch up with him.

Here are five basic patterns:

1. Defenseman who gets possession of the puck passes to wing on the same side. Once in possession, the wing moves, always remembering to keep the head up. Movement is essential. Do not stand still. (See Diagram 6.)

2. If the wing on the same side is covered, pass to the center, who should not be in the slot. (See Diagram 7.)

3. Feed to the opposite wing, preferably through the air or by indirect pass—off the boards. But before doing that, be sure he is free and that no opposing team player is in a position to intercept. Although a direct pass will move the puck faster, an indirect one is preferable because it is safer. It should be a high pass, hitting the boards three inches or more above the ice. (See Diagram 8.)

4. A give-and-go pass. In the give-and-go, the defenseman gets the puck in his own defensive zone. Presume he picked it up near the corner or near his own net. He looks for the stationary wing on the same side. When the wing sees his own defenseman has the puck, he gets out of the slot. The puck holding defenseman passes to the wing at the boards and then starts up the ice, being careful to stay out of the slot himself. The wing returns a lead pass, and the two start up the ice with the wing trailing. This is the best pattern for a breakout if the right men—especially the

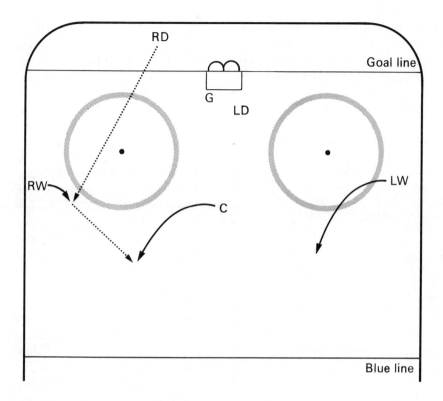

Diagram 6. *Breakout—Defense to Wing. RW bends toward the pass, receives puck, looks up (still skating), and feeds C. RD trails the play.*

defensemen—are available to carry it out. (See Diagram 9.)

5. Peel-off play. Assume a player getting possession of the puck finds himself trapped to a point where he cannot go forward or to the side. Forecheckers are aggressively harassing him. Usually, he should skate behind his net. If he cannot carry the puck out himself, he must get it to a teammate on the same side from which he came. His wing should get to the corner, and the man with the puck should pass it off the boards from behind the net into that corner. There is always the temptation to follow the puck carrier, whether it is expedient or not. Usually it is not. When all players gang up on one man, as a tenacious forechecking team might in harassing a puck carrier, it is fairly easy to break out by shooting into the corner. The player who picks the puck up often has a clear field on his side of the ice. It will not stay that way, of course, but it will get his team out of trouble, while at the same time turning a defensive situation into an attacking one. This maneuver is sometimes referred to as a *peel-off*. (See Diagram 10.)

On breakouts in general, it is helpful to remember that the object of a breakout is defeated if the recipient of the pass tries to save time by skating one way while looking the other. To make sure the pass is safely on his stick before he tries to carry it down the ice, he should bend *toward* the pass even if it takes a

fraction of a second longer to get going. Some pass recipients on breakouts look over their shoulders to where they want to go when they should be looking at the puck. Obviously, once in possession, he must keep his head up and control the puck by feel. But he is asking for trouble if he tries to break out before he has complete control of the puck. If he does that, he will probably be hit by an opponent the second the puck reaches his stick. That kind of check is perfectly legal as long as the recipient has the puck on his stick. Although the passer may not be at fault, this type of situation is often called the *undertaker's pass*. The reason is obvious.

Every player on the bench should be watching the breakout patterns of the other team. These patterns will emerge as the game progresses. When playing a familiar team, they should be known, but it is still a good idea to watch and make sure no changes in the breakout patterns have been developed.

Line Play. Whenever a player enters the attacking zone with the puck, he should be trailed by a teammate. This is not always possible in that the puck carrier has such a big jump on the field that he has had to go down the ice alone. However, it is just as important for someone on his own team to catch up with him as for a member of the opposition. Unless he makes a lone sortie

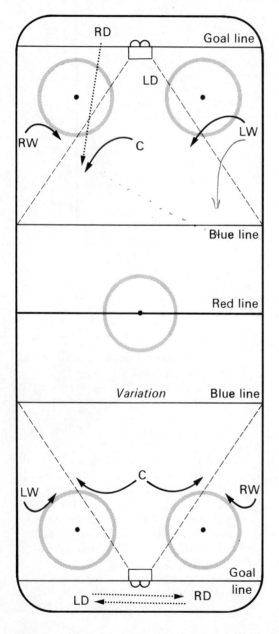

◀ **Diagram 7.**   *Breakout—Defense to Center. RD feeds C—note the pass is made on the outside edge of the slot. C bends toward the pass. Heads must be up, legs in motion, sticks on the ice. Often the LW is posted higher (nearer the blue line) and breaks out fast as the head man.*

climaxing in an actual score, he must have a man to trail him in the event he misses a check or shoots and either misses the net or has his shot stopped by the goalie. If the goalie retains possession of the puck of course, there will be a whistle and a faceoff. If he does not, then someone should have arrived to help in the attacking zone, since there may be a rebound, and the attacking team helper—the trailer under these conditions—should be in a position to take

a shot on the rebound, with a possible goal resulting.

Some coaches maintain that there is really no difference between the center and his wings. This is true only if all are of equal ability. It is also true in cases where one man makes the breakout alone and has a big jump on everyone. Then the man who trails him may be another forward simply because the man who makes the breakout will normally also be a forward.

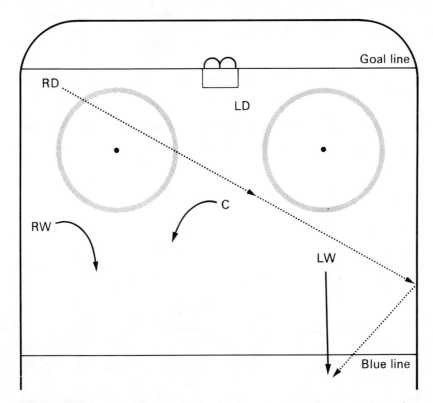

Diagram 8.   *Breakout—Defense to Opposite Wing. This play entails knowing the boards and their angles, looking up to see that the path of the puck is free, and having the puck go at least halfway up the boards as it rebounds off the boards. Play can be used from either side. RD must look up and make sure the path of the hard pass is clear of opponents. Angles and position of RD may vary. This is an effective feeding out play against a 2-1-2 pattern.*

It is a common mistake for young coaches to name their lines by number—first line, second line, and third line. Actually, there should be no distinction among the first three lines—they are all first lines. The best way to differentiate among them is to name them by colors—red line, blue line, or white line, for example. The starting line means nothing. It can only play a few minutes before being replaced. Two good lines are hardly enough. Forwards need frequent rest, and the best way for them to get enough is to have three lines. All should be of roughly equal ability, if possible.

The longer the lines work together, the more effective they will be because each man will learn the moves of his mates, be able to anticipate them, and, if one has a fault, the others can compensate for it. Each knows the others' strengths as well as weaknesses. This common bond among linemen is very important in hockey. It is always better to try to develop a line as a unit than to develop each player as an individual. This is best done by keeping combinations together, working them as a team, and constantly stressing position play. Each man eventually will instinctively make the right move for the other mem-

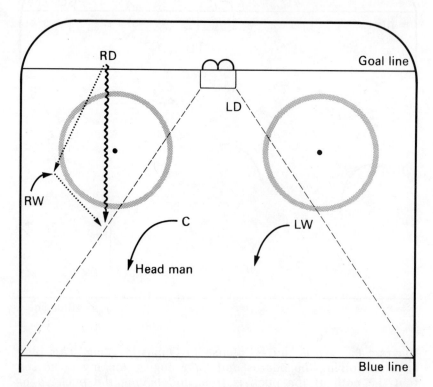

Diagram 9.   *Breakout—Give and Go. RD passes to RW; note how RW bends toward the pass. RD continues in a straight line. RW looks up after receiving the pass and passes ahead and slowly to RD; in fact, RD is led by a soft pass. C bends and does not leave the zone until RD has the puck. RW trails RD.*

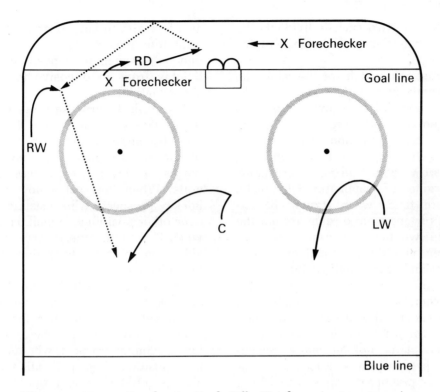

Diagram 10. *Breakout—Peel Off. Used against a tenacious 2-1-2 forechecking pattern. RW goes toward the corner. RD, pressed by a forechecker, skates behind his net where he sees another forechecker; then he passes (high off the boards) at an angle that sends the puck back toward the corner. RW gathers it in, looks up, and can feed C. Timing, angle off the boards, backchecking, accurate passing, and staying in one's lane are very important. Note: Backchecking to position is paramount. Break to positions indicated after puck is controlled. Do not leave zone before passes are made.*

bers of his line. Before they are through, each should know the moves of his mates as well as his own.

Certain players will never be able to work together. This can and should be determined by the coach before the competitive schedule begins. Personality clashes are sure danger signs. Three men on the same line must get along. If they do not, it will be apparent early enough to change them. Sometimes, one

man will want to do all the scoring. Even if he is the best of the three, he should be made to realize that he is helping neither himself nor the team by being a puck hog.

On the other hand, if two men have the tendency to hold the puck rather than pass it, maybe they should be split up. Obviously, the coach must talk to anyone who thinks he is the only man on a line who should do the scoring.

When he has two such individuals, he must separate them for the good of the team.

He must also watch for the men who try to be all over the ice at once—right wings who crowd their own centers and even their own left wings. It is not possible to teach position play without stressing the importance of remaining in one's own zone and not encroaching on the zones of teammates. Obviously, there are times when it may be expedient for one man to roam around the ice, but it will not happen often because few men can do it effectively. Even the Russians have modified their crossover, as they proved in their 1972 series with Team Canada. In this maneuver, forwards roam all over the ice, but compensate for each other's movements. However, it is not normally recommended because amateur teams in general do not practice or play except within certain seasonal limits. Teamwork of the Russian type is developed by practice that lasts about eleven months of the year. Neither American nor Canadian teams have ever operated that long each year, and it is doubtful they ever will.

However, there are ways in which both amateurs and professionals can switch. The center can interchange with either of his wings, a move that is often in the best interests of the team. But the wings should rarely, if ever, interchange. However, a wing and the defenseman on his side can interchange when the defenseman moves up to the forward line by carrying the puck. In other words, the left wing can swap with the left defenseman and the right wing with the right defenseman. This must be done when the defenseman goes up the ice

as a forward, to keep from being caught with four men down the ice and only one defenseman in a position to shift quickly from an offensive to a defensive situation.

These shifts are examples of working together on position play. Team work *must* become second nature to a young player. Many coaches may have to embarrass a player who refuses to cooperate. When they get a boy with fine hockey prospects who insists on taking over other positions as well as his own when it is neither necessary nor advisable, something has to be done to teach him a lesson.

The easiest is to sit him on the bench and keep him there until he gets the point. But there is another, faster, more effective way. Some coaches, when they find a young prospect who is a puck and position hog, pull all the other skaters off the ice and say, "OK, you want to play everywhere. Go ahead." The boy then discovers that, with himself and his goalie the only players on one side, he is smothered by the opposition. It is a pretty sure cure that usually works after only one treatment. Counselling individual players often brings very positive results.

Sometimes a coach will find that he has a three-man line that actually works as two. For example, for one reason or another, the center and the left wing pass the puck only to each other, while the right wing skates aimlessly along up and down the ice. Usually, the reason for freezing out this third man is a past association that he did not share. Perhaps the two friends were schoolboys together, or grew up together, or are related. Sometimes, two are fraternity brothers and the third is not. Or two are seniors and the third a sophomore. And sometimes it is a rut that two forwards get into by accident.

It is not always easy to spot this sort of cooperation between two men at the expense of the third. Unless it is flagrantly obvious, it may not be noticed for some time. Sooner or later, however, the coach will see, for example, the right wing wide open in the offensive zone while the center passes the puck to the left wing. Or he will sense that the left wing is handling the puck a great deal more than the right. This should be corrected as soon as possible.

The surest way to check this out is to assign a team manager the job of counting the times the centers on each line pass to one wing or the other. It will take only a practice session or two to learn if a center is favoring one wing at the expense of the other rather than for the good of the team. Some lines go this way all season without the coach noticing what is happening.

When spotted, the practice must be stopped by the coach. Just how is up to him. As a rule, it is not advisable to break up the line, especially if the two working together have been together a long time. Usually, a threat to break them up is enough. In any event, the coach should talk to both, pointing out that the third man is not being given enough chance to help and that the two-man line does not score many goals. It is also a good idea to talk with the center alone, because he is the key man. And, since skating up and down all through a game without the puck is discouraging to any forward, the odd third man should be given assurance that the situation will change. Only if none of these methods works should the offending center be moved to another line. It is, of course, essential that he be told why.

6

Team Specialties

POWER PLAY

Power plays are situations in which a team has a one or more man advantage over the opposing team.

6-on-5

The most frequent power play is 6-on-5—six men on the attacking team with the defending team one man short. This will happen more often than any other ratio of men in a hockey game because it becomes effective as soon as someone goes to the penalty box.

The attacking team (referred to as the team with the manpower advantage) has two minutes in which to score, assuming it will be at full strength throughout the time the defending team is one man short. Two minutes is a comparatively long time in hockey—one tenth of a period. Since the puck can be brought down the ice in seconds, a team with a good power play should have many

chances to score within that time. When the attacking team does score, it loses its advantage.

Instead of starting a power play with the defensemen back in their own zone and the forwards up front, it is more advisable for the whole team to start together at its own end. In this way, everyone but the goalie is involved in the play from the start, and the one man edge over the other team will be a real offensive advantage. A forward will carry the puck into the attacking zone, and his four teammates will be right with him. The defensemen will take up their positions at the points, and the other two forwards will move to advantageous positions.

They will usually encounter a *box* defense—the conventional defense in a power play situation, which will be discussed later. The offensive center at the first opportunity should move into the middle of the box, taking up a position in front of the net and as close to it as he can. He should keep out of the crease. With only one cover, he has a better chance than usual of converting a pass into a goal. The defensive team cannot afford to put more than one man on him because it must be prepared to cover the other four attackers with only three men when the box bends or is broken.

The wings will be in the corners, and one will probably be in possession of the puck. The defensemen will be in position to shoot or pass—they will have either option—but must lay far enough back to protect the zone. When teams are not at equal strength, icing is not called on the team that is one man short. Therefore, if it gets control of the puck with no chance of carrying it out of its zone, it can be shot the length of the ice. The attacking team will then have to scramble back for it, wasting seconds that become increasingly precious as the penalty time goes on.

In these cases, the attacking team's goalie can be helpful by skating out for the puck himself. As soon as he sees where it is coming, he can save his teammates some of this time by passing the puck out from his own zone to mid-ice, from where the rest of the team can generate another attack.

Assuming the attacking left wing has the puck on the left side, he has several good options. If the angle is right and the way is clear, he can shoot. Otherwise, he can pass across to his right wing on the other side, to his center in the middle of the box, or to one of the defensemen at the points. He might be rushed but there is a chance he will not be. At best, his cover may harass him some, but the cover always has in mind the fact that his is the short-handed team, so he cannot concentrate too heavily on one man. (See Diagram 11.)

The object of the power play is to score, but first it must either break the box defense or bend it so completely

out of shape that it is no longer effective. It is not a perfect box, of course, but a rough one which bends according to the location of the puck.

The attacking defensemen on the power play should not be too defensive-minded. In the power play, the defensemen on the attacking team may be considered forwards. The team will seldom have as good a chance to score. To put defensemen who lack good shots into the game on a power play is a serious mistake. Everyone on the ice except the goalie should be a potential scorer.

Actually, the defensemen should be forwards playing close to where defensemen normally play. In an attacking situation on a power play, the men simulating defensemen must protect the blue line, but should not play as close to it as regular defensemen do. This is too far out—sixty feet—for a power play. The blue line can be guarded as well from half that distance, and it is easier to score from thirty feet out than from sixty.

The cover who goes for the defenseman with the puck will have to leave someone else open. With the defenseman moving in, this gives the attacking team a chance to put more pressure on the goalie. The latter must depend heavily on his own ability to keep the attacking team at bay because he will not get the protection he would normally have with five men in front of him. Therefore, the more shots on goal the attacking team gets, the better the chances of a score.

Sometimes the attacking defenseman —or the man playing defense—can get such a good start with a clear field in front of him when he has possession of the puck that he can score by himself. He will be skating toward the net. The

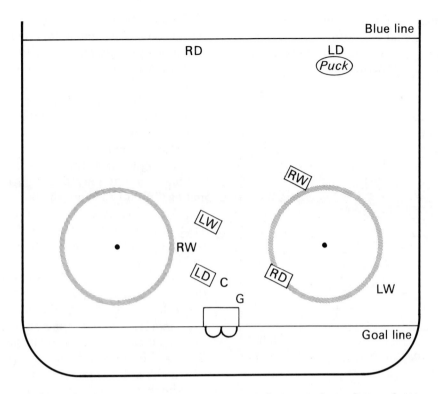

Diagram 11.   *Power Play—6 on 5. This is a bent box; slot is covered by LD. Goalie must cover or intercept passes to offensive RW.*

puck will be extended in front of him and he will be getting set to shoot while watching the opposition as well as the net. If he has a chance to score, his teammates will be screening the rest of the opposition. His center, originally in the middle of the box and close to the net, will get out of his way. If every man on the attacking team carries out his assignment, he may very well have a clear shot at the net, with only the goalie to beat.

The power play, more than any other, is like a game of chess. The attacking team is trying to move all the defenders out of the way while one man is either taking the puck in or passing it to some-

one near the net. These power play scoring attempts are set up in advance by the coach. The skater has all the latitude he wants in deciding how the plays should go. Since he has five skaters to work with against four opponents, the patterns of attack are unlimited. (See Diagram 12.)

In the power play, the defensive covers have to change, a situation which gives the attacking team an additional advantage. It is not possible to set up a real man-to-man defense. The attacking team can always shake somebody loose as long as it is careful to control the puck. To give it up in a power play situation is disastrous. At best, the short-handed team will ice the puck. At worst, it will get a breakout with two men moving in on the opposite net. This is one way in which short-handed teams score goals.

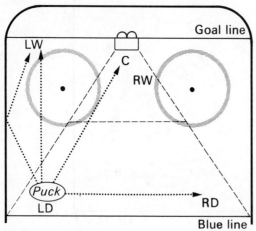

Note: C close to goalie if puck is at the point.

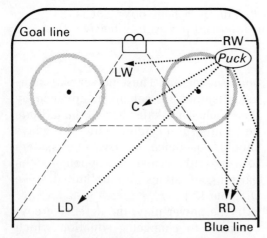

Note: C shakes his cover and moves fifteen feet back if the puck is in either corner. Keep stick on ice and be ready to receive passes or play rebounds. Know where the puck is at all times.

Diagram 12.   *Power Play Variations.*

When the two teams are at full strength, the man with the puck should never let the opposition get closer to him than ten feet. In a power play situation, the attacking puck carrier should try to keep at least fifteen feet from a defender. Anyone closer than that has too good a chance to poke check the puck, or at least tie up the man who has it.

In trying to score in a 6-on-5 situation, too many young players forget that it is just as difficult to shoot the puck through a wall of players with a man advantage as it is when the teams are even. This is a very easy mistake to make. The attacking team is rushing the defending team hard—trying to smother it with that one extra player. But it must always be remembered that there is a time to shoot and a time to pass. Experienced players shoot or pass off *earlier* than the inexperienced player.

If a defender is right in the way, *do not shoot.* The attacking team must keep its head, but too often young players involved in a power play kill their chances of scoring by sheer anxiety. Instead of thinking about how to get the puck into the net, they think about the time element—the two minutes they have in which to take advantage of the fact that the opposition is short-handed. The more time that goes by, the more anxious the attacking team may get. The team that scores on a power play is the one that never loses control of the situation.

True, the clock must be watched. The two minutes will go by, and it is no tragedy if the attacking team fails to score in a 6-on-5 power play situation. It is only a lost opportunity. If the players on the attacking team remember that, they have a better chance to score. They will not waste shots trying to drill the puck through a defender in the way.

6-on-4

The 6-on-4 situation certainly enhances the opportunity for the attacking team. It does not happen often, but when it does, the attacking team will not have very much time—probably a minute at the most. This does not put any more pressure on the attacking team, of course, because it will have at least a one man advantage for something like three minutes instead of two, assuming that the second man on the defending team went into the penalty box approximately one minute after the first one. If neither has served his full time when the attacking team scores, the first man to enter the penalty box returns to the ice, still leaving one man in the box to serve out his penalty.

The alignment of the attacking team in a 6-on-4 situation will be similar to the pattern of 6-on-5. The attacking team should start as a unit down near its own net so that it will be at full speed and will be well-organized when it reaches the defending blue line. With one less man to harass them, the members of the attacking team have more latitude. On the other hand, they must be careful not to give up the puck. The defending team, with only three skaters, will probably be in a triangular rather than a box formation. This will probably include their two best defensemen and a man at the apex who can move around well and has the fortitude to take a shot off any part of his body.

As long as the defending team is minus two men, the attacking team can afford to gamble more. The defensemen (who actually should be either offensive-minded or forwards) are able to position themselves inside the blue line,

closer to the net. The center is generally in the middle of the triangle. The wings are on each side, both nearer the posts of the net and at a scoring angle.

In appearance, the general shape of the offensive alignment will be much like 6-on-5, except that the triangle may be tighter. The puck carrier will pass to an open man if the way to the net is blocked by a defender, or if his shooting angle is poor. It is important not to try to drill the puck through a human wall in a 6-on-4 as in a 6-on-5. If the puck is lost, the opportunity is probably lost because the defender who gets it will hold it as long as he dares, then try to ice it, sending the whole attacking team back beyond the blue line and killing more penalty time.

The two offensive defensemen may be positioned closer together than in a 6-on-5. This will put additional pressure on the goalie, who may have to absorb a lot of shots unless the offensive team fails to take full advantage of the opportunity.

Once again, as in a 6-on-5 situation, the attacking team must not be too anxious. There is a tendency to waste shots when a team has a two man advantage. Every shot the goalie stops is another opportunity gone. If he can control the puck after stopping it, he will force a faceoff, and a faceoff may be to the advantage of the defending team. It has nothing to lose. It is being smothered by the attackers in its own zone. With a faceoff, there is always a chance to ice the puck, or at least to keep control of it for a few more seconds.

It is easy for the attacking team to be careless about forming a screen. It must always be remembered that a screened shot is the toughest for a goalie to stop. He must look through legs, sticks, and skates to find the puck, which he must block almost by instinct. No matter how fast his reactions, the attacking team should be able to beat him as long as the two man advantage remains in effect.

With two more men on the power play, the attacking team can do a good deal more in the corners than under any other conditions. The defending team cannot afford to spend much time in the corners. It must protect its own net or try to get possession of the puck for purposes of getting it out of the zone.

The attacking team can send two men into a corner after the puck. If one defender goes in, one of the two can bluff, playing the puck and going for the man, while the other can go for the puck. His problem then is what to do with it. If his partner can forecheck the man, it will cut the defending team down to two skaters. In that situation, someone with a better shot on goal than the man who has the puck will be free to take a pass and convert it into a score.

Some teams have a tendency not to play the corners properly. Obviously, it is not possible to score from there, but in a power play situation the team that controls the corners controls the game. If the defending team gets the puck, the man who does so may be able to ice it and throw the whole attacking team offside, which happens once the puck crosses the blue line into the middle (neutral) zone. If the attacking team gets the puck, the man with it has plenty of options, depending on where his teammates are and who is in the best position to score. Players should talk to each other.

This does not mean it should be taken for granted that taking over the puck in a corner will stop an individual attacker from scoring. It means only that he can-

not score from there. If he is fast and clever enough with skates and stick, he may bring the puck out to an angle where he *can* take a shot on goal. This is another example of a man not taking a scoring opportunity, but opting to pass instead. If the man in the corner is the team's best shot (he will be in the slot, but it happens if he is drawn away) then he may be the one who should take that shot in a 6-on-4 situation. The coach will know this, as, indeed, will everyone else on the team, so no one will resent his positioning himself for the shot. This is not hogging the puck, but using the best scoring weapon at a team's command.

A coach should drill a power play team incessantly, keeping it together as much as possible. He can combine this with drills for short-handed situations. One of the best is to throw the puck into the single defender, while two attackers come at him. This actually is a 2-on-1 situation, but it is typical of what can happen in a 6-on-4 or even a 6-on-5. If the defender can get out of the corner with the puck or, failing that, shoot it out of the zone, he is showing the kind of initiative a defender needs under those conditions. On the other hand, if one of the attackers can fake going for the puck, then go for the defender while the other attacker takes the puck, the power play men are learning one part of their assignments.

5-on-4

This is similar to 6-on-5, and occurs more often than 6-on-4. As a rule, if a second man on a team is penalized, he takes someone from the other team with him. Rather than give majors for fighting, most officials prefer to call it high sticks on the part of two men in a scuffle, with both going off the ice. The defending team will be in a triangle, with its most maneuverable man at the apex, nearest the blue line.

It is better when using the power play to either carry the puck in or pass it in ahead of a wing who can pick it up. In 5-on-4, as in other power plays, it is not good to dump the puck into a corner, because one man on the defensive team could leave the triangle and go after it. If he gets it, he may have time to ice it or freeze it, and the attacking team wants neither.

In order to integrate defensemen with forwards, as might happen in a power play, a good drill is for two forwards and a defenseman to go down the ice, with the three passing the puck between them. They will go into the offensive zone in this formation and try to break or bend the triangle.

That is the way the attacking team actually should go in on a power play. If it is a 5-on-4, the fourth skater will act as a trailer, either picking up a drop pass in hopes of getting off a shot on goal, or moving slightly to his right or left (he will be the only defenseman on the attacking team). This depends on where the puck is.

The single defenseman will be near the blue line, moving back and forth as the puck moves. He really has a double job —to act as a fourth forward if the occasion arises or to protect the blue line if the defending team tries to ice the puck. However, he must not be timid about going in and joining the attack. A power play is just what it implies—a play wherein extra power is used by the attacking team. It has a good chance of

resulting in a score whether it is 5-on-4 or 6-on-5.

The odds of a score may be a little better if it is 5-on-4 because the defending team, two men short, must rely on a triangular defense, since it does not have enough men for a box. A box is usually more effective and harder to break than a triangle.

MAN SHORT SITUATIONS

One Man Short

Because the team that scores the most goals wins the hockey game, beginning coaches have a tendency to stress offense. They look for the potentially great shooter, the boy who can get the puck into the net, either by outskating the opposition or scoring by the sheer power of his shot. This is their primary objective. In their search, these coaches all too often forget defensive play. Only after some hard experience, losing games by the weight of the numbers of opposing goals, do they begin to realize the importance of stressing defense.

Experienced coaches spend about sixty percent of their time teaching defense. Sometimes, they have to force this instruction on their players because young ones are so offense-minded that they do not want to learn anything else. But the complete hockey player—even a forward —*must* know the principles of defensive play. He *must* understand that defensive play is not for defensemen and goalies alone, and he *must* be prepared to actually play defense from time to time because he will have to swap with the defenseman on his side of the ice who moves in on the attack with the two other forwards when the occasion arises.

This is especially true when his team is a man short. The game for him and his mates then becomes almost entirely defensive, although there are times when his team can break out and score even though short-handed. That is the exception, not the rule. When a team loses a man on a penalty, its first function is not to score, but to keep the attacking team from scoring until the penalty is served and the sixth man is back in action.

The best defensive pattern with a man short is the box (see Diagram 13). Normally, the right defenseman is about twenty feet in front of the net, almost on a line with its right post. The left defenseman is parallel to his partner, but somewhat to the left of the net's left post. The right wing is between the right defenseman and the blue line, and the left wing between the left defenseman and the blue line.

As described and diagrammed, this forms almost a perfect box, but of course it is not. The four players are not equidistant from each other, nor are they on exact lines with each other once the play starts. However, they wait for the offensive sortie in a rough rectangle that is a bit wider than it is long. They will remain in this rough rectangle as long as expedient because that is the best way to keep their net protected and their goalie covered.

There is no compulsion to use the box when one man short, but years of experience have proved it to be the most effective way to stop a power play. Almost all coaches have now adopted it, and beginning young coaches should know the pattern and adopt it.

When one man short, the defense should stay in one place as long as possible. The defensemen should never chase the puck unless they have a sixty percent chance of getting it, since otherwise they will break the pattern.

It is up to the defense to do anything legally possible to get the puck out of its own defensive zone. If the defense gets a breakout, two men can go up the ice together, and if they are fast enough one might even get a shot on goal. But this is not likely, so the defensive team generally must not think offensively.

There are two ways to get the puck out—by icing it, for which there will be no whistle, since the team is short-handed—or by skating it out. It is usually safer and more advisable to ice it. Although that will stop any chance of the short-handed team from scoring, it will throw the power play team offside. Everyone on it will have to backcheck to the neutral zone across the blue line, then start another rush.

Both teams keep one eye on the clock, but this is more important for the defense than the offense. The offense has nothing to lose—only something to gain. The defense has a goal to lose. Each second that goes by is a second less in which to lose it. The passage of time is to the defensive team's advantage.

Although the box is the best defense against the power play, the defensive team must be careful not to become a slave to it. Once the teams make contact with each other, with the puck in the defensive zone and a power play team manipulating it, the box must become flexible. The net must be protected, of course, but the players on the short-handed team should cover their men as closely as possible.

Someone should be at or near the cor-

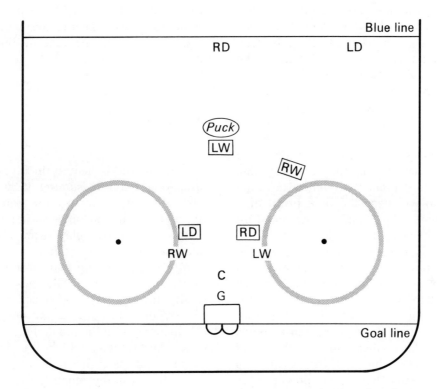

Diagram 13. *The Box for One Man Short. The box has been formed to cover key offensive men. The defending team must not screen the goalie; let him cover the opponent's C if he is within four feet of the crease. If the right point passes to the left point, defending RW moves up and covers him. Defensive LW then drops back to cover in the slot.*

ners if the puck goes in that direction. No one on the attacking team should be left alone. Harassment is the biggest hope the defenders have of staving off a score. Two men should operate right around the nets, particularly watching the attacking center and the wings. The other two should be ready to take the defensemen or, if possible, intercept passes going their way.

A faceoff is to the defending team's advantage. If it can force one, there is at least a chance of getting control of the puck. Therefore, the defense should not

be afraid to freeze the puck against the boards or anywhere else a faceoff can be forced.

It must be borne in mind by the defensive team in getting ready to form the box that only two of their skaters will be in the defensive zone before the puck goes in. This is why the wings who will form the outside edge of the box will be in motion in the neutral zone as the attackers come at them. While there, they should try to force the power play team to dump the puck in, at the same time being sure to move with the puck to complete the box. If the puck is dumped in, the defending team has a better chance of controlling it. One defenseman can go over for it or be ready to take the carom as it sweeps around the boards.

This is one reason why the box must be flexible. No one stands still. Everyone must be moving—moving with an attacker, harassing him, keeping him from shooting or passing, doing everything possible to protect the goalie. He is the man who will bear the final brunt of a power play attack, and he will need all the help he can get.

There is a relationship between delaying a power play before it reaches its offensive blue line and the defenseman's job in stopping an on-coming skater. This is in setting up a one man wall. Before hitting his man, the defenseman who can legally make contact harasses first and keeps between the puck carrier and his net. Forwards harassing power play teams before they reach the blue line have the same job with one essential difference—they do not have to make contact. They are playing a stalling game. Their objective is to gain time. If they succeed in that alone, they are doing their job.

In a man short situation, the goalie must remember his role as another defenseman if the chance arises. Obviously, it is dangerous for him to come too far out of his net, which he has to protect against all odds. However, even remaining just in front of the crease and without skating dangerously far from it, he can use his stick to intercept passes. In the tight scrambles that occur around the net on a power play, the goalie is in the midst of the action. No one has a wider stick than he, and some-

times no one is in a better position to intercept passes. This is not just a bonus arrangement for the rest of the team, but very much a part of the goalie's job in a man short situation.

Two Men Short

With the odds heavily in favor of the attacking team (assuming it is at full strength, setting up a 6-on-4 situation), the defense has a tough assignment. As long as the power play team has a two man advantage, the odds of a score are pretty high. The big man on defense in this case is definitely the goalie. He is really the only one who can stave off the opposition, but even an outstanding goalie cannot do the job alone.

In the triangle, which the defensive team must use, the man at the apex should be a defenseman if the team has one who is fast and good at harassment. At the beginning of the power play, he must be in the neutral zone, since there can be no more than three men, including the goalie, in the defensive zone before the puck gets there. The man at the apex will skate his way into his own defensive zone backward, while doing what he can to distract the puck carrier or whoever seems in the best position to take a pass from him (see Diagram 14.)

However, he must not chase the puck. With only two teammates instead of three to protect the goalie, he has to be very careful not to let the play get away from him. He can handle one man or, with good luck, two, but he must end up at that apex. If he finds himself anywhere else, the attacking team will have

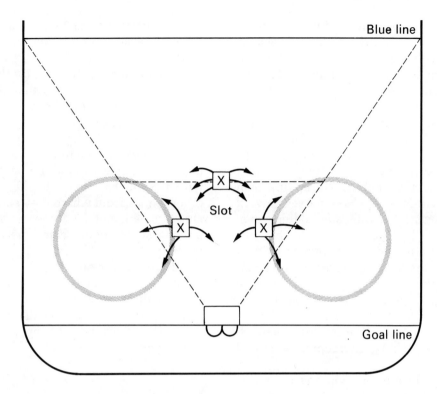

Diagram 14.   *Two Men Short. The triangle must be kept. Goalie also has a man to cover. The slot is the key.*

little trouble getting through the other two defensemen at the base of the triangle.

The defensemen will be placed approximately where they would have been on a one man short situation, the difference being the possibility of their moving closer together. Whether they do or not is usually a matter of personal preference on the coach's part. Some feel it is better for the defensemen to maintain the same distance with two men short as with one. Others prefer the tighter defense, on the theory that this serves as added protection for the goalie.

The job, as always when outmanned, is to beat off the opposition until help comes. Everyone—including the goalie —must cooperate. Aside from the stops he will have to make, the goalie must help with interceptions where he can. He is also usually responsible for any attacker behind the net. He should know who is there and what they are doing. More than one goal has been scored by someone sweeping around from behind and poking the puck into a corner of the net.

The three skaters in front of the goalie will have their hands full. The two defensemen must watch the puck as well as the men. Each will probably have two forwards to cover (assuming the attacking team has put at least one in a defenseman's position), while the apex man should be watching the fifth skater. But he will keep shifting from one opponent to another, harassing and fighting for the puck, hoping for a faceoff or, better still, a chance to ice it.

As pressure is put on by the power play team, both offensive defensemen have moved in closer. As the defensive triangle sags, anyone with the opportunity to get the puck or tie up the man with it will probably have moved toward the boards. The offensive defensemen (probably both are or could be forwards in a 6-on-4 situation such as this) will be moving in closer and closer. The goalie must watch them because if one gets the puck he will be dangerous. As in a one man short situation, it will help if the goalie is clever enough with his stick to intercept any lateral passes.

The goalie's prime function is to stop shots. If the power play is working, he will have his hands full—too full to worry about anything except pucks coming at him. Some goalies, especially tall, powerful professionals like Tony Esposito and Ken Dryden, thrive on this sort of pressure. One goalie of this calibre, most coaches agree, is worth two defensemen. Esposito and Dryden are so big and so agile that they can keep the situation under control even when two men short. But most goalies, amateur and professional, simply cannot cope with every shot that comes their way.

The only saving feature for the defending team is that the ordeal will not last long under normal circumstances. It is not often that a team remains two men short for a full two minutes. One man will almost certainly be back in half that time. With the power play still on, the pressure will continue to be heavy, but the extra man back on the ice will ease the situation for the defenders.

With so much depending on the goalies, it is necessary to see that they get plenty of practice stopping shots coming from several different directions at once. One common drill to sharpen up a goalie's reflexes is to have eight or ten men stand in a semi-circle around the net, some with two pucks. Some should skate in, others shoot from where they stand. The shooters will not be firing all at once, but the shots should come fast enough to keep the goalie stopping shots in rapid-fire succession.

No goalie would be expected to stop every shot under these practice circumstances, nor would any goalie have that many shots to stop with no protection in front of him.

Pull Goalie

Many coaches are inclined to take for granted the pulling of a goalie because it sounds so easy. All the goalie has to do, as they see it, is get off the ice to make room for a skater. They do not bother practicing this maneuver, with the result that, when a goalie leaves the ice, the team, now with six skaters, seldom scores anyhow.

But pulling the goalie is just as much a science as anything else in hockey. The coach who fails to work on it during practice sessions is making a bad mistake. Proper execution on everyone's part —especially the goalie's—is one way a team has a good chance to score.

The goalie must anticipate the situation. He is the man who will make the move, and should understand when and

138

why. As a general rule, however, the goalie should stay where he is except under two conditions:

1. Any time in the game that the referee calls a delayed penalty on the defending team. If the official calls the play properly, complete with a visible arm signal, everyone on the ice will know that the defending team has committed a rule infraction that will result in a penalty as soon as the attacking team loses the puck. Therefore, the attacking team has nothing to lose by pulling the goalie. The responsibility for his coming out of the game should be his alone because there is a time element. His team does not figure to hold the puck very long. If he fails to skate off the ice the instant the delayed penalty is called, it may be too late. By the same token, a forward designated by the coach (in advance, if possible) should be ready to leap the boards as soon as the goalie is on the bench. Someone else—the trainer, manager, another player, or even the coach—should be at the gate holding it open for the goalie. With all his heavy equipment, he cannot jump the boards fast enough. By getting off the ice quickly, the goalie can give his team a sixth skater before that team loses the puck. All six can be on the attack. No one has to defend the open net because it is impossible for the defensive team to score. The moment it gets the puck there will be a whistle stopping play so that the penalty may be activated. Actually, with play moving so rapidly on the ice, this contingency may not often result in a goal. The attacking team must hold the puck for it to be effective.

2. With his team a goal behind and the puck either in the opposite zone or in control of his team in the neutral zone. There should be no more than two minutes left in the game. In those circumstances, pulling the goalie is good only when a goal is needed to *tie the game*. If it is already tied, the goalie should not be pulled. Then there is too much risk of losing on a long shot into an empty net by the opposition.

Either by prearrangement or by signal from the bench, the goalie should know when to start making his move. Whenever it is, he should begin skating out of his net toward his bench as soon as he realizes leaving the net open is fairly safe. The skater who replaces him should be poised at the boards, and jump as soon as the goalie touches the sideboards at the bench.

There is a curious reluctance on the part of many coaches to take the chance of the opposition scoring on an easy goal with the goalie on the bench. They are gambling a chance to smother the opponents at a time when they need a score most, against the possibility of losing the game by two goals instead of one.

At that point in the game, it hardly matters whether the other team scores an extra goal or not. The game will be lost anyhow if a team fails to score with six skaters on the ice. If it is going to take a loss, it might as well do it fighting as hard as possible for a tie, which it is not doing if the coach puts the goalie back in for fear his opponents will scale the puck from their own zone into the empty net.

When the goalie is pulled out of the game, he must be replaced by a shooter. When the sixth skater goes on the ice, the puck has crossed the blue line out of the trailing team's defensive zone, or perhaps it will be in the offensive zone. By the time the sixth man is on the ice, the attack will be going at full swing. The two defensemen will be at their regular posts, guarding the blue line. The three forwards will be driving toward the net, hoping to get in close for a shot on goal.

The sixth man—a forward or a hard-shooting defenseman—will join his mates close by the opposition net. The most popular, and in the opinion of the majority of coaches the most logical, attack will be the formation of a wall across the slot, with four forwards instead of three—much like a power play. This will give the attacking team an extra man, one more than the defending team can play man-to-man. Someone on defense will have to take two men. Again this is similar to a power play.

The difference between this and a regular power play against a short-handed team is that the attacking team *must* score to save the game. In a power play, it is fighting for a goal, but failure to score one will not be disastrous. The pressure under those conditions is on the defending team. Now the pressure is on the attacking team. If it does not score, the game is gone.

The sixth man could enter the game for the goalie at a whistle with the puck in the leading team's territory. In that case, he will come into a faceoff. On his team, the center will be in the circle. The left wing (assuming the faceoff is in the circle to the left of the nets) will be between the circle and the blue line. The right wing, the defensemen, *and* the sixth man will be on a line in the slot, about fifteen feet out from the crease.

The center, as in a normal faceoff in the attacking zone, will try to get the puck to a shooter if he wins the draw.

Chances are that man will be the left wing, who will be skating in from his position as the puck is dropped. If he gets the puck, the whole team can put heavy pressure on the goalie. Five of the six men are in a position to score, and the sixth—the center—will be in the play.

Too often, the problem on the part of the attacking team is timidity—fear that the opposing team will get the puck and either shoot a long one into the open net on the other end or carry it closer for a more accurate shot. The two attacking defensemen will be in close, with the area around the blue line fairly clear.

Under any other conditions, this would be a most dangerous procedure. However, it must be remembered that the attacking team is desperate. It scores, or it loses the game. This is why it must take the chance of losing the puck instead of keeping a tight guard at the blue line. With six men swarming around the net against five defenders and the goalie, there is a good chance for that tying score.

The attacking team must keep the puck because it cannot score the tying goal without it. Therefore, wherever the puck is, the attackers must keep two men on it. By protecting it with two men, the chance of losing it to the other team is reduced. The two men can work together in the event the puck goes into a corner with a defensive man after it. Two men *must* be with him, one to take the man, the other to get the puck. This is a maneuver that should be well-drilled in advance. A good coach will anticipate this as part of the fight for the tying goal with six skaters on the ice.

The secret of scoring in a six man alignment with the goalie out of action is tenacity and determination. The attackers must get used to the idea that there is nothing to be gained by letting up. They must fight for the puck, think offensively, and give every bit of their attention and effort to keeping it.

When defending against a six man attack, it must be borne in mind that the result of the game is at stake. The defenders should be drilled just as hard as the attackers. Since they do not have to score, but simply prevent the other team from scoring, it is not necessary to use forwards if enough defensemen are available. There is no reason all five defenders cannot be defensemen.

It is not necessary to have a good shooter on the defensive team, because that is the team leading by a goal. An extra goal will not change the result of the game. The job is similar to penalty killing. The defensive team is fighting the clock, too. It needs men who are defensive-minded because offense is no longer a factor.

The key man, as almost always, is the goalie. In the last analysis, he is the one who must make the stop that will save the game. It is his responsibility to do anything he can beyond keeping himself set for shots. Under these pressure conditions, this may be confined to yelling for the purpose of keeping his mates in-formed of the total picture as he sees it. He may be able to intercept a pass. He must smother the puck if he can, which will force a faceoff. But his deepest concentration should be on the puck —he must always know where it is. If the screen is so thick he cannot see it, he must rely on his instincts.

The goalie, always important, is never more so than when defending against a six man attack in the last frenetic seconds before a game ends. Since this does amount to a power play, he is under fully as much pressure as though defending against one—probably more. His job is cut out for him. No matter how much help he will get from his teammates, he knows they will not be able to keep him totally free of shots. Furthermore, his stops will be the hardest kind. The puck will probably come out of nowhere, through a screen of legs and sticks, often at full speed and often miscued unintentionally. The chances of a long shot from near the blue line are slim. No one on the attacking team will normally be able to take such a shot because the zone will be too crowded and it could cost the offense the puck. Yet the goalie should be ready for one, just in case.

IV

Organizations

7

Youth Groups

Hockey is the fastest growing sport in the western hemisphere; and the fastest growing group within hockey's framework are the youth programs. They are developing so rapidly and spreading so widely that it is almost impossible to keep up with them.

In 1973 there were over 100,000 young boys playing under the supervision of amateur hockey associations in the United States and Canada. These ranged between the Mite (or Tyke) class, usually aged seven and eight, to Midgets, aged fifteen and sixteen. There were variations from community to community, but the general divisions were fairly constant.

There was some hockey being played in most of the states and all the provinces, but the growth was so fast that the exact number of rinks, players, and coaches was incalculable. The pattern of how these groups started and how they grew was more important than the numbers, for this pattern can be followed anywhere.

A typical example is Natick, Massachusetts, a town of some 30,000 people about fifteen miles west of Boston. Although not a bedroom community, it is within the Boston orbit and its hockey program began in Boston, as did most of the others in the area. After a slow start, the growth of Natick's program has been great.

It started in 1952, when three interested young men took about twelve players of high school age to the Skating Club of Boston for a workout. At that time, the town's only formal hockey program involved the members of the high school varsity team. Its players were part of a suburban league that practiced once a week and played most of its league games in Boston. No one in the group taken to the Skating Club was on the school hockey team, a significant factor in the beginning program then and a significant factor everywhere today. Without a youth program, there was no place for a boy who wanted to play but was not good enough to make the high school varsity. His only hope was natural outdoor ice which, of course, is entirely dependent on the weather.

Almost every youth program starts

with teams of high school age when they should really start with little boys just learning to skate. When a team is started with older boys, there is no source from which to draw future teams.

An interest in hockey needs to be instilled in boys when they are very young, so that many will have the ability to play on a par with others of their own age by the time they are high school freshmen. Only by building up from lower brackets can an effective feeder system be developed in a community.

In 1970, with nearly 400 boys in the ice program, it was obvious that Natick needed a rink of its own. The youth

program had boys from several other communities. None was able to support independent programs, but all had young people who wanted to play hockey. Not only was the parent town near enough and big enough, but its ice program was the fastest growing in the area.

A drive was launched to raise funds for an arena. The bulk of this drive, supervised by parents, was actually done by the children themselves. Both boys and girls raised money in any way they could, including such things as selling candy, running raffles, distributing bumper stickers and decals for automobiles, soliciting money wherever crowds gath-

Figure 7-1.   *Community backing: an essential to a good program.*

ered, and closely covering shopping malls and plazas, while their elders ran luncheons, dances, and other special events.

The money was finally raised and the area had its arena. With it came a greater demand than ever for ice time. The result was another drive, which financed a second arena adjoining the first. The two are connected by an indoor runway. The only difference between them is that the original arena has stands for spectators who pay admission for tournament games, whereas the second rink is for practice and house games only.

Today thousands of boys are in similarly organized hockey programs all over the United States and Canada. If no arena is available, those in cold enough weather zones for ice have makeshift backyard arenas. Wherever there is natural ice, young people are practicing hockey informally. When the weather is too warm for ice, they turn to street, backyard, and playground hockey.

The impetus for this tremendous increase in interest comes primarily from two sources—the widest spread in history of professional hockey at the top level, due to repeated expansion of the National Hockey League and the establishment of the World Hockey Association, plus newly established "minor" leagues everywhere and television's discovery of hockey as a major entertainment in sports. The latter has taken an exciting game once confined only to northern climates into homes from Alaska to southern California and from Nova Scotia to Florida.

From watching either hockey in person or on television to wanting to play it is a short step, especially for young people. In the past years the only comprehensive programs for teaching hockey

were designed for boys with sufficient talent to compete with the best in their age groups. Today, youth programs for everyone who wants to play, regardless of talent, are being planned or have been put into effect. How this is done will be explained in the pages that follow.

GROUP NAMES AND AGE RANGES

Mites

The Mites, known in some areas as Tykes, are the youngest in organized group hockey. Generally—with a few variations depending upon local preferences—they are seven and eight years old. In a well-organized youth program, these boys have already learned the rudiments of skating, handling a hockey stick, and manipulating a puck.

This does not mean that they are good at any of these skills. Obviously, some boys will learn faster than others, while some may never really learn at all. But at seven, if they have had previous instruction, they will know what they are *supposed* to do, and even before seven will know the object of the game and the prime importance of basic skating.

Although many children do not begin to learn to skate until they are seven or eight, those that have can be part of a Mite team organization. These boys will be formed into teams, will be placed at positions whose general requirements have been taught them, and will be part of what are usually called house leagues (local leagues embracing everyone in the program who wants to play hockey, with each boy assigned a team commensurate with his abilities).

In some communities, boys as young as four are accepted into the youth hockey program. Although teaching techniques for the beginner vary somewhat from community to community, there are a few general principles designed to produce the best results.

There was a time when very young children were put on double runners, much as small fry learning to ride bicycles go first on tricycles, then on bikes with training wheels. But there is no real technique for double runners, which, unlike bicycle training devices, do not really help a child learn. Instead, even four-year-olds begin with regular shoe skates. They may hold the hand of an adult at first, but this is discouraged for any length of time. It is more advisable to give a small child a chair or some other object bigger than he to push— almost like a walker. In that way, he takes his first skating strides alone.

Progress varies with the child. Some are so natural on skates they get along without a device like a chair after only a few lessons. Others, lacking the balance, must depend on an object to lean on for longer periods. As soon as he learns to get around on skates by himself, the child should go into a class, under the supervision of a teacher.

Stopping techniques are usually difficult for smaller children. At first, any stop possible is considered better than falling down or skating into the boards. These are the natural tendencies of most children in the early learning stages. One of the best ways to teach stopping is to show little children a stop like a skier's snowplow—toeing in. This will not be the final move in stopping, but it does give a child control of his skates. Once he has that, he forgets the snowplow stop and learns to stop properly on skates.

In order to take the first lessons in hockey, a child should be able to skate forward and backward, and to stop. Only then should he be given a hockey stick and shown how to handle it. Like skating, stick-handling is not a natural function; it must be taught. And, like skating, it is learned with various degrees of facility. Some children pick it up very quickly; others find it more difficult.

If a child is school age and really wants to learn, he may go so far as to take the stick to school with him, carrying it around much the same as an older athlete may carry a football, a baseball, or a basketball. The job of the teacher is to make the child understand the necessity of getting the "feel" of his hockey stick. The sooner a boy has that, the sooner he will be able to grasp the principles of keeping control of a puck.

Squirts

The usual age for Squirts is nine and ten. Since all the youth groups are by age, a boy may start in the Squirts if he is too old for the Mites, but an experienced Mite who has learned the rudiments at five or six and has played two years of organized hockey will be well ahead of a boy who has just begun to learn at Squirt age.

Every youth program should have a place for the beginning Squirt. Once again, it is a matter of putting a boy in with his peers. A late start in learning does not necessarily mean that a boy of Squirt age cannot catch up to his own age group.

Some boys of nine may never have had a previous chance to learn. Possibly, one is new in town and has come from an area where there is no hockey and no youth program. Whatever the reason for his late start, if he has ability it will soon come out. A nine-year-old will normally have more balance than a five-year-old; therefore, it will take him a shorter time to learn to keep his feet on skates. Because of his age, he may well be able to keep up with the best boys in his group if he shows natural ability.

The Squirts will go as far as their own particular program permits. In some programs, Squirt teams are in leagues including communities other than their own. In others, a Squirt will play only so-called house games, in a league that includes only his own town.

Under no circumstances should a boy be pushed too fast, even within his own age group. Not everyone can show unusual hockey talent, or even any at all. This is why it is essential that boys at the Squirt level be kept with their peers not only by age but by ability.

Children of nine and ten are still, essentially, little children. Some will need more help, more encouragement, and more coaching than others. The prime objective of youth groups should be recreation. If a boy (or a girl) wants to play hockey, he should be encouraged to do it for fun, even when he is patently not in the same class as some other boy of his own age.

Squirts should not be handled like grown men. They will sometimes be frustrated, sometimes cry, sometimes "act their age." If they need sympathy —a pat on the back or even an arm around them—their instructors should be prepared to give it to them.

At the same time, it can always be borne in mind that Squirts are older than Mites—the second youngest in the program, not the youngest, which means they have advanced—chronologically, at least. Having advanced, the pride of being a little older may act as an incentive for them to become a little better at playing hockey.

Bantams

The Bantam division, in most cases age eleven and twelve, is often the youngest in which there is competition beyond the local level. This is not a rule of thumb. In many cases, there is outside competition in the younger divisions, too, but the best of the Bantams will always have it if it is available.

It is also at the Bantam level that many boys decide whether they will continue playing hockey for recreation or drop out. Actually, by that age, a boy may either love hockey or want to forget it. There are few in-betweens, and thousands of boys who know by then that they will never be top-level hockey players continue to play because it has become a fun game which they do not want to drop.

The best of the Bantams may be good enough to move up, for, although a boy may not play in an age group younger than his, he is eligible to go into an older one, if he is good enough. Bantam hockey is more competitive than either of the younger groups, but not as competitive as the two oldest groups, which will be discussed later.

No matter how efficient a Bantam player is, it is usually not advisable to move him into an older group. Even Bobby Orr of the Boston Bruins, who was a sure future big leaguer at the age of twelve, was playing Bantam hockey when first seen by Boston officials. He was twelve then, and an outstanding hockey player, but did not move up until he turned thirteen.

A Bantam should know many of the sophisticated aspects of hockey. If he has been playing youth hockey since his years as a Mite, he will probably give some hint of ultimate efficiency beyond the average, as Orr did.

Peewees

In a way, the Peewee division, made up of boys thirteen and fourteen, is the most sensitive of youth hockey groups. One reason may be that it is customary to refer to the whole program as "Peewee hockey." Although the other divisions are rarely mentioned in off-hand discussion of youth hockey, the term "peewee" always seems to come up.

But, more important to the boys themselves, it is in the Peewee division that pressure comes close to reaching its height. By the time a young player is a Peewee he is really neither boy nor man. In age, he is the youngest of adolescents, but as a hockey player—and this is true of other sports which have organized leagues that find young athletes in national or international competition—he is considered practically a man.

The higher the level of play, the more importance is placed on winning. At the lower levels, the emphasis is on fun, with winning more or less incidental. For the good of the boy, it is probable that

this attitude would be best at the Peewee level, because at that age the disaster factor should be kept out of losing. Pressure is one thing most boys of that age can do without.

Pressure often emanates from the people closest to the players—parents, other members of the immediate families, and coaches. Intelligent directors of youth programs must do everything possible to counteract that pressure by fighting any attempts, intentional or otherwise, to make the boys feel they *have* to win.

It is not an easy fight. Too many fathers, in particular, want to see their sons play on winning teams. For this reason alone, without realizing the possible ill effects on their children, many carry their enthusiasm too far.

Directors of youth programs can help to stop this by pointing out to all adults involved the pitfalls that are present. Most believe that if their elders would leave them alone, Peewee hockey players (and some younger players who may be exposed to the same type of pressure) would take their important games in stride. The men in charge of the programs should emphasize that no sleep should be lost nor spirits crushed by defeats.

Since the tournaments rather than the weekly games during the regular season present the most possibilities of heavy pressure, there are those who feel tournament play should be eliminated at the levels of fourteen and younger. Others feel—properly, it appears—that it might do just as much harm to swing in the other direction. To drop tournament play because of increased pressures on the players seems too much like cutting off a finger to cure a hangnail.

One other important element of Peewee hockey is that it, rather than Bantam hockey, often becomes a turning point. A good player will want to keep on, regardless of age. But a boy of lesser talents may decide to go elsewhere for recreation if he cannot make a competitive Peewee team.

However, the boys who play hockey for fun will not stop at the Peewee or any other level. If they enjoy the thrill of playing, they will play somewhere, regardless of age, if ice is available. For this reason alone, many local programs encourage boys to go on, regardless of their ability, by instituting farm teams.

Midgets

The highest level of most youth programs are the Midgets who are fifteen and sixteen (high school ages). Because of the overlap with high school teams, some programs eliminate Midgets altogether. Many strong Midgets make their high school teams and either do not care to continue in an organized youth program or do not have the time for it.

There are two schools of thought with regard to Midget hockey. One group feels that, since it will not attract the best players in a given community—the best will be on the high school team—there should be no formal Midget division within the framework of a youth program. This, they feel, becomes a real problem when the tournaments begin. Obviously, every youth director wants his best players to represent his community in a tournament, but this might mean using high school boys in the Midget age group to replace boys who have been playing all season because they were unable to make their high school teams. Letting Midgets play in-

formally solves that problem. They get in their hockey hours for recreation without being part of the program.

The other group feels that a formal Midget program of any kind is better than none at all. Even though the best players are no longer part of the program, those who remain can enjoy the game and the competition. But if no formal records are kept, something is lost for players of that age.

The result of this philosophy is two-fold. Either the Midgets who played through the season continue in the tournament play which most boys look forward to, or some or all the varsity high school players of fifteen and sixteen are allowed to represent their communities as Midgets. This will leave plenty, if not all, the boys who have performed through the season on the team for tournaments, but some will spend more time than others on the bench.

In some communities, an in-between condition has been reached by permitting varsity high school players who grew up in the local youth program to come back and play as Midgets in the tournaments. That may be the best answer to the problem, since not so many boys will be affected in either direction. There will be only a few high school players eligible, and most of the Midget squad will be made up of boys who have been in the program all season.

Juniors

Juniors are boys over sixteen who continue in formal hockey programs, playing for teams that may be under the auspices of professional organizations.

These are divided into groups by ability, with Junior A the highest, and, except for the colleges, make up most of the pool from which the professional teams draw talent.

There is little Junior hockey in the United States, since most nonschool youth programs end with the Midgets; however, there are Junior hockey programs for boys aged sixteen to twenty in six states: Michigan, Minnesota, Wisconsin, Massachusetts, Rhode Island, and New Hampshire. American hockey players of exceptional ability from other states continue to play in high schools and colleges or apply for Junior hockey membership in Canada. Junior divisions have thrived there for many years. Junior hockey usually ends at twenty, the minimum draft age for professional play.

EQUIPMENT

Skates

In hockey, skates are basic. Unfortunately, conventional shoe skates, whether for boys six or sixteen, are not inexpensive. The prices rise some, but not appreciably, with the age of the boy.

Parents are advised to get their children skates about one size smaller than the regular shoe size. The blades should be stainless steel and the fittings should be made only by experts.

Unfortunately, the need for snugness usually means that a small boy is likely to outgrow his skates after only one season. This presents a potential financial problem, the best solution to which

may be found in a later part of this chapter.

Protective Equipment

Sporting goods houses in general have different prices for different sizes. One sells a set of equipment for boys twelve and under, including shin guards, gloves, and helmet for about $60.00, but because this is inexpensive, it is not the best quality and the company's personnel do not guarantee or advise it.

More realistically, for durability lasting several years, protective equipment, even for smaller boys, should be bought item by item. Good-quality gloves are advisable for $35.00, with shin guards a dollar or two less than that. Helmets, which should be compulsory in all youth programs, can be bought for 30.00 or $35.00, and shoulder guards for about $4 00.

Goal-tending equipment, including skates, is much higher in price than the other skaters' equipment. The special skates a goalie needs are about twice the price of conventional shoe skates. Leg guards and chest protectors start at about $40.00 each. Plastic face masks are about $8.00. Gloves, one a baseball catcher's type and the other for holding the stick, are in the neighborhood of $100.00.

Sticks

In all cases, the price of sticks varies with the age of the boy and the type of stick. Curved sticks, at about $5.00

and not usually recommended at the youth level, cost roughly $3.00 more than straight sticks. It is generally advisable to tape that part of the stick which touches the ice. It not only gives the player better control of the puck, but helps make the stick last longer.

Goal-tending sticks can be purchased for anywhere from $5.00 (for boys' sizes) up to $15.00, $20.00, or even more, depending upon the individual's taste. The less expensive stick is adequate for young goalies, partly because the shooters of the lower age groups lack the strength for hard, twisting shots and partly because a Mite or a Squirt goalie may change to another position when he is older. However, a Bantam, Peewee, or Midget goalie should have a good-quality stick.

MONEY-SAVING DEVICES

Availability of Equipment

All youth programs do whatever possible to help participants' families save money. In virtually all communities, both in the United States and Canada, skates and equipment are owned by the program for indigent boys who want to play hockey. None is turned away because of lack of money.

In any well-developed youth program there should be several sets of goalie equipment, at least two for each age group. Other extra equipment, such as leg guards, gloves, sticks, shoulder pads, and skates should be available. The expense of hockey equipment should never

deter a boy who really wants to play, regardless of his ability or lack of it.

Exchange Systems

An exchange system is the best way to save money for everyone. Increasingly popular in communities that have larger and larger numbers of young hockey players, a good exchange system, usually run by volunteers, is a practical money-saver.

The need for snugness in skating shoes almost always means that a small boy will outgrow his skates after only one season. For the convenience of everyone in the community, rich and poor alike, a nonprofit skate shop can easily be set up. Such a shop can offer skates at reduced prices by accepting used skates for trade-in on larger used skates. These are easily sharpened and reconditioned right on the premises and can be resold at a fraction of their original cost.

Besides alleviating financial problems, a reconditioning skate shop can pay for itself while allowing parents to save by buying reconditioned skates. Volunteer help, often a mother or older brother or sister of a young hockey player, cuts expenses down to the bone. Any profits can be ploughed right back into the program.

A good exchange system can keep even the most indigent hockey player in its program. If a boy cannot earn enough money to pay for equipment, he can use what he needs on a loan basis, turning it back in at the end of the season. In this way, no boy, regardless of age or financial status, need be left out of a youth program. Some sort of work within the program should be found for him. Volunteers are always needed, both in and out of season. The economically disadvantaged boy who wants to play hockey may well be the most enthusiastic volunteer of all, for he benefits directly from the program.

FACILITIES

Private

Since hockey requires ice and there are comparatively few localities where natural ice is regularly available, a comprehensive program must depend on artificial ice. Indoors or outdoors (there can be artificial ice outdoors if it is covered) artificial ice is expensive. It requires underground pipes, automatic freezing units, and spreaders to make new ice from time to time. The ideal arrangement is to have an indoor arena.

Arenas usually have many functions in addition to the youth hockey program. Anyone who likes to skate and is a member is entitled to ice time, especially those in figure skating programs. Competitive games need ice time, for it is through competition that much of the sustaining money is raised.

Even a well-planned youth hockey program is limited by the amount of ice time it can get. When Natick's hockey people discovered this fact shortly after the original arena was built, money was raised to erect the second arena, primarily for practice purposes. The additional building helps make it possible to have a comprehensive youth hockey program.

Another way of getting an indoor arena with a heavy emphasis on youth hockey is to find an "angel." This happened in Sebastopol, California, a community of less than 5,000, where Charles Schulz, creator of the cartoon strip "Peanuts," built an ice arena primarily for hockey. It made possible youth skating and hockey programs that could not have been arranged otherwise.

Very few private arenas in the United States or Canada are, in effect, open to the public. The Skating Club of Boston is probably the oldest, dating back to pre-World War II days. The emphasis there is on figure skating, although it is open for hockey.

Colleges and universities are building more private ice facilities today than ever before, but these are mostly for their own use. Off-hours—midnight to seven in the morning—are open in some of them, but except for boys of high school age, these are impossible times for a youth hockey program embracing younger children.

Adult involvement and good leadership are essential in the construction of a private arena. Any campaign needs both, assuming that the citizens of the community have and are willing to pledge the necessary funds. There is a heavy dependence on volunteers, for these will provide the life-blood of such an ambitious program. Pride in the community, willingness to work together, and, perhaps most important of all, the leadership of someone with experience can combine to give any medium-sized city or town the kind of private facilities for a high-quality, all-embracing youth hockey program.

City or Town

With the tremendously increased interest in ice hockey throughout the country, municipally sponsored arenas have sprung up all over the United States in recent years. Facilities of this type have been available in Canada for many years. Every city of any size throughout the dominion has one or more public arenas, some built as early as the turn of the century.

In one respect, Canada has had a distinct advantage over the United States in that natural ice is available in so many communities. This has meant huge savings, since arenas for public use, including youth hockey programs, often have been unnecessary. In cities where natural ice is available for months every year, the arenas are used almost exclusively for competitive events that attract paying audiences that help pay for projects involving young students of winter sports.

However, even in Canada, there are cities that have no guarantee of natural ice for sustained lengths of time. The big southern cities, such as Toronto, Montreal, Winnipeg, Regina, and Vancouver all have community-owned arenas—in some cases, more than one. Ice time in these is in as great a demand as in the big cities of the United States.

It is here that what amounts to an arena explosion has taken place since 1960. Hundreds of cities and towns that never before needed ice now have indoor facilities, some busy almost twenty-four hours a day. None of the larger cities, such as those that have professional hockey teams, have anywhere near enough room to teach the increasing number of children who have learned to love hockey through the medium of television and in other ways.

Previously unlikely states such as Florida have arenas (and youth programs) as far south as Tampa, St. Petersburg, and Miami. Other states fronting the Gulf of Mexico, as well as Arizona and southern California, are becoming so hockey-minded that there are not nearly enough facilities to handle the demand.

It is impossible for the large northern cities to service the children who want hockey. In Boston, one of the original hockey centers, there is almost as much activity in the old Boston Arena at two in the morning as at two in the afternoon. Some of this ice time is paid for by schools, some by individuals, and some is donated by the city.

Boston is not alone, but is only an example of the rise of hockey as a favored sport for boys. It has not only facilities within the city, but innumerable rinks in the surrounding communities. Actually the core city—and this is largely true all over the country—is an increasingly difficult area for an all-embracing youth hockey program. Everything, including ice time, is more expensive because rink maintenance, the most costly feature of an ice program once the building is erected, is more expensive.

But the problem can be solved, and should be. The day may come in the very near future when no city or town athletic program is complete without a hockey complex of some kind. There are playgrounds for other sports almost everywhere. Ice arenas for hockey should become almost as universal.

Regional

Park and recreational supervisors have become more and more aware of the need for artificial ice facilities. If, within the political structure of a community, it appears difficult or impossible to raise taxes for building arenas of some kind, it may be done through special regional groups such as a Metropolitan District Commission. Facilities are owned, built, and operated by the MDC and are all-purpose and all-seasonal. Some are roofed open-air sheds, some enclosed buildings, some completely outdoors. In most cases, they are used for recreational activities such as roller skating in summer and ice skating and hockey in winter.

These are public facilities, which charge low fees to individuals for their use. In cases of extreme need, children may use them without charge. Youth hockey is one of many activities within the framework of the MDC. The Commission itself is publicly supported, part of a state system.

Some feel that in its recreational activities, the MDC tries to do too much, that it cannot be all things to all people, but it does help fill the type of void that plagues big cities. Any public facility that not only keeps young people off the streets but gives them supervised activity has merit. An MDC ice rink is as good as a full-fledged arena. Thousands of children take advantage of it, with many taking part in youth hockey programs which, although crowded, provide budding young athletes with the chance to develop latent skills or satisfy active desires.

Other

For ice hockey, the only possibilities of building any sort of youth program other than through private, public, or regional rinks are rivers, lakes, or flooded playgrounds in localities that have natural ice.

These are, of course, limited. Once again, Canadian boys have an advantage because so much of Canada has natural ice in the winter. Bobby Orr, for example, learned to skate on Georgian Bay when he was growing up in Parry Sound, about 140 miles north of Toronto.

Comparatively few American boys have this advantage. Except for the northern and the mountainous states, there is very little natural ice that lasts over sustained periods. And, in order to play hockey, natural ice must be present long enough to build up a safety factor in depth. Occasional snowstorms or cold snaps are not enough.

Natural ice is a factor in the Northeast, some of the Canadian border states, and mountainous areas like Colorado. These can and do have youth programs that work when there is ice. But there is no substitute for the dependability of artificial ice!

PERSONNEL

General

Although there is considerable merit in setting up a regular slate of officers and a board of directors to run a youth hockey program, there is no substitute for one enthusiastic, knowledgeable supervisor, preferably a professional teacher, physical educator, or athletic director.

Whatever the official arrangement, most successful projects have one man at the top, either officially or otherwise. He may or may not be paid for running the hockey program. In some communities, he may be hired to run the arena. This man, as a rule, is a hockey enthusiast who once played and probably coached the game somewhere. He will provide the life-blood of the program, for he will be a veteran coach and teacher who enjoys working with boys of all ages.

There are communities all over the United States and Canada where one such man is the central figure in the program. He will know how it should be run, where to get the necessary personnel to run it, and how to teach unprofessionals coaching techniques for everyone from Mites to Midgets.

In some cases, he may be a volunteer, but it will be more effective if he has a job that keeps him around the ice. No youth hockey program can get along without volunteers, but one professional, interested and enthusiastic, can sometimes get more work done than many volunteers.

The professional should supervise the volunteers. Generally, he will not be specifically paid for running the youth hockey program, but that may be part of his regular duties. People who like to work with boys will work with them whether they are paid for it or not. A summer playground director often is a winter arena director, so that he works with boys all year round.

Coaches

Besides the director, the most important volunteers in a youth hockey program are the coaches. Good coaches are not easy to find—on the contrary, obtaining and assigning coaches to the proper age group are among the hardest jobs a youth director might have.

The natural pool from which to draw are older brothers, fathers, or interested relatives of boys in the program. The best are usually those with no vested interests—men who derive real enjoyment from working with boys, especially in hockey.

[handwritten margin note: Parents don't make good coaches]

Close relatives sometimes present problems because of overenthusiasm. They get so wrapped up in their own children—and the teams for which their children play—that they cannot see the forest for the trees. They forget that these boys in whom they are most interested are boys—some very young children—and, without meaning to, they are among those most often guilty of applying heavy pressure.

The younger the boys, the more likely the ill effects of pressure, but fathers and brothers rarely recognize this fact. It is, unfortunately, an occupational disease of all youth athletic programs—baseball and football, as well as hockey. In youth hockey, as in other sports, one of the director's hardest jobs is keeping heavy pressure under control.

A youth coach must not become a one-man cheering section for the team his young relative represents. It is better for him to coach a team that does not include someone in whom he has a close family interest.

[handwritten margin note: Family members should not coach each other]

Inexperienced coaches—or, perhaps, instant coaches—must have at least a few qualifications that coaches of boys in other sports do not need. First and foremost, a hockey coach must know how to skate. It is no more sensible to permit a nonskater to coach hockey than to try to teach a nonskater to play the game.

[handwritten margin note: Coaches should be able to skate]

If an aspiring coach cannot skate, he will probably have to be ruled out. It is hard, if not impossible, to teach an adult enough ice-skating skills to permit him to show others how to play hockey.

Assuming he can skate, a youth coach must learn the fundamentals of hockey. If he already knows them, so much the better. If he does not, the basic fundamentals and coaching techniques given in this text should prove most helpful. Coaching clinics will also be worthwhile to coaches. If no hockey clinics are held, the youth hockey director should organize or promote a local mini-clinic for his youth volunteer coach.

If possible, a good coach should be persuaded to remain in the program even after his own relative has outgrown it. This may or may not happen. Therefore, the youth hockey director is in a never-ending quest of coaches. It is an occupational hazard of which he should be well aware.

Officials

The most important official in hockey is the *referee*. He is in complete charge, presiding at faceoffs, watching for rule infractions, making important decisions, settling controversies, and inflicting penalties.

His penalty powers are an important function. Penalties do not decide hockey games, but they have a profound influence on the play. When a player goes off the ice, his team must play short-handed for two minutes. If it does not have good penalty-killers—players who can keep the puck away from the opposition as long as possible—the price may very well be a goal against it.

By the same token, the team with the one man advantage should have a good power play, with which it can overpower

Figure 7-2.   *Three generations.*

the short-handed team and harass its goalie. Its hope, of course, is to score before the penalized player returns to the ice.

In youth hockey, the results of a penalty may not be too drastic—certainly not among the younger groups. But by Bantam age, it will make a difference because Bantam boys are old enough to take advantage of rule lapses on the part of their opponents.

The referee in youth hockey must use good judgment and understand young people. In the younger groups, a boy may do something wrong without realizing it, or his mistake may be something he could not help. Where the referee may penalize an older boy, he may simply stop the game and warn a younger one rather than send him to the penalty box. Whatever he does, he is in charge of the hockey game. His is a most important role, a fact he must realize without taking advantage of it.

Next in importance to the referee are the *linesmen.* In most youth hockey games, there is only one, whose principal job is to check to see if players stay onside. Although he has no authority to inflict a penalty, he calls offsides whenever he sees them.

Although one linesman is enough for house or even regular season games, in tournaments or playoffs there usually are two. In the case of younger boys, one linesman can usually keep up with the action. But older boys skate faster, work together better, and stick-handle more cleverly. For these reasons, two linesmen are recommended.

The *timer* is exactly what his title implies: His job is to watch for time-outs when the action is stopped, keep track of penalty times, and know when the period or the game should end.

The *scorer* keeps score and also has the responsibility of keeping track of those who scored and those who make assists. These are often, but not always, given him by the referee, who is usually in the best position to judge who should get credit for assists. It is also the scorer's job to total up goals and assists for the game.

In some youth programs, there are *goal judges,* one at each end of the rink. They are posted directly behind the goals and have the job of flashing on the light when the puck goes across the goalline. As a rule, goal judges may not be necessary in youth hockey, but are used in important games and tournaments. The referee may overrule either goal judge.

SYSTEMS OF PAYMENT

Who gets paid and how much varies widely from one youth program to another. If qualified volunteers are available, they are often used as officials. In any case, the one official most likely to be paid is the referee. If a second official is paid, it will be the linesman, who normally receives less than the referee. Normally no other officials are paid.

Obviously, the more volunteers the better, as far as youth hockey is concerned. Unfortunately, however, volunteers cannot always be depended upon, although they usually enjoy their roles as officials.

It is important that the referee have good judgment and that he take a professional attitude toward his job. He must be thoroughly familiar with the

Figure 7-3.   *Clinics—needed for officiating skills and consistency.*

rules, some of which are quite complicated.

His hardest job—meting out penalties—cannot be properly handled if he is unfamiliar with all the nuances of rule violations, as well as the penalties. Aside from every other consideration, a referee in any game above the Squirt level just cannot do the job unless he is very knowledgeable.

PROGRAMS

Practice

Practice in a youth program is much like in any organized hockey program except for one significant difference. In a youth program, especially among the younger groups, nothing can be taken for granted. Older boys report for preseason practice with general ideas of what is expected of them. Younger boys often do not have the slightest idea of what is expected or what to expect.

Preseason practice will differ with the age group. After the Mites, who must be taught to skate, the older groups should work in accordance with their individual abilities. Boys with great natural skill—which will begin to emerge when they are nine or ten—may be given more sophisticated preseason work than those who show no special aptitude for hockey.

One requirement for everybody during the early weeks of preseason practice is as much skating as possible. In youth groups, it can be assumed that the boys have skated little, if any, before beginning a new season. Therefore, practice in starting, forward and backward skating, stopping, and, in the case of older boys, turning, spurting, speed, and endurance work should be stressed.

Even major-league hockey players need plenty of skating before the start of a new season. These men, experienced as they are, cannot swing right into action without getting their so-called "ice legs." If professionals need skating practice when they go into a new season, amateurs, and particularly young amateurs, need even more.

It is a truism in hockey that no player can get too much skating practice. The more time he spends on the ice, the more at home he will feel there. Anyone who plays hockey must feel at home on skates before he can make the next move in his game education.

Older boys may begin working on their passing and shooting techniques during the first week of preseason training. Mites and Squirts who can skate and have had some experience may need more time. In any case, it must be borne in mind that few youth hockey programs allow for more than an hour or two of practice each week, since there usually is no more ice time than that available to them.

It can be assumed that older boys will work alone or in independent groups somewhat more often, especially if they are serious about their hockey. Most boys are willing to work in one way or another—playing street hockey if no ice is available—between early-season practice sessions. If, on the other hand, they do not have the time for even that, preseason practice should start as early as possible, so that the boys will be ready for competition when it is time.

The various phases of hockey techniques, all of which have been previously discussed, apply as well to youth hockey. Younger players have the same obligations to the game as their older brothers. If they wish to play hockey well, they must practice, know their way around a rink, and be willing to work hard.

Groups of boys, such as forward lines who may be working together during the season, should practice together whenever they can. At any level, there are no set forward lines, for the best laid plans are always subject to change without notice. Injuries, nonhockey obligations that conflict with practice, or moves in and out of the area, all have their effect on interfering with the teamwork necessary in developing forward lines.

The same is true of defense combinations. When two defensemen expect to work together, they can profit by practicing together wherever they are. But they, too, are subject to changes. Some boys who want to work together just are not suited to one another. This is something that has to be determined by the coach, who will know what to do when the game season begins.

Budding young goalies can work with anyone except each other. For a goalie, there is no substitute to being "shot at." Whereas other skaters really need ice more than anything else, a goalie can practice on the street, in his backyard, or at a playground. He does not even need a puck, for a ball will do as well.

Obviously once practice sessions begin, a goalie will work with the rest of the team. Properly rigged with protective devices, he must work as hard as everyone else. His objective is to stop the opposition from scoring. The best practice for him is to stand in front of a net and learn to stop shots from all angles and under all conditions.

Games

There is nothing at stake in practice, but there really *is*! For many boys, practice is not much fun. Nothing can be proved and there is no incentive other than dedication.

Games are something else again! The drudgery of practice produces the results of the games. A hockey player, regardless of his ability or age, never wants to lose, any more than an athlete in any other sport does. A game is something the player can really enjoy. It is there that he proves to himself and others what he really can do.

Youth hockey directors always try to match teams of equal strength. An outstanding team should not be pitted against one that has boys of less ability. A bad beating is the worst kind of morale killer in any sport, and hockey is no exception. When teams meet each other within the framework of the same youth program—so-called "house teams" —this can easily be controlled. The coaches know what their own boys can do and, after they have learned the personnel within the age group with which they are working, they should know what other teams can do.

Probably the best way to prepare boys for games is to indicate that practice is comparable to classroom work and that games are similar to examinations. In a game involving teams of equal strength, the best drilled group should usually win.

Very young boys—Mites and Squirts —should not be encouraged to battle for victory to a point where defeat will be a traumatic experience. To them, hockey should be fun. They should try to win, but victory should not and cannot be stressed.

The older the boy, the more important the game, but youth groups should never be given the idea that the world will come to an end if they lose. On the other hand, Peewees, Bantams,

Figure 7-4.   *Skating—great form.*

and Midgets can understand the *relative* importance of winning, for that is the objective of any game.

The farther afield a team goes, the more important the game. If a youth group team plays a team from another community, its boys will be carrying pride in their own town into the game with them. There will be some pressure, but it should not be life-or-death. As long as the boys learn the satisfaction of winning and understand that it is no disgrace to lose, the general objective of youth hockey is accomplished.

Technically, game play is no different from practice. When a youth team plays, it must observe the rules, understand the infractions, expect penalties resulting from any, and put into the game everything taken out of practice.

Hockey is a contact game, and the older youth group teams will be in perpetual contact with opponents. These boys must be made to understand the meaning of contact and the differences between legal and illegal contact.

They will realize in the course of a game just how much or how little they have learned in practice. If the coach is conscientious, he will see the mistakes his boys make in a game and try to correct them in subsequent practice sessions. This is the key to good coaching at any level.

Nothing is quite so satisfying to a young hockey player as seeing what he has learned in practice work in a game. A boy will also probably learn more in one game than in many practice sessions. What the opposition does, which often governs what he does, is something he cannot help but learn.

The experience a boy gets in a game is very important. Every game is a new experience. For a young boy, it may at

first be somewhat frightening, but an older boy will be more interested than frightened and a really promising young player will benefit greatly from every game he plays.

Drafting

In most youth hockey programs, coaches draft the better younger players who move up from one division to the next. This does not include the youngest division. When the Mites, usually age seven and eight, move up to the Squirts (nine and ten), there is not much purpose in drafting because the ability of boys that young is hard to determine.

But Squirts about to move up to Bantams can often be judged by their ability, and coaches of Bantam teams take turns drafting the younger boys. From the Bantam division up, drafting is a regular procedure that helps shape the quality of the teams in the older divisions.

In drafting, there is always one unwritten rule—never hurt a boy by dropping him in mid-season. Since many coaches are themselves inexperienced, their ability to judge a young player will not be flawless. If they draft a boy who does not turn out as well as they think he will, they must live with the error. The alternative—to demote a player to a lower-ranking team—may hurt the boy so much that he may drop out of the program. This is most likely to happen when a Bantam coach drafts a boy moving up from the Squirt division. A ten-year-old is usually not yet old enough to have found his groove in any youth sports program. This is not always true, but when a boy fails to live up to the promise he might have shown as a Squirt, the coach who drafted him is not always to blame.

The safest draft ages are from twelve up. Peewee coaches draft from Bantams and Midget coaches draft from Peewees. The older the boy, the more reliable his performance in the framework of a squad or team.

The purpose of a draft in a youth hockey program is to set up the better teams, those that will compete in games against outsiders and in tournaments. In any division, the oldest boys will be lost because of their ages. They will be replaced by boys coming up from the younger divisions.

The draft is usually the first move as a new season approaches. The coaches meet with the hockey director, or perhaps the board of directors, and choose the new players by lot. In some cases, the best team will draft last, as happens in professional ranks.

No matter how it is done, drafting involves the better players only. If a mistake is made, the player should stay with the team all season and, for his own sake, be allowed to play from time to time. The only possible way to rectify the error is to bring up a boy from a so-called "house" team. In this way, the disappointing player will not be hurt. Actually, he does not even have to know that his team added another boy because of his own inadequacies. It is much better to have one too many players than to drop one and replace him with another from the lower ranks.

In cases where new coaches are brought in, they will not know whom to draft, since they were not part of the program the year before. The experienced coaches can draft for them, since they know which of the younger boys

were the best of the available players in the new draft.

Drafting is part of a good youth hockey program. It not only helps the coach of a team that may not have won often the year before, but it is a source of satisfaction—a reward, if you will—to the boys who are drafted. Since building a boy's morale should be one of the functions of any youth program, the draft is an effective device for that purpose.

MISCELLANEOUS

Fees

Fees for participants in a youth hockey program depend on several factors, some of which are unknown in the beginning. One that is known is the cost of ice time. In smaller communities it is likely to be less than in large cities. In privately owned rinks it probably will be more than in municipally owned rinks.

A variable that cannot be determined for some time after the beginning of the program is the number of boys in it. This could start in the tens or even hundreds and can go into the thousands, depending upon the size of the area from which membership is drawn. It does not follow that the more people in the program the less the cost to each. Obviously, the more boys who play, the more ice time will be needed. It is possible to handle only so many boys per hour. The number is determined by the size of the rink and the number of volunteer coaches.

In Canada, where most boys grow up on skates, this is not as important as in the United States. Many Canadian boys cannot recall when they learned to skate.

The reason is that there are many men available to teach them informally. A father can show a son what he is doing wrong because the father probably skated all his life.

But in the United States, there are just not that many fathers who grew up ice-skating. Those who did can be helpful, and usually are. Generally, however, American boys are not natural skaters and must be given extra instruction.

There are some youth programs in which added expenses, such as using professional coaches and professional referees, are provided. In these circumstances, the cost to each player may be greater than in a program that has more volunteers.

A good rule of thumb at the start is a registration fee of five dollars. It is a fair price that most people can afford. After a year or two of operation, those in charge of the program can determine if it is enough.

When a boy moves from one age group to another, there should be a fee. Generally this is ten dollars. That, too, is fair and will bring in revenue to help with expenses as they come up.

Assuming that after two or three years a thousand boys are in the program, at five dollars a boy, five thousand dollars would be raised in registration fees. This could be a realistic figure even in a small community because it is probable that boys from the surrounding towns may be included.

Out of the registrants, perhaps 300 will move up into the next higher classification every year. At ten dollars per boy, that will raise another three thousand, giving the program a cushion of eight thousand dollars on which to work.

The boys who can afford it will pay for their own ice time. This should be over and above the basic revenues from registrations and promotions because that money must be available for operating expenses.

Ice-time money usually goes directly to the rink. In cases of private ownership, it will help defray operating expenses, but all will not be devoted to the hockey program. Some must go to a figure skating program and to such other expenses as rink personnel, ice machines, upkeep, depreciation, taxes, and rental for an exchange store.

No matter how many people are in the program, there may not be enough money for basic expenses. Both small and large programs should be run as tightly as possible. But in all programs, provision should be made for the family that cannot afford even the modest expenses of a youth hockey program. No boy should be denied the chance to play hockey because his family cannot afford the money. Funds must be allocated to take care of these needs. This is one of the most important items in a youth hockey expense agenda; no good youth program can be complete without income to take care of such matters.

Sponsors

Sponsorship by those who can afford to help should be solicited because no matter how many participants are in a program, they alone cannot support it. The best sources of sponsors are well-to-do families with children in the program or local business firms.

Sponsorship should be sought for the entire program, not for any one group or any one team. No youth hockey program will be fully successful if only one

165

favored group has financial backing. In most cases, a youth hockey director will not accept money for that purpose.

Teams should have uniforms and names or nicknames, but should never advertise on their uniforms a business firm or an individual who has donated money. There may be merchants here and there who refuse to help unless their own companies can be advertised, but experience has shown that most will cooperate.

Money-Raising Plans

There are as many ways to raise money as people in a community with imagination. One of the best methods is to arrange with a big company—a candy producer, for example—to ship his product at cost to a community, with the profits from the same going to the youth program. In that way, the boys themselves can participate in money-raising projects, much as the Girl Scouts raise money through their annual sale of cookies. The product can be sold door-to-door or by solicitation in central areas where the largest crowds usually gather. The drives for money should not be confined to the boys in the hockey program alone. The entire family will benefit, since such programs as figure skating and public skating will be for everyone interested.

In some communities, local merchants will set aside one day's profits for the program. Many of the merchants themselves may have children involved. There are also special drive possibilities, including special sales (commonly known as "short sales") in peak sales periods before Thanksgiving and Christmas. By

asking a whole community to cooperate, considerable money can be raised from the profits of a few hours on a given day.

Printed programs for tournaments can be a source of considerable funds by soliciting advertising among the local merchants. Those who are sponsors can be given credit in the program, and advertising sponsorship can add to their participation.

Wealthy families can help by backing special events. In one community, several thousand dollars is raised by one family that finances an annual horse show. The sale of bumper stickers, automobile and window decals, and other so-called gimmicks are all helpful to the support of an amateur hockey program.

Although admission is usually free to regular games, admission to tournaments adds to the backlog of money for the program.

One thing to bear in mind is that the cost is greater than it might seem. With all expenses, even a comparatively small community will need a budget of from $15,000 to $20,000 annually to sustain a youth hockey program.

Publicity

A youth program should help to generate its own publicity on the local sports pages. Newspapers, both daily and weekly, are dedicated to promoting their own communities and will cover any events that do so. A youth hockey program is a good source of publicity, especially when there is competition.

The broader the competition, the more and better the publicity. But, although some of the more capable teams move into big interstate and national—even international—competition and thereby receive state, national, and international publicity, there is no substitute for comprehensive local publicity. The big-city publicity may be a source of civic pride to the people of a community and of satisfaction to the players and their families, but it does not help much in raising money. It is what the local media do that really counts.

Awards themselves—usually trophies, plaques, or scrolls—should not be expensive, but well-suited for home or rink display. For outstanding players, they often represent the first of a long series of awards later won in high school, college, amateur, or professional play; to others, they may represent the only award the person may ever get.

Every youth hockey program should have a publicity director, a volunteer who is willing to donate his time. In smaller communities this is usually a sportswriter for the local paper. Besides giving the program as much publicity as he or she reasonably can, the person will often keep track of records and statistics, team, division, and league. This help is invaluable and should not be overlooked. Nor should the value of publicity: It is the best way to keep the community informed of every development, from the hockey committee's first meeting of the season to the final game of the last tournament.

Association Suggestions

Groups such as the American and Canadian Hockey Associations suggest procedures helpful to anyone interested in youth hockey programs. Here are some of their suggestions:

1. *Items of expenditure:*
   Ice rental
   Uniform repair and replacement
   Equipment repair and replacement
   Awards
   Transportation charges
   State tournament costs
   Program costs
   Referee charges
   Administrative costs
   Invitational tournament expenses

2. *Fund-raising:*
   Candy sales
   Sponsor assessments
   Voluntary donations
   Player registration and promotion fees
   Game and tournament ticket sales
   Program advertisements
   Service organization contributions

Figure 7-5. *The winners.*

3. *General:*
A publicity program
A code of player conduct
Assignment and duties of: officers, directors, purchasing agents, equipment managers, tournament directors, game directors, scheduling directors, promotion directors, league statisticians, program editors, awards chairmen, team traveling directors, farm system coordinators, and registrars
Honorary officers

Insurance

Insurance is vital because of the possibilities of injury. No matter how careful they are, boys will be hurt playing hockey. This is not only because it is basically a rough game, but because of its speed. Hockey is so fast that no one can control injury possibilities from falling on the ice, getting hit by a puck or stick, crashing into boards or goal uprights, or any one of a dozen other mishaps.

A youth hockey program should provide insurance for its entire membership. This is obtainable from an insurance company that specializes in sports accident insurance. Besides the insurance taken out by the youth program, parents should be encouraged to take whatever conventional accident, health, and hospital insurance may be available to cover their children. Some companies have designated hockey insurance carrying premiums as low as ten dollars a year.

To guard as much as possible against injury, all youth programs should have available protective equipment for boys who cannot afford to buy any. This

should include—and families that can afford it should be prepared to provide—such devices as helmets with built-in nose and mouth guards, shoulder, knee, leg, and body pads, athletic supporters, and gloves.

Number and Size of Teams

The number of teams depends upon the number of registrants. Every boy should be assigned to a team. If his ability is limited, he should still be given a chance to play with and against his peers.

The usual size of a squad is seventeen players. This includes three forward lines of three players each, plus one extra man; two sets of defensemen of two players each, plus one extra man; and two goalies.

For tournament or important game play, a fourth forward line, plus a spare and one more defenseman, is usually recommended. This will allow for injuries or, in the case of Midgets, additional players who may return at the end of their high school hockey season.

Even for house play, a few extra players should be included because the boys of least ability will be left over after all others are assigned.

Summer Camps

As the fame of hockey expands to all geographical areas on the continent, so do the hockey schools—especially the summer hockey schools. The first recognized resident schools began in Canada but the idea rapidly expanded into the United States. In general, the leading instructors in the early summer hockey schools were the big-name professionals. The schools usually opened in the last week of June and concluded around Labor Day, meaning a ten-week operation. Most of the schools today operate from six to eight weeks with instructors from the professional ranks joining college and secondary school coaches. In the early years of hockey camps it was common for two instructors to be on the ice for every twenty-five or thirty campers, whereas today it is not uncommon to find three or even four instructors for thirty to thirty-two young men. One of the instructors is often a specialist such as a goalie coach and in some cases a power skating coach.

Many camps offer at least three hours of hockey instruction on the ice per day, augmented by about one hour of power skating. In addition, the more up-to-date camps offer daily instruction on the "blackboard" plus instructional films. The chalk talks (blackboard) instruction augmented by instructional films are worthwhile because they give the player and instructor time to absorb in detail various patterns and fundamentals of the game. Put a pair of skates on a young man and he wants to move—not to listen to explanations. Instructors or coaches all like to utilize ice time to maximum efficiency and are often too brief in explanations or brush off questions asked by the players. These are just a couple of the numerous reasons why blackboard drills and films are helpful.

Films are particularly effective in instruction. When a young player sees a nationally known star or any hockey player going through the correct drills he will try to emulate him. Films portraying the stars can be most valuable, and the quality of the films is improving each year.

One method is to augment the blackboard talks with actual practices in individual, paired, or team patterns on a gymnasium floor or composite tennis court. The puck moves well and mistakes are easily corrected. By using this method of educating the youngster prior to his actual skating on ice, valuable time is saved and the three hours of daily ice time are used to the best advantage. All instructors have to agree on the teaching philosophy for the school, yet the instructor is not regimented in one type of offense or defense. Elasticity and freedom to teach are recognized.

Supervised outdoor shooting into regulation goals from waxed plywood sections is another valuable teaching aid. The players use their own sticks and are taught the wrist shot as well as the slap shot. The four corners of the goal are emphasized as well as control of the height of the shot. This is taught in groups of fifteen or sixteen and the other fifteen or sixteen members of the section can be doing exercises that will develop the major muscle groups used in hockey. Both activities are supervised by hockey personnel and can be made a fun activity by generating competition. Eight goals are used and only two players are assigned to each goal, with a pair of pucks for each pair of campers. On the surface, one might think that such a hockey school was very regimented, but this is far from the truth. The player and his family pay well for instruction and one cannot get too much training and review of fundamentals.

Free time in any type of boys' camp is always a problem. The parent and the camp want supervision—not regimented supervision, but a healthy use of leisure time. This can be attained by having the campers choose an activity when not scheduled for hockey. Successful summer camps provide activities such as swimming, tennis, golf, baseball, softball, basketball, touch football, fishing, sailing, canoeing, movies, and arts and crafts. Naturally, the environment of the camp often determines the activities.

When choosing a summer hockey camp, a parent should not only look at the teaching personnel but should request information about the following: cabin supervision, free-time activities, experience of staff not on the ice, supervision of activities, health and safety precautions, food service, list of patrons recommending the camp, medical facilities, proximity of doctors and hospitals. Questions to be asked should include: Is there an experienced trainer at all practice sessions? How many students are in each bedroom? How long has the camp been in operation? What percentage of campers return? Is there a snack bar? Can the camper purchase hockey equipment at the camp or nearby? How many instructors are on the ice each session? How many campers are on the ice each session? Is it possible for players to move up or go down to more or less experienced groups? *Will the school provide a detailed report of progress and recommendations at the end of the camper's stay?*

The term "power skating" covers a multitude of ideas but if properly taught is one of the most important facets of the program. It is a rare player who cannot improve his skating. Power skating, taught by an experienced teacher, is most beneficial for proper use of the body muscles and proper use of the body

in skating, especially in hockey. This activity is recommended and it should receive about four hours per week in instruction—it can be made fun.

There is no reason for having poor ice or foggy conditions in a rink. The sophisticated machinery used in rinks today can provide a new ice surface in less than fifteen minutes and dehumidifiers rapidly remove fog and moisture. Another question to be asked might be: "How old is the rink or when was it last brought up to date?"

Excellent hockey players available as instructors are numerous *but hockey players who can teach are not as numerous.* Just because a player is in the headlines does not mean that he can impart his "God-given" ability to a young player. Again, questions should be asked.

The easiest way to conduct a hockey session is to have a scrimmage. The players all want it too. However it is a rare player who does not need fundamentals each day. Why practice mistakes? Therefore a good program does include fundamentals daily—they are varied and can be made into fun sessions. At the conclusion of each session a short scrimmage can be provided. As the week progresses, the scrimmages increase in length and the last day should be a full-fledged scrimmage under game conditions. Chalk talks should cover the rules of hockey, and practices should be conducted under the rules of the game. Instructors are coaches and permissiveness in practices is carried over into games. Coaches and game officials must be strict regarding penalty calls and always cognizant that they must teach *emotional control* as well as skating, passing, and shooting. One week of a hockey camp is fine, but can a group of

TABLE 1. Daily Schedule

	Monday	Tuesday	Wednesday	Thursday	Friday	Saturday	
7:15– 8:00	Breakfast Clean Room	Breakfast Clean Room	Breakfast Clean Room	Breakfast Clean Room	Breakfast Clean Room	Breakfast Clean Room	7:15– 8:00
8:15– 9:15	Hockey Rink	Hockey Rink	Hockey Rink	Hockey Rink	Hockey Rink		8:15– 9:15
9:30–10:30	Outdoor Shooting	Outdoor Shooting	Outdoor Shooting	Outdoor Shooting	Outdoor Shooting	GAME 10:15	9:30–10:30
10:45–11:30	Weights Rink	Weights Rink	Weights Rink	Weights Rink	Weights Rink		10:45–11:30
12:00 Noon	Lunch	Lunch	Lunch	Lunch	Lunch	Lunch	12:00 Noon
12:45– 2:30	Indoor Hockey-Gym	Indoor Hockey-Gym	Indoor Hockey-Gym	Indoor Hockey-Gym	Indoor Hockey-Gym	Check Out	12:45– 2:30
2:45– 4:15	Hockey Rink	Hockey Rink	Hockey Rink	Hockey Rink	Hockey Rink		2:45– 4:15
4:30– 5:30	Instructional Film	Instructional Film	Instructional Film	Instructional Film	Instructional Film		4:30– 5:30
5:30– 6:00	Dinner	Dinner	Dinner	Dinner	Dinner		5:30– 6:00
6:15– 7:45	Softball Game	Movie	Basketball Game	Movie	Softball Game		6:15– 7:45
8:00– 9:00	Power Skating	Power Skating	Power Skating	Power Skating	Power Skating		8:00– 9:00
9:15–10:00	Room & Lights Out	Room & Lights Out	Room & Lights Out	Room & Lights Out	Room & Lights Out		9:15–10:00

coaches really teach enough in that time? A two-week session should be the minimum and four weeks the maximum.

The question often comes up, "How old should my son be when I first send him to a hockey camp?" It depends on the experience the young man has had: If he is a good skater and has been in a good youth program, then six to eight years of age may be all right. If the young man has not had much hockey, then he should not be sent before he is eight or nine years of age. He should be taught to skate at his home rink plus do some shooting and passing—then he can be sent to camp.

The equipment needed at the camp is usually emphasized in brochures. Certainly *all safety equipment has to be purchased* such as shin pads, good skates, padded pants that fit, and sticks. Too often a youngster arrives at camp with inadequate equipment or poor fitting skates, and this becomes a serious problem. For instance, skates must be fitted for the season he is in, *not two years hence.* Weak ankles are generally a figment of the imagination. Poor fitting skates at the ankles, in length and width, plus dull blades and no rocker all contribute to poor skating. A skater should have good skates and a good fit. Well-used skates that fit are better than the purchase of new cheap skates.

If a boy is a goalie, he should get instruction from a goalie coach. This facet of the game has been overlooked for too long. The proper equipment should be in his possession before going to camp. Goal-tenders should spend as much time skating as possible and certainly should take the power skating classes.

Classes should not have more than six lines, six sets of defensemen, and three or four goalers. This is a total of thirty-three or thirty-four to a class and is the ideal setup for drills (using both ends of the ice) and scrimmages. More than three lines on any team means that much less ice time when scrimmaging. Boys do not go to camp to sit on the bench.

A typical daily schedule is presented in Table 1. The youngest classes generally meet from 8:30 A.M. to 10:30 A.M. The older campers finish the program off from 9:00 P.M. to 10:00 P.M. This particular schedule was planned for the nine- to eleven-year-old group. It is recommended that *all* goalies have a joint session each morning at 6:30 A.M. or at least every other morning in addition to their regular class schedule.

8

Secondary School Hockey

RESPONSIBILITIES OF THE COACH

It is helpful but not absolutely necessary that the hockey coach should have played the game. The coach should be able to skate because he should be on the ice, especially with younger players. There have been exceptions to both of these conditions but most people agree that playing the game gives experience that is immeasurable. A coach should meet the educational requirements of any faculty member. A background in selected courses in psychology, growth and development, and teaching techniques help to make a better coach.

Experience in the game of hockey helps a coach to know which basic fundamentals should be stressed to players as well as the patterns of the game. A coach makes the patterns fit the personnel, not vice versa. It is a cardinal error to insist that players, regardless of age, play a hard and fast system. Each year the coach will find that his material changes and he, through experi-

ence, should study each player and utilize individual strengths. Too often outstanding material has not been utilized properly.

The coach should have administrative training and experience. The game of hockey as far as the coach is concerned is not just the actual time on the ice. The time expended in administration is at least double that spent on the ice. For instance the following categories take considerable time and are most important:

1. Equipment and supplies—recommended athletic gear to be purchased, such as sticks and pucks;
2. Ice time—practice and games;
3. Daily schedule planning—line personnel, defense pairs, goalies, drills;
4. Meetings—with parents, school officials, league officials, referees, service clubs that help the programs;
5. Scouting reports;
6. Information—to the squad about practices, trips, and regulations;
7. Publicity—with the school newspaper as well as the local members of the fourth estate and other media.

One can readily understand the complexities of the coach's job and the need for administrative experience.

It is of paramount importance that the coach and his staff be very familiar with the athletic and academic codes prescribed by their school league and state. There is no excuse for ignorance of rules and regulations any more than not knowing the actual playing rules on the ice. In the past, too many players, schools, and teams have been unnecessarily hurt by forfeitures due to the coach's ignorance of codes and regulations.

The future secondary school players are generally found in youth hockey programs as well as in primary school programs. Therefore, it is important for the coach to have good rapport with youth groups. If possible, he should convey to the coaches of youth programs his philosophy of the game and some of the basic patterns he will use plus the basic fundamentals he would like to have stressed. The coach must sell himself to these groups, because in reality they are his "farm system." He cannot alienate such groups and expect to have a complete program nor can he be dictatorial.

Sponsors of youth programs and economic backers of good secondary programs are the town fathers who are in such service groups as Rotary, Kiwanis, and Lions. In addition to the service organizations are the church affiliations, PTA groups, and athletic groups. The coach should work with these organizations through good public relations.

Within the school the coach should work closely with the teachers because the onus is on the coach to know the academic rating of each of his players. He is akin to a "chaplain" because in addition to the faculty advisors and school counselors, the coach enters the advanced educational plans of his players through meetings with parents, college coaches, and alumni of recruiting colleges. One can readily see that the coach should be familiar with each of his players' academic progress as well as their future plans. It is important for the coach to work closely and harmoniously with the counseling department.

School organizations such as the band, newspaper, and key societies are a great help to a coach and he should avail himself of their cooperation in helping the hockey program.

The size of a hockey squad is generally the prerogative of the coach. Economics enter the picture relative to the number of uniforms available but it should be up to the coach to determine the size of his squad. Some coaches have to work alone and want only eighteen players; other coaches working alone may accommodate a squad of twenty-five. In general, the varsity squad ranges between eighteen and twenty-five players, whether or not there are assistant coaches.

Prior to the first workout, the contending players should all be given a thorough physical examination. The hockey season is long, difficult, and the game is a contact sport. The coach should be familiar with the physical examination results and if in doubt about any particular phase of the examination, he should confer with the proper medical authorities. Glasses or contact lenses worn by players should conform to safety codes.

Some coaches desire to have about one-third of their team seniors, one-third juniors, and the other third sophomores. Other coaches take the best eighteen players and put them into suitable playing positions. There is no hard and fast rule but, in general, some underclassmen should be carried unless the coach is fortunate enough to have an excellent JV and/or freshman program.

Each player should be given a fair opportunity to make the squad. The coach should notify prospective players well in advance when the first practice is scheduled and make sure this information is disseminated to all.

After the squad has been chosen, the coach should decide the offensive and defensive patterns he will use. In other words, if he has fast skaters, the patterns used will be different from those used if he has slower skaters. The physical size of the players will also affect the choice of patterns. Care must be taken not to choose lines or defensive pairs too soon. The players should be interspersed to get balance and harmony. The coach should have a preplanned practice schedule before going on the ice with his squad. This rule should be adhered to each day because all facets of the game must eventually be covered and constant review of weaknesses practiced as well as the strengths. The coach and assistant coaches should meet after each practice to evaluate that practice and plan for the next day's practice. Lack of communication from coach to coach and coach to player has caused many failures in coaching and in the success of the team. The coaches should try to set aside some time each day for players to have an opportunity to "rap."

When planning the daily schedule, the coach should make sure each player is utilized as well as each coach and be doubly certain that the ice time and ice areas are used to the utmost efficiency.

Use of blackboard talks and films are important. Many coaches hold blackboard talks daily, especially during the early part of the season. Once the players are on the ice, action and movement are paramount. It is the wise coach who utilizes every minute of ice time!

Some excellent hockey films can be used as teaching aids. These films are available at little or no cost. The American Hockey Coaches Association and the education departments of the various Canadian provinces have excellent listings of films and where they can be procured. In recent years the use of films, filmstrips, and loop films has grown. Videotaping of both practices and games is currently being used for the teaching and analysis of skills.

Some coaches scrimmage the first few days of practice and each day thereafter; others stress more time on the basic fundamentals and group patterns. Coaches who have used both philosophies seem to have been successful. The daily practices should be varied to make hockey interesting rather than a routine of the same drills every day. Many drills will accomplish the same objectives.

Ice demonstrations can be performed by capable coaches with young legs or by preplanned use of squad personnel with the coach identifying each move. It is unfortunate that many inexperienced coaches try to get into the practice sessions as players and therefore do not observe what *each* squad member is doing. The players should *play* and the coach should coach.

Televised games of professional hockey have been both helpful and detrimental. The game has grown through exposure through TV but, unfortunately, some

177

youngsters try to emulate certain players and it definitely has a poor effect on their play. For instance, in the professional game there may be "fights" whereas in most secondary school rules a fighting penalty is "immediate game expulsion" plus "exclusion from the next game." Another example is when a professional hockey player carries the puck out in front of his own goalie. This is considered a bad move. The "hero" or sports idol can do no wrong in the eyes of his worshipper, but the fundamental is opposed to that of the secondary school coach and, if emulated by the young player, will result in chaos.

Scouting reports are most valuable. The coach or his assistant whenever possible should scout all future opponents as near to his team's scheduled game with them as possible. Scouting reports should bring out the strengths and weaknesses of opponents.

Unfortunately, in some leagues, when playoff teams are tied in wins and losses, teams are selected by total goals scored. This policy generally means that the coach tries to roll up the scores in all games. This system is wrong. When it is not used, the coach may substitute freely when he has an adequate lead. Players should be rewarded by playing and game experience is still the best teacher. Next year's players must get into the games.

The coach must have his penalty killers and power play units preplanned and trained in special practice periods.

Each practice scrimmage and the drill should be at full speed and under game conditions.

Substitute plans may have to be used if players become injured or are out ill. The experienced coach trains players for several positions for all emergencies and for all game situations.

Coaches should preplan trip schedules so that leg stamina is not left in the vehicles prior to going on the ice. And at least three hours are needed to digest a pregame meal. Use of water, milk, synthetic liquid-ades, sugar, and fruit should be regulated.

It is imperative that the coach be aware of the health of his team. Colds, lack of sleep, injuries, family or personal problems—all can take their toll, but the coach who is cognizant of these problems will usually have a healthier squad both mentally and physically.

THE PLAYERS' BENCH

During a game, players on the bench should be seated according to lines, defense pairs, and spares. The players move on the bench as lines change. In most rinks there is at least one door to the players' bench (opening inward to the bench) and often two doors—one for leaving and one for entering. If there is only one door it is important that the relief players get on the ice first and that those players being relieved be at the door, alert to the location of the puck to make certain it is nowhere near their body or skates. If the puck hits a player who is waiting to enter the players' bench, the team may be called for having too many men on the ice.

Players should relieve each other only when the puck is moving toward the opponents' end of the ice—it is foolhardy to change personnel when the puck is controlled by an opponent moving toward one's own goal.

Coaches differ in their philosophy about the length of time a line should stay on the ice. One system is to have the relieving line stand up at the one-minute mark and each player call to his counterpart being relieved. The onus is on the skating player to come off. A student-manager on the bench might tap the coach on the shoulder at the end of each minute. The lines in the *third* person might shift at the forty-five second mark.

Speed is the name of the game and one must be in excellent physical condition to go at full speed for three periods. Hence, shorter shifts should be maintained in the third period.

Conversation on the bench (players' box) should always be of a positive and encouraging nature. This applies both to the coach, his staff, and the players. Hockey is an emotional game, and tempers are short-fused. There should never be any derogatory comments, allegations, inferences, or name calling directed at opponents, referees, or spectators from the bench. This philosophy should be adamantly enforced by the coach. The coach or his assistant should never make comments to the opponents.

The *head* coach should be the only one to make comments to the referee or linesmen but these should never be abusive comments, since his assistant or players may follow his lead—with trouble resulting. The players' sticks should be held more or less uniformly with the handles up. They should never be extended over or on the sideboards to interfere with the players or officials on the ice. Well-disciplined teams have good bench decorum. The rule books state

that no more than one coach, one manager, and one trainer be allowed on the bench, although often an assistant coach replaces the manager. Most coaches concur that three, or at the most four, non-playing personnel are sufficient.

Players on the bench, once they have regained normal breathing, should study the strengths and weaknesses of the opponent. Most teams have an "Achilles heel." Players who are slow, injured, out of position, or overskate show it, and smart teams pick up these weaknesses and utilize them to their own advantage. Conversely, teams have strong points and it is usually self-defeating to attack constantly the strength of the opposing team. Players should always be studying and thinking about their opponents.

Before the game and before each period, the players' box should be policed for tape, paper cups, and gum. Players' spare sticks should be clearly marked and in a stick rack that is specifically and strategically placed for efficiency and protected from pilferage by souvenir hunters.

The doctor assigned for the game should be located near the bench so that he can efficiently go to the ice, players' room, or first aid room when needed.

If the game is being played in a rink always used by the home team, it is only good manners and sportsmanship to greet the visitors and try to provide, within reason, whatever services they request.

A good policy is to have parents or rooters assigned to seats behind and adjacent to the home team, and visiting parents and guests assigned to seats behind and adjacent to the visitors' bench.

The *home team* should provide protection and preserve decorum. Too often at "big games," there is not enough thought given to this matter. Whenever possible it is both a wise and kindly gesture to provide the visitor with coin boxes or canvas bags or some such suitable receptacle in which to keep the players' valuables during the game.

The locker rooms, toilets, showers, and parking areas should be inspected long before the teams arrive. It is most annoying and confusing for a team to arrive at the game site and find that these advance preparations have not been made.

V

Conditioning
and
Testing

9

Conditioning

Before playing hockey, an athlete must master the art of skating, an acquired function. Off-season conditioning for hockey is not like off-season conditioning for practically any other sport.

Special exercises have been devised by Bill Head, a veteran physical therapist and former trainer of the Montreal Canadiens. Throughout his years with the Canadiens, Head also worked with many other hockey teams in the Montreal area, including amateurs of all ages. His findings and conditioning routines are applicable to them as well as to professionals. This section of the book is based on his conditioning manual for hockey players.

Most sports other than hockey demand muscular power and reflexes that cannot be easily adapted to skating and carrying a puck. Even the simple process of running requires the development of muscles that may interfere with the peculiar dexterity needed in hockey.

In other sports, the leg propels the body forward or backward by raising the heel and transferring the weight to the ball of the foot. This is the basis of

almost all leg movements in other sports. In skating, this type of muscular coordination is not used at all. On the contrary, it is impossible to raise the heel and transfer weight to the ball of the foot because that would mean lifting each foot off the ice altogether.

A trap that many hockey players fall into during their off-season is the fact that they can do as much without skates as any other athlete. On the other hand, without previous experience on ice, performers in other sports cannot even stand steadily on skates, let alone move around with any degree of balance. The muscles of the leg and thigh are unable to control the skate-shod foot.

The hockey player develops other muscles that enable him to maneuver gracefully and effectively on skates. Because he does not use these muscles when not on skates, they relax if he goes too long without skating. Without proper corrective exercises then, he may suffer unnecessary problems when he starts skating again. Some could be serious enough to keep him incapacitated for short or long periods of time.

Hockey players of ages from about twelve on are particularly prone to groin injuries when they resume skating after long layoffs. These groin injuries are caused by strain on muscles especially used in skating. Many normally unused groups of muscles are brought into play when skating while at the same time many normally used muscles are actually relaxed. Overdevelopment of nonskating muscles combined with underdevelopment of skating muscles is the basis of groin injuries.

The muscles affected one way or the other are at different levels of the thigh bone and attach to the bone at the base of the abdomen. Muscles on the front and outside of the thigh, regardless of how powerful they may be, are completely governed by the flexibility of the muscles of the inner and back part of the thigh. This lack of flexibility, a characteristic of nonskating athletes, is what keeps the most physically powerful nonskaters from doing well when they first try to move around on skates.

Some very strong skaters have surprisingly weak shots. This is because they have poor balance in trying to transmit their power through the arm and hand to the hockey stick.

Actual participation in other sports during the off-season is not likely to have adverse effects on hockey players if they devote a few minutes every day to special exercises that will keep the muscles they use in hockey supple and strong. The person who follows this regi-

Figure 9-1.   *Conditioning prior to practice. Note use of sticks as part of drill.*

men throughout the off-season should have little trouble readjusting to hockey when he resumes playing it, no matter what activity or sport he turns to when the hockey season is over.

FEET

The feet are the foundation for human balance. Although skating is considered almost a flat-footed function, the spring effect of the arches is a governing factor. In order to keep the arches flexible, holding the foot steady and curling the toes downward until there is a cramp under the foot at the arch is an excellent exercise for skating. Eventually, a hockey player will find that he can curl his toes as sharply as he can without suffering the cramp. This maximum curling will keep the arch loose, improve the spring effect of the feet, and maintain control and flexibility of the leg muscles.

ANKLES

A hockey player needs special ankle strength, for the ankles are the first to go when learning to skate and are the weakest part of the leg even for expert skaters. Everyone loses some ankle flexibility with maturity. The ankle moves in four directions—up, down, out, and in. All but the inner movement, which becomes exaggerated, especially among hockey players, loses flexibility. Most ankle sprains are at the outer part of the ankle, since this joint flexes inward with little or no provocation.

In order to minimize ankle sprains, a hockey player should lie flat and move his ankles, one at a time, in all directions except inward. In each case, he should move with force as far as he can, with the most important part of the exercises being the outward or eversion.

Besides minimizing the ill effects of a sprain (no exercise will *prevent* sprains altogether), these exercises help maintain greater balance and control when skating. In some cases, they may even prevent a fracture.

KNEES

In all sports, the knees are the most vulnerable part of the legs. There are all sorts of knee injuries because the knee is made up of a complicated network of tendons, ligaments, and muscles, all potential trouble spots. It is possible that knee ailments have caused athletes more trouble than any other injuries. The knee usually takes longer to heal than even the most serious fracture and, once hurt, the knee's vulnerability to reinjury is so great that many athletes with knee problems must go through years of their careers wearing specially built knee braces.

Because of the speed of the action, hockey players are particular targets of knee injuries. Therefore, anything they do to strengthen their knees in the off-season will be helpful in mitigating the effects of injury. Certain exercises will help any hockey player, whether or not he suffers from a chronic knee problem.

Despite the power that hockey players develop in their thighs, many cannot use it effectively because they have so little knee joint flexibility. This is not caused by the knee joint, but by the muscles at the back of the thigh. These run from the buttock down to the hamstrings, three powerful tendons easily discerned behind the knee.

A good exercise to build these tendons and develop more knee flexibility is to lie on the back and try to kick the buttock with the heel of the foot. Most athletes should not find this too hard.

More difficult, but very effective in developing flexibility of the muscles at the front of the thigh and knee is an exercise which, in the beginning at least, may take help from someone else. Lying face downward, try to get the heel up to the buttock. Although someone else may have to help at first, a player eventually should be able to do it alone, bringing his foot up to where he can reach it with his arm, then moving it to the buttock. At the start, there may be a painful pulling toward the upper front of the thigh. If this exercise is repeated often enough, the pulling will ease and finally stop altogether. It, as well as the similar exercise of lying on the back, strengthens the knee because the extreme bending gives it flexibility.

An exercise especially beneficial to hockey players, since it gives them a feeling of well-being and what they themselves refer to as "looseness," is also helpful for the leg, thigh and hip, and the lower part of the back. In this one, the athlete sits on the floor with both feet flat against the wall, with the heels touching it evenly. The arms should be stretched out in front with the hands open. While breathing out through the mouth after taking a deep breath in through the nose, the exerciser should bend forward and touch the wall with his hands.

Most essential is that, while bending forward and right up to the time contact with the wall is made, the backs of both knees remain flush to the floor. It is better not to touch the wall at all than to bend the knees. After a few minutes of this daily, an athlete should be able to *punch* the wall while keeping his knees flat on the floor.

This will not only strengthen the knees, but create suppleness and flexibility in muscles and tendons from the waist down.

PULLED GROIN

Rather than suffer the groin pull that is so common among hockey players when they first resume skating after a long hiatus, it is a good idea to do an exercise that actually *causes* a slightly pulled groin. It is better to pull a groin with a controlled exercise than to suffer a more serious groin injury while playing hockey. The deliberately pulled groin will be slight and easily controlled. The accidental groin injury that comes in a hockey game or practice might be serious enough to keep a player off the ice indefinitely.

When he first resumes skating, even a player with strong buttocks and thighs is likely to find it hard to skate freely and loosely. A hockey player's legs do not move forward, only his body. During a stride forward on skates, three well-developed buttock muscles will be brought into play.

Unless these muscles are so conditioned to permit stretching to their maximum, the skater will not be able to move with the freedom he needs. In order to develop that quickly, while at the same time minimizing the risk of a serious groin pull, an exercise has been devised that gives freedom and control to the outer and inner movements. It will also increase speed and dexterity.

The starting position of the exercise is lying flat on the floor and doing the "split." While keeping the legs flat on the floor, they should be spread as far apart as possible. The first time this is done, it is a good idea to measure the distance between both heels. Later measurements should find that the split will be considerably wider after the exercise.

The deliberately pulled groin will be more the *feeling* of a pulled groin than an actual pull. It will be a vague but unmistakable feeling and will do no harm. In fact, it is better to get the feeling than not. If, after moving the legs to maximum width apart there is no pulled groin feeling, the adductor muscles must be tighter than the average.

For best results, it is recommended that one leg be anchored to a heavy object, so that only the other will move. When maximum width is achieved (with both legs always flat on the floor), the slight groin pull should be felt on the side of the free leg. The anchored leg will give a feeling of pressure against the stationary object.

After moving the free leg back and forth to complete the split movement, the legs should be reversed. The free leg should be anchored and the anchored leg free. In this manner, both legs will be moving.

Eventually, the exerciser should feel the slight groin pull first on one side, then on the other. And it should not be long before he will find that his split will be considerably wider after the exercise than it was before.

The pain of the slight groin pull is really a thigh condition—almost a simulated groin pull. And the exercise will make a real groin pull suffered while playing hockey much easier to heal than it might have been otherwise.

SHOULDER

Shooting the puck appears to be little more than a simple flick of the wrist, but it incorporates the coordination of muscles of the hand, arm, and shoulder, as well as those as far down as the middle of the chest and the top of the hip bone. The person who has that remarkable coordination can indeed seem to use just a flick of the wrist to snap the puck past a goalie. Without the coordination, the flick of the wrist is not only not so easy, but, depending upon the individual, almost impossible.

Without proper muscle coordination, a hockey player might receive a pass and be in a perfect position to score, but then fail because he cannot move fast enough. Before shooting, he must brace himself to get his body into a convenient position. Hockey is too fast a game for this to work very often. By the time the uncoordinated player has all conditions for shooting just right, he usually will have lost his opportunity.

The best test of the muscles of the shoulder or upper arm is to ask a player to put one arm around him, with the back of his hand as close as he can between the shoulder blades. That in itself is not too difficult. But then ask him to reach from above with the other hand and touch the tips of his fingers. If, with the first hand flat against his spine between his shoulders, he is able to overlap it with the fingers of his other hand reaching down from the top, he should have good muscle coordination of that part of his body.

In the case of a thick-set person, touching fingertips might be impossible. But even with that sort of build, a boy or a man should at least be able to lie his first hand flat against his spine. Regardless of the ability to make the connection between the fingers behind the back, there are good exercises designed to achieve coordination and flexibility of those muscles used most often in shooting the puck.

To start, the athlete should lie flat on the floor with his hands palms down and his arms beside his thigh. Keeping the muscles loose, he then throws first one arm and then the other above his head without bending the elbow. The entire arm and the back of the hand should lie against the head, not away from it.

Still flat on the floor, first one arm, then the other should be stretched out at right angles to the body. Then, barely bending the elbow, the arm should be thrown across the chest so that the hand touches the floor on the opposite side. The upper arm should be directly across and in contact with the chest.

In another exercise from the same position, the arms in turn should be flung out straight, then, with the elbow at right angles to the upper arm, the forearm moved upward until the hand is pointing toward the ceiling and the palm facing the feet.

From the same basic position—as are all these shoulder exercises—with the elbow bent, rotate the upper arm at the shoulder until the hand can be slapped flat on the floor near the hip line. Then the arm should be brought back up with

the same shoulder rotation until the back of the hand can be slapped to the floor above the head. As soon as contact with the floor is made, the arm should be swung across the body to the opposite side, then returned to its original position.

Having done each maneuver with each arm, all the upper body muscles and most particularly the shoulder will become more and more flexible. This will help strengthen the muscles brought into play when shooting a puck. There is no reason why anyone able to handle a hockey stick cannot achieve this flexibility.

NECK

Flexibility of the neck is essential because it is so often necessary to change direction suddenly in hockey. Although the actual movement is made by the body, it is initiated more or less subconsciously by the head. If the head does not turn, the body will not turn either.

Free head movement depends entirely upon the muscle balance of the neck. Although neck injuries are rare in hockey, they do occur. Any athlete is badly hampered by a sore neck. A hockey player is so handicapped by one that he can hardly function at all.

Two exercises will help keep the neck pliable and comfortable. Both are simple and require little more than a minute or two to complete. In both, the subject stands in front of a mirror.

First, he stands with the mirror at his side, then swivels his neck until he is actually facing it. He does this from both directions, right and left. If he does not find it easy and comfortable, he should make this part of his daily regimen. Repetitiveness eventually will give him the flexibility he seeks.

In the other neck exercise, he faces the mirror and, without turning his body, leans his head as though trying to touch his shoulder with his ear. As in the other maneuver, he should do this on both sides. If he has difficulty at the beginning he will, with repeated practice, be able to move his head back and forth without limitation or discomfort.

ELBOW

Previous injury or overdevelopment of the biceps sometimes causes loss of flexibility in the elbow. But even young amateurs who have never been injured or have not had time to overdevelop the biceps will find this exercise useful.

The athlete lies flat on the floor with the arm slightly away from the body and the palm of the hand turned up. A rolled towel or some other type of soft pad should then be placed on the floor beneath the upper arm, just above the elbow. This will keep the hand from actually touching the floor, thus allowing complete extension.

From this position, the elbow should be bent until the forearm has reached a point where the fingers touch the shoulder. The hand should then be dropped back to its original position, with the movement started by very slight pressure but completed by the natural weight of the arm. It should land at a point somewhat below that from which the exercise started.

It is essential that no muscle control be used. The secret of the success of the exercise is in letting the force of gravity do all the work. If the arm will not go up far enough to enable the fingers to touch the shoulder, gentle pressure with the other hand will help complete the maneuver.

The exercise should be performed alternately with each arm. It will help stretch the triceps muscle at the back of the arm, which is the opponent of the biceps. The ultimate result will be complete flexibility in the elbow and correction of loss of extension resulting from injury or overdevelopment of the biceps.

WRISTS

In a sense, the wrist is one of the most important parts of the body for a hockey player. All the strength and dexterity of a fine skater and stick-handler can be lost if, because of injury or lack of flexibility, the wrist will not function effectively.

Stick-handling is controlled almost entirely by the wrist. The hockey player who can do everything else correctly is unable to complete his job if he cannot or will not use his wrists properly.

The wrist controls the shot—not simply the shot on goal, but the passing shot as well. It also controls such maneuvers as "deking" (faking an opponent out of position while keeping possession of the puck), and almost all other stratagems that hockey demands.

With poor wrist movement, shooting, passing, everything a hockey player must do suffers. Proper wrist control and function can be not only the difference between victory and defeat, but even the difference between making and not making the team.

It is not a question of power, but of control—in a sense, of harnessing that power. In order to perfect freedom of wrist action there are six different movements that are necessary.

The first two go together. With the elbow on a table or some other object comfortably used while sitting on a chair, the elbow should be placed with the hands together and the fingers pointing to the ceiling. Using pressure on one hand, the other should be pushed backward until it is at right angles to the wrist. Using the same type of pressure from the same position, one hand should push the other *forward* until it is at right angles to the wrist. These two movements are extension and flexion. When the wrist is forced into one direction or the other (usually extension) during heavy contact, it can cause a ligament sprain or even a wrist fracture.

There is no question that the exercise just described minimizes or even eliminates the possibility of serious wrist injury. Presuming that in the exercise a person is able to extend his wrist only eighty-five degrees instead of ninety (the maximum that can be achieved with gentle pressure from the other hand), he may be badly hurt by those last five degrees. In the exercise, he will first feel real discomfort in making his wrist bend those five degrees, but if he continues the exercise day after day he will eventually be able to make the move easily and without pain.

Assuming that he has not succeeded in doing so in the exercise, the probability of wrist injury in a game is obvious. When being checked hard into the boards by an opponent, a hockey player instinctively extends his arm to min-

imize the force. He does not have time to think of the position of his hand or wrist on contact with the boards. If it is not awkward or does not take the full force of the blow, he may not suffer any injury. But if he hits the boards in a position where the hand and wrist take all the force, he will almost surely injure his wrist in some way—either by a sprain or break—unless he has succeeded in achieving maximum (ninety degree) freedom of movement in his wrist exercises.

The next two exercises also go together. These are designed to prevent or minimize wrist injuries by forced rotation—actually turning the wrist by heavy pressure on contact during a game.

The flexed forearm should be placed on the table, thumb upward and completely relaxed. In the first movement, the hand should be turned quickly and loosely until the table can be slapped with the palm of the hand.

The second movement is quickly and loosely not only returning the hand to its original position but bringing it all the way around until the table may be slapped by the back of the hand.

Since this is a wrist exercise, the elbow must always remain stationary. All the pressure on the wrist may cause initial discomfort, but the two simple exercises will strengthen wrist rotation, thus enabling it to take a strong rotating blow in a game with little or no injury.

The fifth of the six wrist exercises looks easy but really is not. The forearm should be placed on the table palm down. Then, without moving anything but the wrist and keeping the palm flush to the table, move the hand back and forth. Although this, too, may be quite difficult at first, it will eventually come easily and naturally.

The sixth wrist exercise should be

done with a hockey stick. While in a standing position, the stick should be held in the hand, with the palm up and at shoulder level away from the body. The weight of the stick will force the wrist down until the stick points to the ground. Then, slowly flexing the wrist—but no other part of the arm—the stick should be moved until it is pointing to the ceiling. Then, in the same manner, start with the palm of the hand down and, still using only the wrist, move the stick from the down position to the up. For younger boys who may find the stick too heavy, something lighter, such as a walking cane or a golf putter, can be used.

Of course, all these wrist exercises should be performed with both hands. Faithfully executed on a day-to-day basis, they will strengthen that most important part of the arm and help control and harness the strength in all other parts of the body. Most of all, they will increase the efficiency of the shot. And that, after all, is the primary purpose of hockey.

LOW BACK

Because low back troubles are usually confined to veteran players, the final exercise was originally designed for them. However, these players derive so much benefit from it that it is now considered as valuable preventively as it is therapeutic. It will help everyone who plays hockey, whether or not he has ever had lower back problems.

It begins by lying flat on the floor, with the body straight out, the knees bent and the arms at the side. Without bending the elbow, the right arm should

be slowly lifted while at the same time the left thigh should be flexed toward the abdomen. As the right arm moves, the left should be placed on the left knee, thus forcing the thigh further into the abdomen than it would normally go.

The right arm continues to move until it is flat on the floor, now above the head, and touching the right ear.

Then, without changing the position of any of the four limbs (all of which are moving in perfect coordination) the right arm should slowly be brought back while the left, having released the left knee, moves up in the same manner as the right had been. Instead of being returned to its original position flat on the floor, the right arm should stop at the knee, with the right hand touching it, just as the left had touched the left knee when the exercise began.

Breathing is also a factor in this exercise. When the hand is not at the knee, breathing in at the nose should take place. When either hand touches either knee, the person doing the exercise should breathe out at the mouth.

At the completion of each movement, the lumbar (lower) spine will be felt pressing against the floor. Normally, when lying down, there is a discernible arch between the lumbar part of the back and the floor.

GENERAL CONDITIONING RULES

There is little need for very young players to do these exercises. If they wish to play hockey, they must learn all the basics first—to skate, to hold a stick, to control a puck, to skate backward as well as forward, and to stop.

By about the age of twelve, a boy playing hockey is risking many of the same injuries as a grown man. He probably will not suffer really serious injuries because his body and its components are all naturally flexible, and flexibility is of primary value in playing hockey.

The older a player gets, the more vulnerable he becomes to the type of injuries peculiar to hockey players. If he is serious about hockey but likes other sports, too, this regimen of exercises in the off-season will help keep his hockey muscle tone and make it that much easier for him to resume the game after months away from it.

The exercises are all fairly simple. Once in a groove of doing them daily, the entire regimen should not consume more than five or ten minutes. It is a small price to pay for increased safety in playing the world's fastest team game.

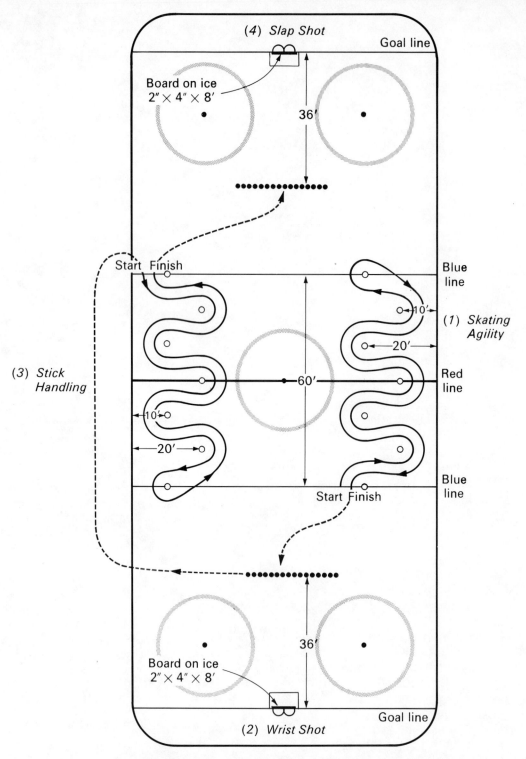

Diagram 15. *Rink with Test Stations.*

10

A Battery of Hockey Skill Tests

To help coaches efficiently evaluate the large number of hockey players who try out for teams, a battery of hockey skill tests has been developed.[1] It was initially used to determine the proficiency of players at the Bantam, senior high school, college, and professional levels.

The full hockey battery includes seven tests. Those starred (*) are in the mini-battery.

1. Skating agility*
2. Wrist shot*
3. Stick-handling*
4. Slap shot*
5. Starts-stops-turns
6. Speed skating
7. Passing

Due to the limited time for testing in youth or secondary school hockey, a mini-battery of four tests may be administered. A four-station design makes maximum use of the total rink ice surface. (See Diagram 15.) The layout can

[1] Edmund F. Enos, Jr., Boston University.

be used for testing and/or for teaching the skills. Players rotate from station to station, practicing the skills or being tested at each station. Following are the skills used in the mini-battery:

1. *Skating agility:* While carrying a stick, player weaves in and out around each tire in accordance with the diagram. One to three trials with the lowest time to the nearest tenth of a second recorded as the score.
2. *Wrist shot:* Sixteen pucks are placed on painted spots one inch apart at thirty-five feet from goal; a 2″ x 4″ x 8′ timber is placed across goal-mouth with two-inch side on ice; using a wrist shot, player makes as many shots on goal as possible within a ten-second period. One point scored for each puck entering the net during the ten-second period.
3. *Stick-handling:* Player, using stick and puck, weaves in and out around tires in accordance with diagram.

One to three trials with the lowest time to the nearest tenth of a second recorded as the score.

4. *Slap shot:* Same procedure and scoring as in number two except player uses a slap shot.

TABLE 2.   Rating Scale

Groups	Skating Agility[a]			Wrist Shot[b]			Stick-handling[a]			Slap Shot[b]		
	Good	Very Good	Superior	Good	Very Good	Superior	Good	Very Good	Superior	Good	Very Good	Superior
Bantam	21	20	19	6	7	8	25	24	23	7	8	9
High School	19	18	17	8	9	10	22	21	20	9	10	11
College	17	16.5	16	10	11	12	20	19	18	11	12	13
Professional	16	15.5	15	13	14	15	18	17	16	14	15	16

[a] In seconds.
[b] Pucks entering net.

Bibliography

Compiled by E. F. Enos, Jr.

Aldcorn, Gary, ed. *Coaches Handbook.* Toronto: Hockey Canada, 1970.

Andrews, Ron, ed. *1969–1970 National Hockey League Guide.* Montreal: National Hockey League, 1969.

Angell, K. *Hockey for the Beginner.* Burlington, Ontario: K. Angell, 1964.

Bathgate, Andy, and Wolff, Bob. *Andy Bathgate's Hockey Secrets.* Englewood Cliffs, N.J.: Prentice-Hall, Inc., 1963.

Blake, "Toe." *Hockey Hints.* Clarkson, Ontario: Ralston-Purina Company of Canada Limited, 1964.

Brodrick, Robert. *Ice Hockey.* London: Nicolas Kaye Limited, 1951.

Canadian Amateur Hockey Association. *Leadership Institute National Hockey Handbook.* Montreal: Canadian Amateur Hockey Association Publication, 1969.

Caswell, "Bing," and Life, Jack. *Coach's Manual: The Fundamentals of Ice Hockey.* Hidland, Canada: The Mc-Mart Press, 1950.

Coleman, Charles L. *The Trail of the Stanley Cup.* Montreal: National Hockey League, 1966.

Crown Life Insurance Company. *Helpful Hints for Hockey Coaches.* Toronto: Head Office, 1968.

Dutton, Marvyn ("Red"). *Hockey, The Fastest Game on Earth.* New York: Funk and Wagnalls Company, 1938.

Farrell, Arthur. *Handbook of Hockey.* Montreal: C. R. Corneil, 1899.

Farrell, Arthur. *How to Play Ice Hockey.* New York: American Publishing Company, 1907.

Farrington, S. Kip, Jr. *Skates, Sticks, and Men.* New York: McKay Company, Inc., 1972.

Fisher, Thomas Knight. *Ice Hockey.* New York: Charles Scribner's Sons, 1926.

Fitness and Amateur Sport Directorate. *Hockey Manual.* Ottawa: Department of National Health and Welfare, January 1969.

Gilbert, Rod. *Goal! My Life on Ice.* New York: Hawthorn Books, Inc., 1968.

Gitler, Ira. *Make the Team in Ice Hockey.*

New York: Grosset and Dunlap, 1968.

Hendy, James C. *National Hockey Guide.* Minneapolis: Can-Am Sports Publications, 1948.

Hicks, S. Trafford. *How to Play Ice Hockey.* New York: American Sports Publication Company, 1912.

Howe, Gordon. *Here's Howe.* Toronto: The Copp Clark Publishing Company Limited, 1963.

Hull, Bobby. *Hockey is My Game.* Don Mills, Ontario: Longman's Canada Limited, 1968.

Hull, Bobby. *Tips on Power Hockey.* Weston, Ontario: C.C.M., 1970.

Johnson, Bob. *Hockey.* Mankato, Minnesota: Creative Education Society, Incorporated, 1969.

Lariviere, Georges, and Bournival, Justin. *Hockey the Right Start.* Toronto: Holt, Rinehart and Winston of Canada, Limited, 1969.

LeBow, Guy, and Saplin, Stan. *The Hockey Scene.* New York: Homecrafts Sports Division, 1966.

L'Heureux, Bill. *Hockey for Boys.* Chicago: Follett Publishing Company, 1962.

McLeneham, R. J., ed. *The Hockey Handbook: Pee Wees to Pro.* Fredericton, N.B.: The Government of New Brunswick, 1963.

Mahovlich, Frank. *Ice Hockey.* London: Pelham Books, 1964.

Nevin, Bob, and Laperriere, Jacques. *All-Stars Hockey Guidebook.* New York: McGraw-Hill Book Company, 1967.

O'Brien, Andy. *Young Hockey Champions.* New York: W. W. Norton and Company, Incorporated, 1969.

Patrick, Lynn, and Monahan, D. Leo. *Let's Play Hockey!* Toronto: Macmillan and Company, 1957.

Percival, Lloyd. *The Hockey Handbook,* revised edition. Toronto: The Copp Clarke Publishing Company, Limited, 1956.

Recreation Branch Department of Youth. *Hockey Coaches' Manual.* Level One. The Government of Alberta, 1968.

Riley, Jack. *The Young Sportsman's Guide to Ice Hockey.* New York: Thomas Nelson and Sons, 1961.

Roche, Wilfred Victor. *The Hockey Book.* Toronto: McLellen and Stewart Limited, 1963.

Ross, Larry. *Hockey for Everyone.* Minneapolis: Burgess Publishing Company, 1968.

Sullivan, George. *Better Ice Hockey for Boys.* New York: Dodd, Mead and Company, 1965.

Sullivan, George, and Francis, Emile. *Face-Off.* New York: D. Van Nostrand Co., Inc., 1968.

Tarasov, Anatoli. *Road to Olympus.* Toronto: Griffin House, 1969.

Vaughn, Richard. *Hockey.* New York: McGraw-Hill Book Company, 1939.

Whitehead, Eric. *Ice Hockey.* New York: Franklin Watts Inc., 1969.

Woodcock, Tommy. *Hockey from the Ice Up.* Trainer St. Louis Blues, privately published, 1973.

Glossary

Backcheck. Skate back toward own goal, carrying out defensive assignments.

Backhand pass. As the lower hand moves the puck, go to the back of the hand.

Backhand shot. The upper hand pushes the stick and the lower hand pulls the stick with a hard follow through making a shot.

Bantams. Ages eleven and twelve.

Boarding. One player forcing the opponent into the boards legally.

Bodycheck. Placing body in the way of on-coming opponent in a legal manner to prevent any further motion.

Box. Generally a defensive formation of four teammates in a rectangle in front of the goalie.

Blue line. A blue line one foot wide parallel to and sixty feet in front of the goal line.

Breakout. A play getting the puck out of your defensive zone.

Charging. Taking more than two steps and hitting an opponent.

Clearing pass. Passing the puck out of your end or from in front of your net.

Close-in shot. Generally any shot within fifteen feet of the goalie.

Crease. A rectangle eight feet wide and four feet deep in front of the net.

Cross check. Thrusting of the stick across an opponent's head or body with no part of the stick on the ice.

Crossover turn. If turning to the right, bring in the left leg over the right leg—just the opposite to the left.

Deke. The puck carrier faking a man out of position.

Delayed call. Generally a penalty by the defensive team but signaled by the referee.

Draw. On faceoffs, succeeding in getting puck to a teammate.

Drop pass. Puck carrier stops puck dead, trailing teammate to pick it up.

Elbowing. Illegal use of elbows on anatomy of opponent.

Faceoff. Puck dropped between two players to start or resume play.

Flip pass. A wrist motion on the stick to lift the puck over an opponent or his stick.

Forechecking. Checking opponents in their defensive zone.

Forehand pass. Pushing with the lower hand on the stick to propel the puck forward or laterally.

Front-foot stop. If one turns to the right, places his weight on the front (left) foot.

Garbage goal. Goal scored from a scrambling in front of the net.

Goal judge. Person assigned behind the net who signals the referee when the puck enters the net.

Hanger. Generally has two meanings:
a) A player getting behind the opponent's defense in the neutral zone.
b) An opponent stationing himself on the off-post (behind) the goalie.

Heavy stick. Player exerting considerable pressure on his stick.

High sticking. Carrying stick above shoulder height.

Holding. Illegal use of hands or stick on an opponent to prevent his movement.

Hooking. Using stick illegally to prevent opponent from moving.

Icing. Both teams have the same number of players on ice. One team propels the puck from their defensive zone to opposite end and puck crosses goal line extended. If there are two blue lines separated by a red line and the puck crosses more than two lines and goes beyond the goal line extended it is icing. (Professional rules.)

Interference. a) Offensive interference is interference with an opponent in playing the puck in the sense of making interference or protection for a teammate by personal contact. b) Defensive interference—A player in the act of covering or being covered may never illegally interfere with an opponent.

Juniors. Boys over sixteen years of age.

Lie of a stick. Angle between the blade and the handle constitutes the lie.

Linesman. An official on the ice calling offsides.

Midgets. Ages fifteen and sixteen.

Misconduct. Generally a penalty of ten minutes with a substitute allowed to go on the ice immediately.

Mites. Generally seven and eight years of age.

Offside. A player preceding the puck into the offensive zone.

Off-the-board pass. A player passing the puck at an angle off the boards to a teammate or recovering himself.

Overloading. Generally means placing two or more of your players in a designated area.

Peewees. Ages thirteen and fourteen.

Penalty shot. The fouled play allowed to shoot unimpeded from mid-ice to opponent's goal taking one shot and no rebound.

Poke check. To make a sudden jab at the puck with your stick.

Power shot. A hard wrist shot.

Power skating. Usually refers to the snap as the knee and hip lock at the end of a skating stride pushing off the inside edge of the skate near the toe.

Rear-foot stop. If turning to the left, the weight is placed on the rear or left foot and lean backward with knees bent.

Referee. Has the sole authority and control of the game.

Scorer. Is a statistician compiling goals, assists, penalties, and times.

Screen. One player blocking the vision of another player.

Shoulder check. Hitting opponent with your shoulder.

Slap shot. Raising the stick to shoulder height (or lower) and bringing it down to meet the puck with a low follow through.

Slashing. Raising the stick above the shoulders and hitting an opponent or his stick.

Slot. Area formed by a rectangle in front of net thirty to forty feet out in front of goalie.

Snap shot. A quick wrist shot.

Spearing. One or two hands on your stick and spearing the opponent in the stomach area.

Special spot faceoff. Special spots located midway between sideboards and goal cage fifteen feet out from the goal line used for faceoffs.

Squirts. Nine and ten-year-old players.

Timer. Person who times the games and penalties.

Tripping. Player falls to ice as a result of illegal use of stick or body.

Two-foot stop. Turning to right or left with weight equally divided on both skates.

Wrist shot. Puck propelled by snapping the wrist.

Index